OFF THE BEATEN PATH® SERIES

Chicago

Off the Beaten Path®

D0097387

by Cliff Terry

The Globe Pequot Press

Guilford, Connecticut

*To Pat, my wonderful wife, best friend, and companion
on excursions from Peruvian Amazon rain forests
to Minnesota hiking trails,
who enthusiastically suggested many great ideas
for this book and later doubled
as a diligent proofreader.*

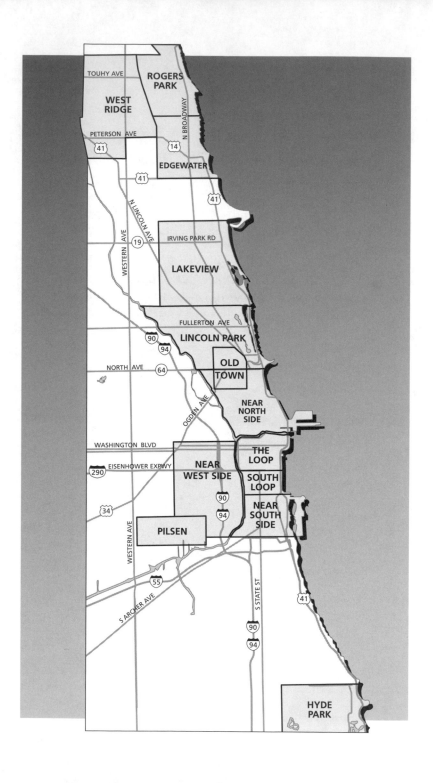

Contents

Acknowledgments

Besides my wife, Pat, I'd like to thank others who ventured forth with great ideas for this book, including our sons, Christopher and Scott, who brought a youthful perspective to these attractions, and many friends, particularly Julia Winn, Esther Manewith, Janet Treuhaft, Bob and Sharon Barton, and Greg and Kris Gleason. Also to the superb staff at the Chicago Office of Tourism, especially Dorothy Coyle and Donna Metz. And last, but by no means least, The Globe Pequot Press, particularly Laura Strom and Himeka Curiel for shepherding this guide from embryo to birth.

Introduction

"When friends from abroad come to the U.S., I always send them to Chicago, or try to," R. W. Apple, chief correspondent of the *New York Times'* Washington bureau, once wrote. "It is the quintessential American city: muscular, inventive, wonderfully diverse, worldly-wise (if a bit oafish at times), and as unpretentious as its prairie-flat vowels."

Ranking Chicago as the best place to live in the Midwest, *Money* magazine stated: "What makes Chicago so great is that it looks and acts like a big city, but it doesn't feel like one." And a journalist from, yes, France has called Chicago "a Midwestern metropolis that is perhaps one of America's secret gardens."

Chicago is a city where they dye the sluggish Chicago River green on St. Patrick's Day, where bridges tie up traffic on lovely warm summer afternoons as they're raised for a couple of sailboats slowly making their way on that river toward, or back from, Lake Michigan. It's a place where trees decorated with white Christmas lights on winter nights brighten the sky along North Michigan Avenue ("The Magnificent Mile") as a kind of electronic lace. It's a place that is trying to leave behind memories of Al Capone and the 1968 Democratic National Convention riots, a sometimes insecure place where the Second City complex—Chicago's long-standing feeling of inferiority toward New York—lingers despite quick denials. And it's a city where its sports teams lose more than they win (where have you gone, Michael Jordan?), a city where its mayors blithely create their own free-for-all grammatical rules.

Chicagoans love superlatives because, well, so many apply to their home. For instance, Chicago is the site of the world's largest public library (the Harold Washington Library Center), the world's largest indoor marine mammal pavilion (Shedd Aquarium), the world's largest Polish population outside of Warsaw, the world's largest chewing gum manufacturer (Wrigley), and—arguably—the world's best pizza. It came as no surprise that the city went absolutely bonkers in the mid-'80s when "Da Bears" won, yes, the *Super* Bowl.

The purpose of this book is to explore some of the city's many (seventy-seven) neighborhoods—the ones that offer the most attractions, are reasonably easy to reach by public transportation, and are relatively safe—and to search out often overlooked and perhaps unsung stores, restaurants, and museums that may not rank at the top of Must See tourist attractions. That's why it doesn't cover the usual-suspect attractions like Sears Tower, the Art Institute, and Navy Pier. They've been covered enough. On the other hand, it doesn't seek out the really scummy places or dangerous communities where visitors would make inviting targets.

History

When the first Europeans arrived during the 1600s at what is now Chicago, they found the Pottawatomie Indians living near the river they called the Cecagou or, as some believe, Cicagoua, which apparently was a form of wild garlic that grew along its banks. Or maybe it was wild onion. (Local historians have had trouble getting in sync.) The first resident of Chicago was Jean Baptiste Pointe DuSable, a prosperous black fur trader from New Orleans, who built a settlement in 1779 at the mouth of that river. In 1830 lots were sold to finance construction of what would become the Illinois and Michigan Canal, connecting Chicago with the Mississippi River, and in 1837 Chicago—with a population of about 4,000—was incorporated as a city. With the 100-mile canal completed in 1848 and with the arrival of the first locomotive from the Galena & Chicago Union Railroad that same year, Chicago had become a major transportation hub. In 1865 the sprawling Union Stock Yards were completed.

Then came the Great Fire of 1871—which actually provided an opportunity to rebuild the whole city. One of the local heroes was architect Daniel Burnham, who created a unique comprehensive plan that is responsible today for the unobstructed lakefront (perhaps the loveliest in the world), citywide system of parks, and green belt of forest preserves. "Make no little plans," Burnham declared, "for they have no magic to stir men's blood. . . ." In 1884 William Le Baron Jenney built the world's first skyscraper, and Chicago was the country's architectural center. Later, during the Roaring '20s, it became known as the country's machine-gun center, but also a fine place for jazz, blues, and literature. As for those original Pottawatomie, they were sent packing. In 1834 and 1835, the U.S. government forced them and neighboring tribes to sell their land. More than 3,000 wound up on reservations—in Kansas.

Transportation

In 1893 Chicago hosted the World's Columbian Exposition, which drew almost 26 million visitors. In order to handle the crowds, the Chicago Transit Authority introduced the first elevated trains to the city. Today,

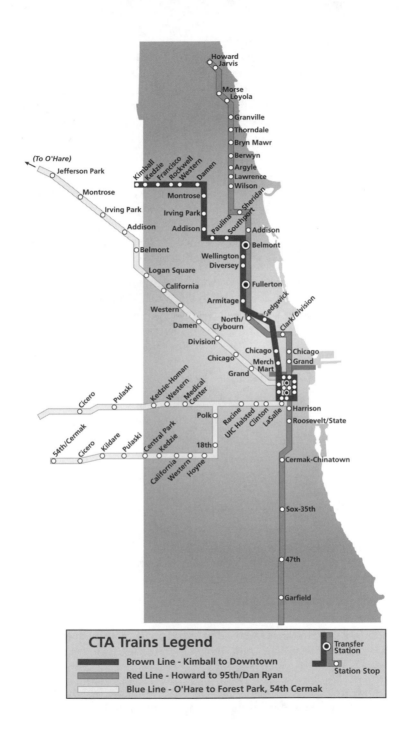

the elevated or "L" trains provide fine public transportation, as do the dozens of bus lines. Each train line has a different color name, the main ones for readers of this book being the Red Line, which runs from Howard Street at the city's northern boundary south to the Loop and on down to 95th Street, and the Brown Line, which begins in the Loop and runs north and then northwest, ending at Kimball Avenue. To get to the Museum Campus, board the #146 Marine–Michigan bus along the west side of State Street in the Loop.

The fare on both "L" and bus, as of this writing, was $1.50 (exact fare only), with transfers—good for two more rides within two hours—available for 30 cents extra. Visitor passes also may be purchased at such places as the city's visitor information centers (see "Sources of Information" next page) and Union Station. (Price: $5.00 one day, $9.00 two days, $12.00 three days, $18.00 five days.) For CTA information phone (312) 836–7000.

Taxis are plentiful and relatively reasonable (although fares keep escalating), and for some of the attractions in this book, it's advised to hail one. Or, in other cases, drive your own vehicle. Above all, Chicago—like Boston, New York, and San Francisco—is a great walking city.

Fees, Prices, and Rates

Many of Chicago's attractions are free, and many museums charge nominal entrance fees, with discounts for young children, students, and seniors.

Fares at restaurants vary all over the place. Ethnic spots (well, maybe not French) can be quite reasonable. This guide will give a rough, ballpark-type indication of what you might expect to pay for a meal per person: Under $15 is considered inexpensive, $15 to $35 moderate, and over $35 expensive.

As for lodging, for a standard double (and not during special events like World Cup games, conventions, when they jack up the rates, or, heh-heh, a World Series), make it $125 and under as inexpensive, $125 to $200 as moderate, and $200 and up as expensive.

At the end of each chapter are lists of suggested "Places to Stay" and "Places to Eat" in the area. I've tried to list off-the-beaten-path establishments wherever possible, but in many cases, the best options available were more mainstream businesses.

Bed-and-breakfast establishments are also available, although such places often come and go, so it's difficult to make recommendations.

One good idea, though, is to check with *Bed & Breakfast/Chicago,* a reservation service that lists guesthouses and inns, self-catering apartments, and rooms in private homes. Most accommodations are located downtown, and in the Near North, Old Town, and Lincoln Park neighborhoods, and most require a minimum stay of two or three nights. Rates vary widely, from $85 to $350 per night. Phone (773) 248–0005, or log onto www.chicago-bed-breakfast.com.

Area Codes

The city of Chicago has two area codes—312 and 773—and just to make it more confusing, you can't figure them out logically by geography. A store or restaurant on one block may have a different code from another on an adjoining block.

Sources of Information

You'll have several sources to find out what's happening while you're in Chicago. There is the ubiquitous *Chicago Reader,* a free weekly newspaper that serves as a bible for many Chicagoans regarding movies, theater, and various music events (www.chicagoreader.com). There is also the "Weekend Plus" section (which comes out on Friday) of the *Chicago Sun-Times* (www.suntimes.com) and the "Friday" section of the *Chicago Tribune* (www.chicagotribune.com). You might also check out another free weekly, *New City* (www.newcity.com), which, like the *Reader,* is found in many stores, restaurants, and bars. Then there's *Chicago* (www.chicagomag.com), a slick monthly magazine most valuable for its listings/rankings of restaurants.

Last, and perhaps most helpful, all kinds of information is available from the efficient *Chicago Office of Tourism,* which maintains two visitor information centers, one at its headquarters at the Chicago Cultural Center (Michigan Avenue and Randolph Street), the other at the Chicago Water Works Building, Michigan and Pearson Street. Its Web site is www.cityofchicago/Tourism. To receive a free information packet, phone (877) CHICAGO. The TTY number for individuals who are deaf or hard of hearing is (800) 406–6418.

Other Attractions

Appendix B, Farther Off the Beaten Path, includes sites on the West and South Sides in neighborhoods that, because of space limitations, don't have enough points of interest for visitors to warrant separate chapters. Consult this section for more suggestions.

Tour Groups and Organizers

Although many private companies offer tours of the city, both on land (buses, trolleys) and on water (boats on the Chicago River), tours offered by two organizations are especially recommended.

The *Chicago Office of Tourism* sponsors inventive tours of some of the city's communities, such as South Side/Bronzeville, Chinatown/Pilsen, and Andersonville/Lincoln Square. Trips are given throughout the year, although they're sporadic in certain months. The majority are scheduled from May through October. Information may be obtained, and reservations made, by calling (312) 742–1190 or by stopping in person at the Shop at the Cultural Center, 77 East Randolph, on the first floor. (The tour Web site is www.chgocitytours.com.) The price, as of this writing, was $25 for adults, and $20 for seniors over 65, children ages 8 to 18, and students with valid ID. Special tours are also given from February through December, covering such subjects as "Roots of Chicago Blues and Gospel," "Threads of Ireland," "A Jewish Legacy," and "Literary Chicago." Price: $50 for adults, $45 for the others named above.

Underground Chicago

A report by Chicago's Municipal Reference Library noted, among other things, that the city, at the end of the twentieth century, had approximately 4,300 miles of sewer mains, about 230,000 catch basins, and somewhere close to 148,000 manholes.

The *Chicago Architectural Foundation,* which maintains centers at 224 South Michigan Avenue and in the John Hancock Center (875 North Michigan), offers a wonderful architectural river cruise, spotlighting over fifty historic and architecturally significant sites. Cruises run several times daily from May through October, with information available at (312) 922–3432, ext. 226. (Price, as of this writing: $21.) Also recommended are the foundation's walking tours, covering such subjects as "Historic Skyscrapers," "Modern Skyscrapers," and "Greater North Michigan Avenue." (Web site: www.architecture.org. Cost: $8.00 to $10.00.)

The Loop Tour Train, sponsored in partnership with the Chicago Architecture Foundation, Chicago Transit Authority, and Chicago Office of Tourism, is a Chicago-only experience in which visitors learn the history of the downtown area and elevated train system while riding the trains themselves. For information on the forty-minute trip, available May through September, call the Architectural Foundation or the Office of Tourism.

Also available throughout the year are tours of such places as:

Chicago Board of Trade (312) 435–3590

Chicago Stock Exchange (312) 666–2980

Eli's Cheesecake Factory (773) 736–3417

Merchandise Mart/World Trade Center (312) 644–4664

Newberry Library (312) 255–3700

The prices and rates listed in this guidebook were confirmed at press time. We recommend, however, that you call establishments to obtain current information before traveling.

Help Us Keep This Guide Up to Date

Every effort has been made by the author and editors to make this guide as accurate and useful as possible. However, many things can change after a guide is published—establishments close, phone numbers change, facilities come under new management, etc.

We would love to hear from you concerning your experiences with this guide and how you feel it could be improved and kept up to date. While we may not be able to respond to all comments and suggestions, we'll take them to heart and we'll also make certain to share them with the author. Please send your comments and suggestions to the following address:

The Globe Pequot Press
Reader Response/Editorial Department
P.O. Box 480
Guilford, CT 06437

Or you may e-mail us at:
editorial@globe-pequot.com

Thanks for your input, and happy travels!

The Loop

*C*hicago's central business district, the Loop, was built over the site of the original settlement. (Plates in the sidewalks near the intersection of Michigan Avenue and Wacker Drive show the location of the original Fort Dearborn.) In 1837 the newly incorporated city of Chicago had a population of 4,179, most of which lived in the central area. In 1853 the first combined City Hall–County Court House building was opened, and in 1860 the Republican National Convention met in a huge, boxlike wooden structure called the Wigwam, a temporary building at Lake Street and Wacker, and nominated, of course, a lanky, young, rustic lawyer from Springfield named Lincoln. In the late 1860s, local mover and shaker Potter Palmer built a large department store at Randolph and State Streets that would become Marshall Field's, and a fancy hotel, the Palmer House, opened in 1870.

After the Great Fire of 1871, the business structures were quickly rebuilt, with the new fire code prohibiting the construction of wooden buildings—effectively ending the Loop's other status as a residential area. The Chicago School of Architecture emerged in the Loop from the early 1880s to 1910. Designers included Burnham & Root, Holabird & Roche, William Le Baron Jenney, and, best known of all, Louis H. Sullivan, who decreed, "Form follows function."

The Loop is the site of some of the city's prized cultural institutions: the Art Institute of Chicago (1893) and Orchestra Hall (1905), both based on Michigan Avenue, and the Civic Opera House on Wacker Drive (1929), now home of the Lyric Opera of Chicago. The Loop is also where you'll find the 110-story Sears Tower, built from 1968 to 1974 and designed by Skidmore, Owings, and Merrill. It is also home to numerous public works of art, such as Marc Chagall's *The Four Seasons,* Jean Dubuffet's *Monument with Standing Beast,* Alexander Calder's *Flamingo,* Joan Miró's *Miró's Chicago,* and Pablo Picasso's controversial Cor-Ten head, *Untitled Sculpture.*

Long playing bridesmaid to the outlying Off-Loop theaters, the Loop itself has created a burgeoning *theater district.* The dazzling new

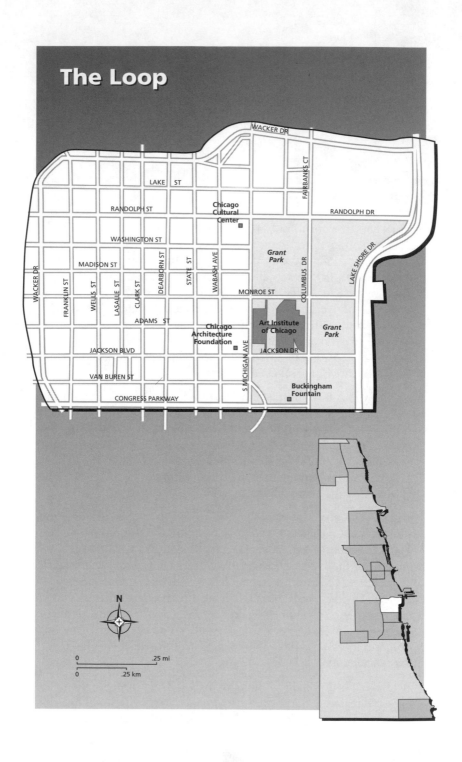

The Loop

WACKER DR

LAKE ST

RANDOLPH ST

Chicago
Cultural
Center

RANDOLPH DR

WASHINGTON ST

FAIRBANKS CT

WACKER DR

MADISON ST

DEARBORN ST

STATE ST

WABASH AVE

Grant
Park

COLUMBUS DR

LAKE SHORE DR

FRANKLIN ST

WELLS ST

LASALLE ST

CLARK ST

MONROE ST

ADAMS ST

Chicago
Architecture
Foundation

Art Institute
of Chicago

Grant
Park

JACKSON BLVD

S. MICHIGAN AVE

JACKSON DR

VAN BUREN ST

CONGRESS PARKWAY

Buckingham
Fountain

N

0   .25 mi
0   .25 km

THE LOOP

TOP ATTRACTIONS IN THE LOOP

Chicago Cultural Center

The Pedway

ECHO at Symphony Center

Thomas Hughes Children's Library

The Rookery

Federal Reserve Bank of Chicago

Goodman Theater, which opened in 2000 on Dearborn Street between Randolph and Lake, joined the Chicago Theatre at 175 North State and the more lately renovated Ford Center for the Performing Arts (Oriental Theatre), at 24 West Randolph; the Cadillac Palace, at 151 West Randolph; and the long-established Shubert, at 22 West Monroe Street.

The Loop's showcase boulevard, with its shops and hotels, is **Michigan Avenue,** which runs along lovely Grant Park, home of free summer concerts and internationally known Buckingham Fountain. The heart of the Loop is the intersection of State and Madison Avenue, which neatly forms the base of the city's street-numbering system. Madison, which runs east-west, divides the north and south numbers. (Thus, the restaurant Trattoria No. 10, for instance, is located at 10 North Dearborn Street, a few doors north of Madison.) State, running north-south, divides the east and west numbers. It is known, in song, of course, as "that Great Street," but State has seen better days. Once the prime shopping center, home to half a dozen big department stores, it now is home only to Marshall Field's, Carson Pirie Scott, and Sears, as well as a decidedly tacky-looking Old Navy. A while back, the city fathers tried turning State into a traffic-free mall, but that bombed, and traffic, the merchants are pleased to see, is back. At the south end of the Loop, State is anchored by the Harold Washington Library Center, as well as the innovative Chicago Music Mart.

Three blocks to the west of State is **LaSalle Street,** the haughty "canyon" that forms the city's financial district. Wacker—a name TV host David Letterman positively loved when he broadcast his show from Chicago (he kept grinning and saying, "Whack-er, whack-er")—is a double-decker affair that winds along the Chicago River and its south branch. (A warning: Starting in February 2001, an almost two-year-long scheduled Wacker reconstruction project was begun; check bus routes for temporary changes.)

Many of the major Chicago Transit Authority (CTA) bus lines run down Michigan Avenue and State Street in the Loop, and the stations for the CTA's elevated and subway lines may be found along State and Wabash.

Probably the main attraction in the area is the Museum Campus (Shedd Aquarium, Adler Planetarium, Field Museum). To get there, you can board the #146 Marine–Michigan bus on State.

To start off your tour of the Loop, walk south of the Chicago River on Michigan Avenue and take the elevator up to the fourth floor of 168 North Michigan, where you'll find the *Hellenic Museum and Cultural Center.* Opened in 1992, its purpose is to document and preserve the history of the Greek immigrant experience in this country, to showcase the Hellenic culture of antiquity, and to provide a cultural venue for contemporary Greek-Americans. On display are such exhibits of paintings with titles like "Landscapes of Impression: Ganos, Karras, and Stamos." The tiny gift shop sells a variety of items: toy Greek soldiers, a Greek column clock, books, notepaper, Byzantine jewelry, frescoes, T-shirts, tote bags, and sterling silver icons. Open Monday through Friday 10:00 A.M. to 4:00 P.M. Phone (312) 726–1234. Suggested donation.

Head south on Michigan, then turn onto Randolph Street for the *Gallery 37 Store,* part of the Gallery 37 Center for the Arts at 66 East Randolph. The store sells original creations by participants in Gallery 37, the city of Chicago's nationally recognized job-training program—through paid apprenticeships in the visual, literary, and performing arts—for Chicagoans ages 14 to 21. Among the unusual items in the store—its motto is "Imagination Is on the Loose"—are brightly colored tables, chairs, and benches; paintings; dinnerware; vases; note cards; jewelry; and even decorative mouse pads for the computer. Proceeds are put back into the Gallery 37 program, which, since being launched in 1991, has provided over 15,000 jobs for Chicago youths. The store is open Monday through Saturday from 10:00 A.M. to 6:00 P.M. Phone (312) 744–8925.

Across the street, between Randolph and Washington Streets on Michigan, is the *Chicago Cultural Center,* originally the home of the first Central Library for Chicago (where, toward the end of its tenure, more books seemed to be missing than present). It has since been turned into a residence for various functions, including eight exhibition spaces, two concert halls, two theaters, a cabaret performing space, dance studio, senior center, cafe, shop, and the Chicago Office of Tourism Visitor Information Center. Following the library years, it was dedicated in 1991 as a place where arts would be celebrated free of charge and accessible to all.

Making good on that charge, the center offers extremely popular daily programs of music, dance, theater, literary arts, and films, as well as exhibitions—more than 1,000 annually. Sponsored by the Chicago Department of Cultural Affairs, the programs are held at noon and in the early evening on weekdays, and sometimes on Saturday and Sunday, and include performances, concerts, screenings, lectures, and workshops. Musical events range from performances by the Chicago

Chamber Orchestra, Chicago Opera Theater, and Chinese Fine Arts Society to the annual Jazz Fair (January) and the Live Music Now! Programs for Children. Among theater groups have been Shaw-Chicago (staged readings), Studio Theater productions by Off-Loop companies, and Puppetropolis Chicago, a collaboration by local, national, and international artists. Wide-ranging exhibitions of traditional and new media include painting, sculpture, photography, graphics, and architecture, and related lectures, panel discussions, and gallery talks are often scheduled. The eclectic exhibits have included "Kandinsky, Malevich, and the Russian Avant-Garde" and "Contemporary Art and the World of Plants."

An architectural showplace, the beaux arts–style building was completed in 1897, inspired by the neoclassical style of the World's Columbian Exposition, held in Chicago in 1893. Formerly known as the "People's Palace," it features wonderful inlaid mosaics, rare imported marbles, and, it is believed, the world's largest (38 feet) Tiffany stained-glass dome, valued at an estimated $35 million. (It's in the Preston Bradley Hall.) The walls of the opulent G.A.R. (Grand Army of the Republic) Rotunda contain names of Civil War battles—Cold Harbor,

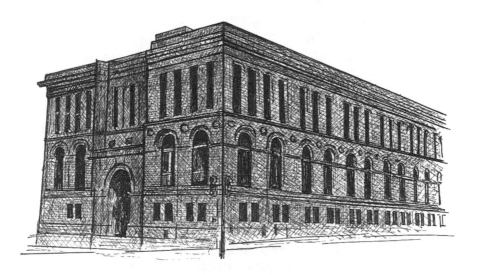

Chicago Cultural Center

Wilderness Campaign, Manassas—in which the Union army fought. The large room is used for exhibitions, performances, weddings, city receptions, corporate events, and, in one case I can remember, a dance rehearsal hall for the stage musical *Miss Saigon*.

Guided tours are available Tuesday through Saturday at 1:15 P.M., leaving from the Randolph Street lobby. Cultural Center hours are Monday through Wednesday from 10:00 A.M. to 7:00 P.M., Thursday from 10:00 A.M. to 9:00 P.M., Friday from 10:00 A.M. to 6:00 P.M., Saturday from 10:00 A.M. to 5:00 P.M., Sunday from 11:00 A.M. to 5:00 P.M. Closed holidays. Free. Phone (312) 744–6630, or visit the Web site at www.cityofchicago.org/Tour/Cultural Center/ for more information or for a list of events and concerts.

On the Randolph Street ground floor there's a lunch or coffee break opportunity at the **Corner Bakery** restaurant, serving soups, salads, and tasty, hefty sandwiches. Fine noon-hour entertainment is provided during the "Lunchbreak" series, featuring pop, jazz, and classical performers.

The Cultural Center is also home to the fascinating, innovative **Museum of Broadcast Communications** (MBC), which set up shop in 1987 and is one of only two broadcast museums in the country. It's a wonderful place for radio and TV nostalgia buffs, with all kinds of vintage radios and television sets, including the kind with the round screens that presented shows in—if you can believe it, kids—*black and white*.

The MBC also serves up such exhibits as mock-ups of "tightwad" Jack Benny's vault and Fibber McGee and Molly's hideously cluttered closet (complete with Molly exclaiming, as always, "No, don't open that door, McGee! . . . Heavenly days!"). Also on hand are the "prime minister" jacket worn by Frazier Thomas, host of the kids' show "Garfield Goose," and a puppet of Garfield himself; the bell rung at the opening of "Ding Dong School" hosted by "Miss Francis" (Dr. Francis Horwich, former head of the education department of the Loop's Roosevelt University); the bandleader's uniform and boots worn on "Super Circus" by blonde, leggy Mary Hartline, one of TV's earliest sex symbols; the CBS camera used to televise the first "Great Debate" in 1960 between John Kennedy and Richard Nixon (and a video of the debate showing a cool Kennedy and a perspiring Nixon); the six original, battered buckets used on "Bozo's Circus"; Charlie McCarthy and Mortimer Snerd ventriloquist dummies; and a "Little Orphan Annie" Ovaltine mug. For something completely different, there are posters of present-day stars such as Rush Limbaugh, Larry King, Charles Osgood, and Don Imus, who have been elected to, yes, the "Radio Hall of Fame."

The museum also offers the unique opportunity to become a news anchor. For about $20 (as of this writing) you can don the anchor jacket, sit behind the desk of a simulated television news set, and read the Chicago evening news. A director and computerized TelePromTer are provided, and you can take home a VHS copy. (Phone 312–629–6010 to make an appointment.) Also, on Saturday afternoons you can join the studio audience for a live broadcast of radio historian Chuck Schaden's "Those Were the Days" program, and on Sundays listen in on a re-creation of a classic radio program such as "The Thin Man" or "The Life of Riley," read by Chicago professional actors. Up on the second floor is a public archive collection of more than 10,000 TV shows, 50,000 hours of radio, 2,500 newscasts, and even 9,000 television commercials, all available for viewing in cubicles for a small fee. Downstairs is the museum store, where you can buy everything from old Superman and Ozzie and Harriet radio tapes to a Lucy clock, "The Young and the Restless" baseball caps, and "Seinfeld" T-shirts.

The MBC is open from 10:00 A.M. to 4:30 P.M. Monday through Saturday, Sunday from noon to 5:00 P.M. Closed holidays. Hour-long tours, conducted Monday through Friday, must be scheduled in advance (312–629–6016). For more information, phone (312) 629–6000. Free.

Years ago, when the word *underworld* was mentioned in Chicago, thoughts immediately turned to Al Capone, "Bugs" Moran, "Machine

Higher Platitudes and Other Daleyisms

*C*hicago's city hall, located in the Loop on LaSalle Street between Randolph and Washington Streets, was the former urban kingdom of Richard J. Daley, mayor of Chicago (1955–1976) and father of the present mayor Richard M. Daley. The "original" Mayor Daley was known for his malapropisms (such as "walking pedestrians") and mangled syntax, collected by journalists and casual observers alike. Among the Daley dealings:

• "The policeman isn't there to create disorder. The policeman is there to preserve *disorder.*"

• "There's no regard for the Rules of Order by the gentleman from the Fifth Ward. Go on with your disorder."

• "Ladies and gentlemen of the League of Women Voters. . . ."

• "Together we must rise to ever higher and higher platitudes."

• "They have vilified me. They have crucified me. Yes, they have even criticized me."

Gun" Jack McGurn, and their playmates. Today, it applies to something more, well, pedestrian—an innovative downtown underground walkway system called the **Pedway.** It consists of a network of underground tunnels—built over a forty-year period—linking over 40 blocks in the central business district. Obviously, the biggest advantage to using Pedway is during rotten weather, although it also was designed to handle what the city tactfully calls the "conflict" between pedestrian and vehicle.

Sometimes the entries to the Pedway are hard to find. Perhaps the easiest way is to start at the Cultural Center on the Randolph side and take the "Pedway" elevator down a floor, or go to the basement level of Marshall Field's and follow the signs to the Pedway. Other venues connected by the system include the Fairmont Hotel, City Hall–County Court House Building, and subway lines. You can find a number of small shops down there, too, from flowers to dry cleaning to shoe and watch repair, and you'll also find the ubiquitous street musicians. There are maps posted on the walls; for your own map, drop in during weekday business hours at the Chicago Department of Transportation, 30 North LaSalle Street, Suite 1100 (phone 312–744–3600).

Pedway development was started by the city in 1951, and private developers, looking for amenities for future tenants, joined in. (A good example is Illinois Center, linking offices, hotels, and residential buildings east of Michigan Avenue and south of Wacker Drive.) One more recent Pedway segment is the Randolph Street Pedestrianway, opened in 1988 and running between Michigan Avenue and State Street. It links the Chicago Transit Authority's State Street subway with Metra's Randolph Street train station and passes through the lower levels of Marshall Field's and the

Under the . . . What Exactly?

*I*t was put up in 1967 to a great hue and cry, and Pablo Picasso's controversial Cor-Ten head, Untitled Sculpture, 50 feet high and weighing 162 tons, is still a subject of controversy. (Is it his wife or his afghan hound?) There is no debate, however, about the city's free "Under the Picasso" programs weekdays at noon in the Daley Civic Center, 50 West Washington Street. Presented by the Department of Cultural Affairs in cooperation with the Public Building Commission, the programs in a typical week have run from "Studio Steppin'" (the public is invited to waltz, fox trot, swing, and salsa to taped music) to the St. Ignatius College Prep Concert Band to a performance by an "Elvis Presley stylist." Phone (312) 346–3278 for information.

Cultural Center. Pedway doors are open Monday through Friday from 6:00 A.M. to 7:30 P.M., Saturday from 8:00 A.M. to 6:30 P.M. Closed Sunday.

How do you get to Symphony Hall besides "practice, practice, practice"? Well, you can walk farther south down Michigan Avenue and find it between Adams Street and Jackson Boulevard. The world-renowned symphony is decidedly *on* the beaten path, of course, but there's a different kind of related attraction just around the corner at a facility known as *ECHO* (67 East Adams), the music education center of the Chicago Symphony Orchestra (CSO). Formally known as the Eloise W. Martin Center, it is located in the sparkling Symphony Center, which opened in 1998.

What ECHO does is utilize interactive technology for both adults and children, especially the latter, and was inspired by CSO music director Daniel Barenboim's vision to make music accessible to everyone. A staff member explains that ECHO is designed for children ages 8 and up, from third graders who may take music only once a week to older youths who belong to school orchestras. Adults also use the facility, perhaps participating as part of a team-building activity.

In the A-Musing Room on Symphony Center's second-floor education and administration wing, you can explore "music through themes, which are relevant to their everyday experiences"—which isn't as fancy-schmancy or intimidating as it sounds. You can explore a series of computer-assisted experiences, set in London-style telephone booths, that illustrate aspects of music, such as "Celebrations and Time," which is about the use of music in various cultures, and "Sounds and Silence," which explores how sounds are made and how they're combined. You'll be given a handheld "instrument box," which may sound like a violin, clarinet, or timpani, which you can plug into a console in each booth. As

Why the Name?

*E*ven before the Great Fire of 1871, downtown Chicago was a booming business area, and horse-drawn omnibuses were introduced on State Street in 1859. In the 1880s cable car lines came into play, circling the area and giving it its name, "the Loop." This was solidified with the construction of the Union Loop Elevated Railway, completed in 1897. The first L line, in fact, was erected to transport visitors to the World's Columbian Exposition of 1893. As anyone who has ever seen a movie filmed in Chicago knows, the elevated trains still run along a rectangular loop over Wells, Van Buren, and Lake Streets, and Wabash Avenue.

you're introduced to concepts like timing, pitch, rhythm, tone, and vibration, the box records some of the musical experimentation. You can then plug the box into the "Orchestra Wall," which lets you hear the "solos" you created incorporated into a group piece, whimsically entitled "Off the Wall" and composed by CSO violinist Max Raimi. When it plays, your name is displayed in lights.

For groups only, ECHO also provides Music Labs, which have a variety of percussion instruments, including Orff instruments (similar to large wooden xylophones), drums from around the world, bells, and cymbals. The forty-five-minute sessions are led by a teaching artist. Session activities range from making instruments to learning a rhythm pattern on an instrument and playing it as part of a group.

The A-Musing Room experience, which lasts ninety minutes, is available for walk-in visits. Reservations are not required but are strongly suggested. Reservations are required for the Music Labs and are for groups of twelve or more. Nominal admission prices vary. ECHO is open Tuesday through Saturday from 10:00 A.M. to 5:00 P.M., Sunday from 11:00 A.M. to 5:00 P.M. Closed Monday. Summer hours differ. Phone (312) 294–3000 or (800) 223–7114, or check out www.chicago symphony.org.

A good choice for a convenient lunch spot, comrades, is **Russian Tea Time** at 77 East Adams Street, which serves "classic dishes of the Russian Czarist court and traditional specialties of the former Soviet Union." The restaurant is a short walk to places like Symphony Hall and the Art Institute, but a strategic setting is only one of its pluses. Besides location, location, location, it serves hearty, delicious meals in a woody, intimate atmosphere. Try the chicken breast roulade with oyster mushrooms a la St. Petersburg or the Uzbek vegetarian "layer" stew. Other items include two classics—chicken Kiev and beef Stroganoff—as well as Georgian chicken breast kebab, grilled quail with dried cherries, and chicken croquettes Pozharski. At the front of the menu are detailed instructions on how to drink a shot of vodka "the proper Russian way." (A sampling: "Breathe out loudly, producing a sound just short of a full whistle. . . . Repeat the round in 10–15 minutes. But make sure to desist and retire as soon as your performance becomes blemished in any way.") Open Monday from 11:00 A.M. to 7:00 P.M., Tuesday through Thursday from 11:00 A.M. to 9:00 P.M., Friday and Saturday from 11:00 A.M. to midnight, Sunday from 11:00 A.M. to 9:00 P.M. Phone (312) 360–0000. Moderate.

Besides providing wonderful, fruitful tours of the city—on foot, by bus, and on the river—the **Chicago Architecture Foundation** operates two stores, one in the John Hancock Center on North Michigan, the other in the Loop at 224 South Michigan. The store features an extensive assortment of books on architecture, as well as everything from Frank Lloyd Wright magnets to videos on gargoyles, dinnerware designed by architect Philip Johnson (whose only Chicago building, incidentally, is 190 South LaSalle Street), and designer martini glasses and toothpaste caps. My personal quirky favorite item for Someone Who Has Everything: a *Mouse House* book that contains five cardboard houses (including Chartres Cathedral, the Taj Mahal, and the Parthenon) that you can make and use as a kind of shelter for your computer mouse. The foundation also sponsors free lunchtime lectures Wednesdays from 12:15 to 1:00 P.M. in its lecture hall in the South Michigan Avenue location. Topics range from "Frank Lloyd Wright's Kentuck Knob" to "A New Park on Prairie Avenue: The Hillary Rodham Clinton Park." There are also evening lectures at 6:00 P.M. The store is open Monday through Saturday from 9:00 A.M. to 7:00 P.M., Sunday from 9:30 A.M. to 6:00 P.M. Phone (312) 922–3432, or check out www.architecture.org.

A great spot for travelers in the know is the **Savvy Traveller,** 310 South Michigan, which sells all kinds of books and maps as well as luggage, travel accessories, hats, umbrellas, multipocketed vests, kids' stuff, and even inflatable globes, a personal water filtration system, and aromatherapy travel candles. On Thursdays, starting at 5:30 P.M., the store also hosts an Open Forum, an informal discussion on a specific topic, ranging from riding the train in Europe, to—for those so inclined—traveling with your pet. (Check the Web site at www.thesavvytraveller.com.) Open Monday through Saturday from 10:00 A.M. to 7:30 P.M., Sunday from noon to 5:00 P.M. Phone (312) 913–9800 or (888) 666–6200.

One of Chicago's most intriguing places, the **Fine Arts Building,** at 410 South Michigan, is an unknown quantity to the majority of Chicagoans. Some might have known it for its onetime ground-floor movie theater, the Fine Arts, which showed art films, but it was shuttered a while back. Walk into the building during the day and you're likely to hear gossamer soprano and resonant baritone voices drifting down the halls. The Fine Arts Building is a crazy-quilt home to many voice and instrumental music teachers (who, during the Depression, rumor has it, would supplement their incomes by panhandling in the lobby), as well as an assortment of other tenants. These range from architects to a literary agent and clinical psychologists to a company dedicated to "integrated

Fine Arts Building

body therapy." Businesses include Bein & Fushi, which specializes in rare violins, violas, cellos, and bows, and the Harrington Institute of Design, which spreads over several floors. It is also headquarters for such organizations as the Chicago Music Alliance, the Chicago Youth Symphony Orchestra (described by the *Chicago Tribune* as "one of the best in the nation"), the Jazz Institute of Chicago, and the Hungarian Opera Workshop, as well as nonmusical groups like the Institute of Divine Metaphysical Research and the United Planetary Association. At one point, the building reportedly was owned by Al Capone's former lawyer. During the late 1950s and 1960s, things became pretty run down, and one observer remembered, "The boiler room/basement looked like a museum of old equipment. They actually had an old lawn mower running pumps."

The Fine Arts Building, renovated in the early 1980s, is also fascinating from an architectural point of view. Those entering the front doors walk under lettering that reads ALL PASSES—ART ALONE ENDURES. Originally, the

1885 edifice with the Romanesque facade was built for the assemblage and display of carriages and wagon parts for the Studebaker company of South Bend, Indiana. When Studebaker moved to newer quarters for more space, it was transformed into the Fine Arts Building. It is a place where old-fashioned elevators are manned by real, live operators. The elevators feature glass-and-statuary bronze fronts ornamented with the forms of musical instruments, and on each floor there are lovely wooden clocks and sturdy, venerable wooden benches on which students may sit while waiting for their lessons. On the top floor, the tenth, there are 23-foot ceilings and skylights and (now-fading) murals done by artists who had studios on the floor.

"Every floor is different," says one tenant. "It's like going to a museum. You find little treasures—a painting, a special door." On the fourth floor—alongside the (open-in-warm-weather) fountain-dominated Venetian court, part of a famous tea room that closed in the mid-1950s—is a gallery showcasing Chicago artists. (Open Wednesday through Saturday from noon to 6:00 P.M. Phone 312–913–0537.) On the ninth floor is Performers Music Store, specializing in classic sheet music and books. (Open Monday through Friday from 10:00 A.M. to 7:00 P.M., Saturday from 9:00 A.M. to 5:00 P.M. Phone 312–987–1196.) On the ground floor is the inexpensive *Artists' Restaurant,* which was established in the early 1960s and serves sandwiches/salad fare along with Greek-flavored entrees. Over the years it has billed itself as "a favorite gathering place for many local and international celebrities—from Nureyev and Baryshnikov to Maria Tallchief and Mike Ditka." (Never characterized as an arty type, football's Ditka, you probably know, is the former coach of "Da Bears.") The restaurant is open every day from 7:30 A.M. to 11:00 P.M. Phone (312) 939–7855. The Fine Arts Building itself is open Monday through Friday from 7:00 A.M. to 10:00 P.M., Saturday from 7:00 A.M. to 9:00 P.M., Sunday from 10:00 A.M. to 4:00 P.M. Phone (312) 987–1196.

Now walk south to Congress, and go west (away from the lake) for a block until you get to Wabash Avenue, and take a right. Located in charming, spacious rooms, the *Prairie Avenue Bookshop* at 418 South Wabash has staked out a decided niche—books and publications about architecture. The store contains some 14,000 volumes ranging from *Country Houses of Majorca* to *Progressive Design in the Midwest,* from *Foundation Design* to, if you really want to know, *How to Design a Successful Petrol Station.* There's also an out-of-print section and periodicals from around the world. Open Monday through Friday from 10:00 A.M. to 6:00 P.M., Saturday from 10:00 A.M. to 4:00 P.M. Phone (800) 474–2724 or (312) 922–8311, or visit www.pabook.com.

Smoking may be "out" in many places these days, but it's been decidedly in since 1857 at *Iwan Ries,* 19 South Wabash (second floor), which advertises itself as "the oldest family-owned tobacconists in the country." In addition to the 12,000 pipes and dozens of brands of cigars for sale, there are all kinds of humidors, pipe racks, and lighters, and the store offers pipe repairs, in-store pipe polishing, and samples of its private-label pipe tobacco. Even nonsmokers might enjoy checking out the display of antique pieces, from Chinese "fairy" pipes to European cigar holders to American Indian tobacco pouches. Open Monday through Friday from 9:00 A.M. to 5:30 P.M., Saturday from 9:00 A.M. to 5:00 P.M. Phone (800) 621–1457 or (312) 372–1306, or visit the Web site at www/iwanries.com.

Located in a compact, somewhat spartan but appealing space on the seventh floor of, all things, a Loop office building (111 North Wabash), *Heaven on Seven* restaurant serves up Cajun/Creole cooking at modest prices. Dishes include what founder Jimmy Bannos calls "Jimmy's New Orleans-style food. It's a Creoleization of modern cuisine. Like, instead of just regular chicken, I'll put a crawfish in there, or Alabama rock shrimp." Other dishes include a fine gumbo, a soft-shell po'boy sandwich, pasta shrimp remoulade, Mardi Gras jambalaya, Baton Rouge

We Should Have Looked for Florida

*Jacques Marquette, a French Jesuit explorer and missionary, was Chicago's first known European inhabitant. On December 4, 1674, his expedition reached the Chicago River, which was snow-covered and frozen to a depth of 6 inches. (So what else is new?) Marquette's exploits are vividly depicted in the **Marquette Building** (140 South Dearborn Street), a fine example of Chicago's turn-of-the-twentieth-century "Chicago school" of architecture. Designed by the noted firm of Holabird & Roche and built in 1894, the building represents one of the few remaining examples of an innovative window treatment known as "Chicago windows," which, unlike the narrow windows of the time, were designed horizontally to let the light stream in.*

Of more interest to visitors, though, are the historic panels and mosaics. Bronze panels over the main entrance show the launching of Marquette's canoe, an attack by Indians, the campsite near the Chicago River (now the intersection of Damen Avenue and 26th Street), and the missionary's burial. In the splendid two-story lobby is a series of mosaic panels of the exploration, and, above the elevator doors, are sculptured heads of both expedition members and Native American chiefs of the Mississippi Valley. The building, incidentally, was restored in 1980 by a company owned by John D. MacArthur, and is now owned by the John D. and Catherine T. MacArthur Foundation, sponsors of those so-called genius awards.

omelet, and—if you're ready for this—shrimp cheese grits. On display on wall racks are dozens of hot sauce bottles, with labels like "Fire Eater Cajun Rush," "Arizona Gunslinger," "Tangy Bang," "Jump Up and Kiss Me," and "Bat's Brew." Be forewarned. Open Monday through Friday from 8:30 A.M. to 5:00 P.M., Saturday from 10:30 A.M. to 3:00 P.M., also dinner the first and third Friday of the month, from 5:30 to 9:00 P.M. Cash only. Phone (312) 263–6443. Moderate.

Those in the know who are looking for the *exact* button or bead head for **International Importing Bead and Novelty Company** at 111 North Wabash, on the seventh floor—just down the hall, in fact, from Heaven on Seven. Established in 1918, the company for years operated out of the venerable Stevens Building and moved to its new, nearby location in 1998. The move involved literally millions of items, including buttons from the '30s to the '50s, ribbons, natural pheasant and turkey plumage feathers, bugle beads and seed beads, hat pins, rhinestones, and, of course, beads. Among the store's customers have been famed fan dancer Sally Rand, a woman who glues beads in patterns on the outside of her cars, and a Chicago seamstress who buys rhinestones to make jumpsuits for Elvis impersonators. Open Monday through Friday from 10:00 A.M. to 5:30 P.M., Saturday from 10:00 A.M. to 4:00 P.M. Phone (312) 332–0061.

On State Street, there are a couple of things worth checking out. Among the many establishments in the Chicago Music Mart—"Stores of Note" at State and Jackson Boulevard—is **Carl Fischer Music,** which for years had been located on Wabash. Known throughout the city for its sheet music for instruments and voice, the store carries copies of everything from individual songs like "Winter Wonderland" to scores from *Carousel* and *Jelly's Last Jam*, from collections such as *Polka All-Timers*

Big House on Van Buren

*P*erhaps the most incongruous building in the heart of the Loop is the **Chicago Metropolitan Correctional Center** at 71 West Van Buren Street. Built in 1975 and designed by the prestigious architectural firm of Harry Weese & Associates, the twenty-seven-story triangular building serves as the federal detention center, housing indicted criminals waiting for trial.

The building is distinguished by its long, thin slit windows—reportedly, an escape route for some prisoners before bars were added. Coincidentally, the center is within a tear gas canister's throw from the Chicago Board of Trade—which might have caused its "inmates," especially in the late '80s and '90s, to have second thoughts about insider trading.

to *Motown Guitar Classics*. Other classics get widespread attention, too, including sacred piano music and scores of operas. There are titles like *Blues Piano* and *Jazz Improvisation* and, my personal favorite (as a lapsed piano player), *The Real Little Best Fake Book Ever*. Carl Fischer also sells guitars, harmonicas, and conducting batons. On the concourse level, it's open Monday through Friday from 9:00 A.M. to 5:30 P.M., Saturday from 9:00 A.M. to 5:00 P.M. Phone (312) 427–6652. For those shopping for instruments, check out other stores in the impressive Chicago Music Mart complex such as Abbey Strings ("The Bass Place"), Karnes Music (grand pianos), and The Chicago String Shop. Or just drop in for free "Tunes at Noon" classical and jazz vocal and instrumental concerts on the Mart's concourse level by individuals and groups, including high school bands. For more information, phone (312) 362–6700.

One of the few nonmusical places in the Chicago Music Mart is the **Afrocentric Bookstore** on the ground level. Featured in the store with the African-American focus are not only all kinds of literary offerings under headings like "Women's Studies," "History," and "Inspirational," but also posters (Malcolm X to Billie Holiday) and Kwanzaa items. There's also a sign that pointedly reads, WE ENCOURAGE BROWSING *BUT* DISCOURAGE READING. Open Monday through Friday from 10:00 A.M. to 6:00 P.M., Saturday from 10:00 A.M. to 4:30 P.M. Closed Sunday. Phone (312) 939–1956.

Although not off the beaten path, the **Harold Washington Library Center,** 400 South State, the largest municipal library in the United States and named for Chicago's late (and first African-American) mayor, contains some often overlooked segments. One is the **Thomas Hughes Children's Library** on the second floor. A warm and welcoming space with soft lighting, it is full of attractive table-and-chair settings, brightly colored exhibits, computers and copiers, magazine displays, and, of course, books—more than 125,000 volumes. It is named for a member of the British Parliament and author of *Tom Brown's School Days*. Shocked by the tragedy of the Chicago fire of 1871, Hughes organized a campaign in England to gather donations of books for the city. Almost every living English author made a contribution of his or her own works, and the 8,000 volumes collected were the beginning of the Chicago Public Library. Not surprisingly, the Children's Library houses the largest collection of children's books in the city and serves youngsters from preschoolers to age 14. The 18,000-square-foot area includes NatureConnections, a project that provides books, materials, and programs related to natural history and "connects" the library with events and exhibitions in institutions throughout the area. The Thomas Hughes Library also presents a wide variety of programs each month, including puppet plays and stories, library orientation, musical events, and videos. Open Monday through Thursday from 9:00 A.M. to 7:00 P.M., Friday and Saturday from 9:00 A.M. to 5:00 P.M., Sunday from 1:00 to 5:00 P.M. For program information, phone (312) 747–4647.

While in the library, you might head for the ninth floor and check out the *Beyond Words Cafe,* a lovely place for lunch that calls itself, accurately enough, "one of Chicago's best secrets." To enter the restaurant, walk through the delightfully peaceful Winter Garden, a large public space that rises over 100 feet through the tenth floor to a skylight and that is available for private functions. Operated by George L. Jewell, a highly respected local caterer, the cafe features lovely views (from some tables) and a pleasing menu that may offer a self-described "decadent" buffet, as well as such items as deep-dish quiche and Mandarin chicken salad, and, for dessert, pecan bourbon pie and chocolate toffee mousse. Open Monday through Saturday from 11:00 A.M. to 3:00 P.M. Phone (312) 747–4680. Inexpensive.

One final suggestion: As you leave the library, exit on the Plymouth Court side and take a look, across the way, at the *Old Colony Building* (407 South Dearborn Street). Designed by the ubiquitous Holabird & Roche and completed in 1894, it's the last surviving example of a "Chicago school" skyscraper and features rounded corner bays. Even nonarchitectural buffs will realize what a magnificent, stylish structure it is.

Walk farther west in the Loop, and both north and south, and you'll find other interesting spots. The *Illinois Artisans Shop* is located on the second level off the soaring seventeen-floor atrium of the controversial but decidedly eye-catching Helmut Jahn–designed, salmon-silver-blue-colored James R. Thompson Center, 100 West Randolph Street, formerly known as the State of Illinois Center. (Is it dazzling or just tacky?) The not-for-profit shop sells traditional, contemporary, ethnic, and folk art items created by some of the best artisans from around the state. These include dolls, hand-painted silk, collage cards, carvings, birdhouses, kids' apparel, pottery, toy cars, dinnerware, baskets, picture frames, clocks, and ceramic floral jewelry. Open Monday through Friday from 9:00 A.M. to 5:00 P.M. Closed weekends. Phone (312) 814–5321.

Largely unnoticed by hard-charging pedestrians working their way through one of the busiest intersections in the Loop, *Chicago Temple* (1923), at 77 West Washington Street, is an architectural gem. If you look up after negotiating a favorable angle, you can see that the twenty-one-story office tower is topped by an eight-story spire—the downtown area's only church spire. The building is the home of the

Best Name in the Loop

Stocks & Blondes Bar & Grille

(36 North Wells Street)

First United Methodist Church, which maintains an ornate wood-and-stained-glass sanctuary on the ground floor and a chapel in the spire. Services are held on Wednesday from 12:10 to 12:30 P.M., with Holy Communion Wednesday at 7:30 A.M. The church also presents the William D. White Fine Arts Series, which includes artists and groups, a noontime concert series, puppets, a choir festival, and art displays. For more information, phone (312) 236–4548.

Located next door at 31 North Clark Street is ***Harlan J. Berk, Ltd.***—"The Art and Science of Numismatics"—a rare coins store, although there are other items. For instance, on display a while back were checks signed by Harry Caray, the late, ultra-popular Chicago Cubs announcer, selling for $75 each ("Holy Cow!" as Harry was wont to say), and an autographed portrait of President William Howard Taft. There are also ancient coins, U.S. and world coins, paintings, and books, and thirteen floors above there's a research center that houses a 10,000-volume library and photo file. It's open "to any customer who wishes to pursue private research or to view coins in our buy or bid sales." The store, opened in 1964, is open Monday through Friday from 9:00 A.M. to 4:45 P.M. Closed weekends. Phone (312) 609–0016 or check out www.harlanjberk.com.

Another bookstore with a specialty—a rather unusual one—is the ***Psychology Bookstore*** at 20 South Clark (second floor). Run by the Illinois School of Professional Psychology but open to the public, it contains dozens of books under such headings as "Treating the Self," "Family Issues," "Social and Cultural Issues," "Therapy," "Trauma," and "Dysfunction." Open Monday through Thursday from 10:00 A.M. to 6:00 P.M., Friday and Saturday from 10:00 A.M. to 3:00 P.M. Phone (312) 279–3954.

The historic building ***The Rookery*** (209 South LaSalle Street) got its name from the former building on its site, a temporary city hall (following the 1871 fire) that served as a roosting spot for pigeons—which, as any disgusted pedestrian will tell you, is still the Loop's most prevalent bird. (Stone-carved birds, it should be noted, flank the entrance, and the elevator doors also feature an avian motif.) Designed by Daniel H. Burnham and John W. Root, The Rookery was built from 1885 to 1888 and incorporated such innovations as plate glass and the hydraulic passenger elevator. In 1905 Frank Lloyd Wright was brought in to redesign the ground story of the court. Restored in 1992, the building today is most notable for its striking, light-filled central court, with a skylight above the second story, a walkway around the mezzanine level, and terrific stairways. Commercial tenants around the court wildly range from Brooks Brothers to a delicatessen.

When you take a free tour at the *Federal Reserve Bank of Chicago* (230 South LaSalle), you walk away with a hundred bucks. There's a catch, of course. The bag you're handed as a souvenir contains *shredded* old bills, once worth $100. The shredded stuff not given to visitors ends up in landfills in the suburbs. So said our guide, who filled the hour with lots of facts and figures and a few scattered corny jokes. If you're paying attention, you get to find out how the process works. As of this writing, the visitor center in the lobby was being restructured. (The previous center contained such attractions as exhibits of old bills and counterfeit money.) Tours are available for groups (call in advance) and for individuals Tuesdays at 1:00 P.M. Phone (312) 322–2400. Oh, yes, the most commonly asked question on the tour (besides the location of the rest rooms): Has anyone ever knocked over the Chicago Fed? Answer: No. Not even Al Capone.

PLACES TO STAY IN
THE LOOP

Hotel Allegro Chicago,
171 West Randolph Street;
(800) 643–1500 or
(312) 236–0123.
For years, in the days when Chicago "cuisine" ran the gamut from steak to potatoes, this was the Bismarck Hotel, an old-fashioned, favorite hangout of local pols. For a while the hotel had a dark, secluded lounge—"a perfect place to go if you were having an affair," a friend ventured, "because you'd never run into anyone you knew." These days, don't try it. That lounge is now a bright restaurant with large street-side windows (hard

to hide *here*), and the hotel is now the completely renovated Allegro, a spiffy art deco place located next door to the completely renovated Cadillac Palace Theatre, a "legitimate" house that's replaced the old Palace movie house. The Allegro boasts an appealing lobby, complete with an assortment of modern paintings, 483 dazzling rooms (with fax machine) and 31 suites (with Jacuzzi), and a fitness center. Web site: www.allegrochicago.com.
Expensive.

Hotel Burnham,
1 West Washington Street;
(877) 294–9712 or
(312) 782–1111.
Located near the burgeoning theater district, including the Goodman, this

charming hotel, opened in the fall of 1999, is situated in the historic Reliance Building (1891–1895), which formerly housed doctors' and dentists' offices and rather tacky retail shops. Now wonderfully restored, it contains 122 rooms, including 19 suites, all of which include a multiline speaker phone, data port, and fax machine. The Burnham also advertises itself as being "distinctively pet-friendly," with "pampered pet programs." On the ground floor is the gracious seventy-five-seat Atwood Cafe (presumably named for the building's designer, Charles Atwood), featuring art deco design and contemporary American cuisine. Open for dinner every day from 5:00 to 10:00 P.M., for lunch from 11:30 A.M. to 3:45 P.M., and for Sunday brunch from 8:00 A.M. to 3:00 P.M. Expensive.

Hyatt Regency Chicago,
151 East Wacker Drive;
(312) 565–1234.
With a great location just east of Michigan Avenue and sitting just above the lovely Riverwalk along the Chicago River, the Hyatt is an always-bustling hotel, especially popular with various groups from the well-known International Housewares Show to the, well, lesser known Narcotics Anonymous. The thirty-six-story hotel maintains a whopping 2,019, good-sized rooms, including 175 suites, and is adjacent to the Athletic Club in Illinois Center, which offers exercise facilities and, if you really want to know, rock climbing. The atrium lobby is airy and sprawling, dotted with several bars and restaurants, including the wonderfully named Knuckles Sports Bar. Moderate to expensive.

The Palmer House Hilton,
17 East Monroe Street;
(312) 726–7500.
A Chicago institution, this large hotel has more than 1,550 rooms and suites, at least some of them refreshingly old-fashioned. The public places are classically ornate, especially the lobby. The Palmer House attracts a large number of conventioneers, which means the place often has a frantic feeling. In-house features include an indoor pool, barbershop, sauna and steam room, business services, and three restaurants, including a seems-like-it's-always-been there throwback, Trader Vic's, home of "pleasantly potent cocktails." Expensive.

PLACES TO EAT IN THE LOOP

Artists' Restaurant,
410 South Michigan Avenue;
(312) 987–1196.
See page 13 for full description.

The Berghoff,
17 West Adams Street; (312) 427–3170.
Established in 1898, this Chicago institution draws long lines most of the time. It's known for its simple fare and testy waiters—who really don't appreciate your lingering over the menu. (My wife and I once told a waiter we needed a few minutes, and he returned in about thirty seconds. You *will* order.) The Berghoff serves its own great beer and is one of the few places in the city where you can still get currently nontrendy German dishes such as thueringer, knockwurst, and wiener schnitzel. There's also a long, old-fashioned stand-up bar with steam table sandwiches. Open Monday through Thursday from 11:00 A.M. to 9:00 P.M., Friday from 11:00 A.M. to 9:30 P.M., Saturday from 11:00 A.M. to 10:00 P.M. Moderate.

Beyond Words Cafe,
Harold Washington Library Center,
400 South State Street;
(312) 747–4680.
See page 17 for full description.

Heaven on Seven,
111 North Wabash Avenue;
(312) 263–6443.
See page 14 for full description.

Miller's Pub,
134 South Wabash Avenue;
(312) 263–4988.
Another local favorite—over fifty years old—this sprawling, homey, no-nonsense restaurant is known for its Canadian baby back ribs, along with other standard fare, such as roast prime rib, broiled chicken, and fresh fish of the day. The long, woody bar is a popular spot to wait for a table, and the late hours are also popular. The restaurant is open every day from 11:00 A.M. to 2:00 A.M.; the bar closes an hour later. Moderate.

Russian Tea Time,
77 East Adams Street;
(312) 360–0000.
See page 10 for full
description.

Trattoria No. 10,
10 North Dearborn Street;
(312) 984–1718.
Extremely popular with
locals for business lunches
and romantic dinners, this
below-level restaurant featuring contemporary Ital-
ian cuisine is dark and, for
its size, surprisingly intimate. The excellent menu
includes pasta dishes such
as ravioli with asparagus
tips and linguine with
roasted eggplant, seafood
(grilled mahi-mahi and
Chilean sea bass), veal
scallopini, and breast of
duck. Open for lunch Mon-
day through Friday from
11:30 A.M. to 2:00 P.M., and
dinner Monday through
Thursday from 5:30 to 9:00
P.M., Friday and Saturday
from 5:30 to 10:00 P.M.
Expensive.

Near West Side and Pilsen

The Near West Side, which encompasses the area just west of the Loop and the Chicago River, forms a colorful mix of ethnic cultures, serving as an excellent touring base for three vibrant communities: Greektown and Little Italy, along with adjacent Pilsen (a Mexican neighborhood officially a part of the Lower West Side).

The Near West has the dubious distinction of being the place where the Great Fire of 1871 originated. For more than a century, it also served as the entry place for immigrants. As the area developed in the 1840s as a manufacturing center—lumberyards, foundries, flour mills—Irish workers moved into wooden cottages along the Chicago River, and were later joined by those from Germany and the Scandinavian countries. The first Greeks also came over in the 1840s, starting out as food peddlers and eventually becoming restaurant owners. Around 1900 they concentrated around the Harrison Street/Halsted Street area, originally known as "the Delta" but later renamed "Greektown." After the fire, newcomers from southern and eastern Europe arrived, and the intersection of Halsted and Maxwell became the center of the Jewish business community—a legendary area known simply as Maxwell Street. As the Near West Side became more crowded and impoverished, the area in the 1880s attracted social worker Jane Addams, whose settlement house served as a refuge for residents of the neighboring slums. After 1900 the Jews began to move out, replaced by blacks and Mexicans. In the first three decades of the twentieth century, Taylor Street was the magnet for tens of thousands of Italian immigrants.

The year 1941 saw the establishment of the Medical Center District, which included Cook County Hospital, Presbyterian–St. Luke's (now Rush–Presbyterian) Hospital, and the Research Hospital and Medical School of the University of Illinois. Madison Street west of Halsted was known as Skid Row. But Madison in recent years has experienced a startling gentrification, as has the sprawling Medical Center area along with the Randolph Street Market area (metamorphosing from meat and produce wholesalers to tony restaurants, residential/business lofts, and art galleries).

Near West Side and Pilsen

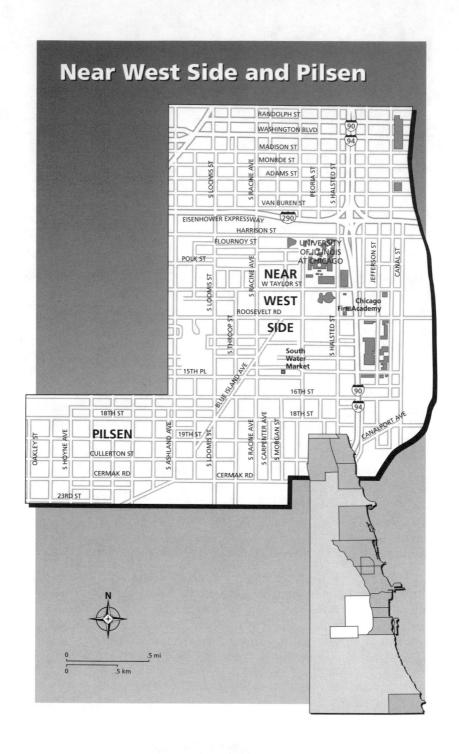

NEAR WEST SIDE AND PILSEN

Top Attractions on the
Near West Side and in Pilsen

Museum of Holography
Jane Addams Hull-House
Museum
Chicago Fire Academy
Mexican Fine Arts Center
Museum

In the 1950s the Greek settlement was largely knocked out by devastating urban renewal projects, such as construction of the Eisenhower, Northwest (later renamed the Kennedy), and Dan Ryan expressways, then got blasted again in the early 1960s with the controversial building of the University of Illinois at Chicago campus in the Halsted–Harrison area. Much of the Italian district was also demolished. Today, the Greek community largely exists in what remains of Greektown: basically, a collection of restaurants in a strip along Halsted. Though greatly diminished, Taylor Street–centered Little Italy is a charming area of houses and cul-de-sacs. Unfortunately, it's all becoming overwhelmed by condo clusters with names like "University Village."

Roughly bounded by Morgan Street on the east, 16th Street on the north, Oakley Avenue on the west, and 23rd Street on the south, the Pilsen community has a core of attractions centering around 18th Street and Ashland Avenue. Because of the influence of Czech immigrants around 22nd Street, Pilsen was named for the city in their native Bohemia. In the early 1950s Mexicans and Puerto Ricans began moving in as the city's demographic flux continued. These days, Pilsen is a poor but proud neighborhood that is desperately striving to upgrade. Still, a visitor may sense that there's a crackling energy in the air, as well as sharp visual stimuli, such as the occasional brightly painted buildings on 18th and the residential side streets that shockingly stand out from the otherwise drab surroundings. (A caveat: Although my wife, who has worked with Habitat for Humanity in Pilsen, and I have never had a problem in that neighborhood, "Pilsen can be tough," says a community activist. "But at least the chance of someone stealing something when your back is turned is far greater than your being personally assaulted.")

Attractions on the Near West Side are widely scattered and require strategic public transportation planning—or a cab. For those just west of the Loop—such as the Bat Column, Old St. Pat's, and Lou Mitchell's restaurant—walking is sufficient. Those heading for Greektown restaurants may take the #20 bus going west along Madison Avenue to Halsted Street (then walk 2 or 3 blocks south), or the #126 bus (board at State and Adams Streets) going west on Jackson to Van Buren Street (then walk a block north). For Little Italy, you can take the #37 bus that curves around out of the Loop and winds up heading west on Taylor Street, but it's tricky figuring out the route. Anyway, cab fare isn't that much. The best way to get to Pilsen is by taxi or car, although a faster approach is to take the 54th/Cermak Blue Line in the Loop to 18th Street and Ashland Avenue, where the station is painted with wonderful Mexican art.

Here's a possible place to start a Near West excursion: just west of the Metra train station on Madison Street. Standing brazenly in front of the institutionally bland architecture of the Harold Washington Social Security Center (600 West Madison), where aging citizens step up to the plate, is Claes Oldenburg's 100-foot-tall *Bat Column* (1976), one of the city's numerous and distinctive public sculptures. Originally, the whimsical Oldenburg—whose gigantic sculptures include an ashtray and a clothespin—looked for "a kind of icon from daily life," and considered an inverted fireplug and then a huge spoon, but, inspired by a tall, ground-level chimney nearby, finally settled on a baseball bat. The 20-ton bat, made of Cor-Ten steel, features a diamond-patterned surface pocked with hundreds of holes and, hey, no cracks about Chicago Cubs hitters.

Walk a little west and north and you'll come to *St. Patrick's Roman Catholic Church,* fondly dubbed "Old St. Pat's," Chicago's oldest church and one of the few buildings to survive the Great Fire. Built from 1852 to 1856, it features a simple facade of limestone and brick. Its onion dome symbolizes the Church in the East and its spire the Church in the West. The interior has been agreeably modernized, from its pews to its vaulted ceiling. Located at 140 South Desplaines Street, the church is known throughout the city for its various social and volunteering events. For a listing of events, check the FUNN Committee Web site at http://members.uss.net/jk-zentano.

Farther out—you can walk north to Madison, take the #20 bus west, then walk north to Washington Boulevard—there's *The Museum of Holography,* at 1134 West Washington, a short distance from Harpo Studios, Oprah Winfrey's television and film production center and home of her talk show. (Trivia alert: "Harpo" spelled backwards is you-know-what.) Right off, you get a personal lesson in how to look at a hologram ("Stand back 3 or 4 feet . . ."), then a description of a hologram: "a recording on a light-sensitive medium of the light waves that reflect from an object illuminated with laser light, forming in complete and full dimension an image of that original object." Whether you quite understand that or not, it doesn't matter. Just walk around and marvel at the exceptionally impressive three-dimensional images— some of them rotating—created by lasers. Subjects range from cats and dogs to a cello, a golf ball, a tarantula, a Buddha, the head of Medusa, Albert Einstein, and hometown favorite Michael Jordan. At one point, a young woman is transformed into a skeleton. At another, planets seem to be hanging out in the middle of the room. (Cleverest touch of all: The donation box itself is a hologram.) One of the three rooms is devoted to holograms created by physicians as diagnostic and teaching tools. Thus, there are such daunting titles as "Retinal Angiograms" and "Lumbar Spine with Severe Scoliosis." However lofty its reach and however dauntingly scientific the brochure that explains everything you wanted to know about "holographic achievements," the museum is not above crass

St. Patrick's Roman Catholic Church

Second City "Firsts"

*C*hicago has been the site of the first steel-frame skyscraper, railroad sleeping car, grain reaper, cafeteria, coeducational public high school, winding watch, Shrimp de Jonghe, and Butterfinger candy bar. It also boasts one of the world's last free major zoos (in Lincoln Park) and the only river in the world that runs backwards—the Chicago River, reversed in 1900 by engineers for sanitary purposes.

commercialism. Among the items for sale are hologram bookmarks, hologram key chains, and hologram earrings. Open Wednesday through Sunday, 12:30 to 5:00 P.M. Admission. Phone (312) 226–1007.

Next, you can walk back to Madison and take the #20 bus east to Halsted, then walk 2 blocks to the assortment of Greektown restaurants. Named for the beautiful, favorite winged mount of Apollo and the Muses, *Pegasus,* at 130 South Halsted, is a delight year-round, but especially in the warmer weather (basically, it is hoped, May through September), when the restaurant opens its rooftop garden—affording some of the best, and often overlooked, views of the city. The roof menu offers drinks, appetizers like char-broiled lamb riblets, baby octopus, and garlicky eggplant spread, and desserts such as galactoboureko, a lemon custard in phyllo dough with light honey syrup (and, according to the house linguists, "the longest Greek word"). Items downstairs in the dining room include the usual Greek standards, but there are also Greek pastas (some with lamb, others with shrimp); pork tenderloin, chicken breast, and swordfish kebabs; char-grilled veal chops; and pan-fried smelts (a Chicago favorite). Family-style dinners are also available. The decor is relaxingly charming, with white-and-pastel murals of Grecian seaside villages. Pegasus is especially popular with Greektown and Loop office workers noontime on

Opaaa!

*A*ccording to local historians, in 1968 gyros and saganaki (flaming cheese) were introduced for the first time in the United States by Chicago's Greektown restaurants. When they are served at the table, the custom has been for the diners to enthusiastically exclaim, "Opaaa!" While this is optional, those who decline may be immediately labeled bad sports.

weekdays. Some Greektown restaurants encourage "Opaaa!"-shouting audience participation when flaming dishes are brought forth, but at Pegasus, happily, there seems to be little (sorry about this) *horsing* around. Open Monday through Thursday from 11:00 A.M. to midnight, Friday and Saturday from 11:00 A.M. to 1:00 A.M., Sunday from noon to midnight. Phone (312) 226–4972. Moderate.

You want candles? Boy, does the **Athenian Candle Company** (300 South Halsted) have candles: candles with saints on them, candles with serpents, candles with cats, candles with Native American heads, candles with the zodiac signs, candles with the devil, votive candles, beeswax candles, floating candles, three-wick candles, and fifty-hour candles. But that's not all. This packed store sells everything from incense to greeting cards, prayer cards, religious paintings, guardian angel magnets, Buddhas, Miraculous Crying icon key chains, bath salts, floor wash, crucifixes, and signs that read PARKING FOR GREEKS ONLY. ALL OTHERS WILL BE TOWED. Actually, says the owner, the biggest sellers are the religious icons, along with items for baptismal and wedding gifts. Open from 9:30 A.M. to 6:00 P.M. Monday through Friday (closed Wednesday), 9:30 A.M. to 5:00 P.M. Saturday. Phone (312) 332–6988.

It was known as the Near West Side's "cathedral of compassion," which one historical observer has described as "more than a reform outpost in the slums. It helped lead a cultural renaissance in Chicago." During

Wanna Buy Back Your Hubcap?

*S**tarting around the turn of the twentieth century, the legendary* **Maxwell Street Market***—evoking Old World flea markets—was the place to go on Sunday morning/early afternoon. Merchants (many of them Jewish immigrants, and later Hispanics) offered fruits and vegetables and anything and everything, new and used, from their pushcarts and street stands. Musicians, especially practitioners of the blues—Muddy Waters and Little Walter reportedly played on Maxwell—and quick-sketch artists were also heavily on the scene, peddling their wares. "If you recently 'lost' a hubcap," someone once cracked, "you may just 'find' it here." Maxwell Street was eviscerated in 1994 for still more development by the University of Illinois at Chicago, and many vendors scrawled MOVED TO . . . signs on their space, but there still is a skeletal scene. The New Maxwell Street Market is open year-round Sunday from 7:00 A.M. to 3:00 P.M. on Canal Street between Taylor and 16th Streets. On a fine summer day, it attracts up to 20,000 people. Phone (312) 922-3100.*

the fifteen-minute slide show at the *Jane Addams Hull-House Museum,* located at 800 South Halsted on the University of Illinois at Chicago (UIC) campus, one learns that Hull-House was the first social settlement house in Chicago (the teeming, multicultural Near West Side neighborhood was crammed with factories and tenement houses), that it established the city's first playground and gymnasium for the public, and that a neighborhood resident named Benny Goodman, son of a Jewish stockyards worker, studied the clarinet there and played in the marching band. (Nit-picking note: One thing never explained is why there's a hyphen between *Hull* and *House.*)

The museum—overwhelmed by the hulking modern buildings on the campus—is one of two surviving structures from the original thirteen-building Hull-House complex, along with the Residents' Dining Hall (1905), currently closed for renovation. The other eleven were torn down in 1963 to make way for UIC, which, ironically, preserves and operates the museum. Located in the Hull Mansion, built in 1856 by the Charles J. Hull family, and occupied in 1889 by social welfare pioneer Addams and college friend Ellen Gates Starr (Addams's career choice was inspired by a visit to a social settlement house in London), the museum consists of several preserved rooms filled with venerable furniture and furnishings, including bookcases and lamps and a wonderful Oliver "visible writer" (i.e., typewriter). There is also a scale model of the Hull-House complex from 1908 to 1963 and dozens of old photographs, newspaper clippings, and copies of such documents as an 1894 "Special Investigation of the Slums of Great Cities," prepared by a special federal agent who resided at Hull-House. Among the items is an advertisement for the resident Coffee House ("Orders taken and dinners outside at schools, factories, etc."), exhibits of the Hull-House Bookbindery and open-to-the-public classes like manual education and art education, and notices of various lectures such as architects Louis Sullivan on "Arts and Crafts in Commercial Architecture" and Frank Lloyd Wright on "Art and the Machine."

Frankly, it is all rather overwhelming, but the slide presentation is illuminating, as it reveals that more than nineteen nationalities lived within blocks of Hull-House, that more than 9,000 people a week used the facilities, and that the tireless Addams (who was awarded the Nobel Peace Prize in 1931 and died four years later) crusaded for such causes as child labor laws, compulsory education, and women's suffrage—and drew flack for being a pacifist during World War I. Open from 10:00 A.M. to 4:00 P.M. Monday through Saturday, noon to 5:00 P.M. Sunday. Special programs on Hull-House and neighborhood history are available to groups making advance reservations. Admission is free (donations are welcomed), and the museum sells such items as Hull-House T-shirts, magnets, and coffee mugs. Phone (312) 413–5353.

Before heading for Little Italy, there are a couple of side diversions. Walk south a block on Halsted to Taylor Street, then east 2 blocks to Jefferson Street, and turn south to DeKoven Street. The **Chicago Fire Academy** (558 West DeKoven at Jefferson), not so coincidentally, sits on the site of the Patrick O'Leary barn, where, on October 8, 1871, a cow reportedly kicked over a lantern at 8:40 P.M., triggering the Great Fire. The spot is marked outside by *Pillar of Fire,* Egon Weiner's sculpture in the shape of

Chicago Fire Academy

a flame. Inside the academy—where future firefighters take such classes as "Firefighting Tactics" and "Fire Causes and Arson Investigation"—there's a model of a 1900 firehouse (the original was made from over 4,000 hand-cast, terra-cotta bricks), a vintage fire pumper, old boots and helmets, a plaque honoring African-American firefighters, and a memorial to the city's fallen firefighters. There's also a pictorial exhibit of Chicago Fire Department history that includes the volunteer fire department in 1835, the paid department's "Long John" steam fire engine in 1858, the 1903 Iroquois Theater Fire (in which 600 died), and the 1910 Stockyards fire (which killed twenty-three firemen). Open Monday through Friday from 8:00 A.M. to 4:00 P.M. Closed holidays. Phone (312) 747–7238.

Need a food break? Walk a block south. A highly diverse mix of customers lines up at **Manny's Coffee Shop** (1141 South Jefferson Street) starting at 5:00 A.M. every day except Sunday. It's an incredibly old-fashioned deli—one of the few in Chicago that hasn't gone blandly upscale, as you can instantly tell from the dismal decor. Even the fading printing over the cafeterialike steam table looks old and worn, but the food keeps them coming back. Granted, it's not exactly heart-healthy (you wouldn't line up at Manny's if you cared): corned beef, pastrami, beef stew, liver and onions, ox tail stew, short ribs. One Saturday morning a short, heavy-set man with a cigar about a foot long lined up to pay his bill on the way out. "Good morning, Judge," said the cashier, who later explained that this magistrate and other political types grew up in this working-class neighborhood, moved to the ritzy suburbs, but still come back regularly for a touch of Manny's food (and, presumably, a reality check). Open Monday through Saturday from 5:00 A.M. to 4:00 P.M. Phone (312) 939–2855. Inexpensive.

Chicago's Own . . . Well, Maybe Not

*O*n the north side of the street, about 1400 West Taylor—directly across from the impending National Italian-American Sports Hall of Fame (it's slated to open late in 2002)—is **Plaza DiMaggio**, dominated by a statue of "Joltin' Joe," the late, graceful New York Yankees star/Mr. Coffee spokesman. "No son of an Italian immigrant lived a greater American dream than Joe DiMaggio, flawless ballplayer, true gentleman, and heroic Italian-American," reads the plaque, which fails to point out that DiMaggio grew up in San Francisco, and, as a recent biography reveals, wasn't exactly flawless and heroic in his off-the-field persona.

Now it's out to Little Italy. Either prepare for an ambitious walk or go back to Taylor Street and take the #37 bus west on Taylor, then get off at Morgan Street. Hard by the futuristically sterile University of Illinois at Chicago (UIC) campus, with its vertical architectural style that might be described as Buck Rogers Stonehenge, *Tuscany* (1014 West Taylor) is a visual treat. The easternmost restaurant on Taylor, it has a charming, copper pots/dried flowers kind of decor, along with a fine Northern Italian menu. Try the ravioli stuffed with asparagus and cheese, or perhaps the fettucine with mixed grill, sautéed veal medallions, sautéed salmon, grilled bass, grilled veal chops, or the several varieties of pizza. There's also an extensive wine list. Opened in 1990, it's one of four Tuscany establishments (the others are on North Clark Street and in the suburbs), and it attracts a lively (sometimes rather noisy) lunch and dinner crowd. (The big talkers may be either local politicians or faculty members from UIC.) Open Monday through Thursday from 11:00 A.M. to 11:00 P.M., Friday from 11:00 A.M. to midnight, Saturday from 5:00 P.M. to midnight, Sunday from 4:00 to 9:30 P.M. Phone (312) 829–1990. Moderate.

There's another choice. When Frank Sinatra was in town, so the rumor went, he would stop in at *Tufano's Vernon Park Tap* (1073 West Vernon Park Place), and chow down in a private second-floor dining room. Not quite true, a waiter says today: "It actually wasn't a private room. The owner just locked the door." Those days, of course, are gone, but if Ol' Blue Eyes is no longer around, Ol' Red Sauce remains. The plain, Southern Italian cooking is still a big draw at the restaurant, located in a nondescript building and so tucked away on a side street, it's hard to find for even longtime Chicagoans. It doesn't help that there isn't any signage to identify the place, other than on the valet parking sign, because, as a staffer simply says, "We've never needed it." (Unless you have a neighborhood parking permit, forget parking in the area yourself.) The food is abundant and good: lemon chicken, pork chops with peppers, veal marsala, lasagna ("Grandma's favorite four-layer, meatless recipe"), pasta shells and broccoli, sausage and peppers, and tripe ("sautéed in Grandma's best marinara"), and desserts such as cannoli, tiramisu, and raspberry tartufo. There's a throwback feeling about the family-owned place, which has been around over seventy years—such as the conversation at the bar one afternoon as one customer was talking about "broads" and saying to a buddy, "How long was I married? Technically, in my eyes, *never*. But *she* thought so." Open Tuesday through Thursday from 11:00 A.M. to 10:00 P.M., Friday from 11:00 A.M. to 11:00 P.M., Saturday from 4:00 to 11:00 P.M., Sunday from 3:00 to 9:00 P.M. Phone (312) 733–3393. Moderate. Cash only.

For even less expensive fare, cut back to Taylor. With its bold name, no-frills *Al's #1 Italian Beef* (1079 West Taylor Street) delivers the goods, drawing a steady influx of satisfied customers who hungrily devour the beef, Italian sausage, Polish sausage, and fries. On the walls are photos of the owners and various celebrities, including Muhammad Ali, baseball's Tommy Lasorda, Frankie Avalon, and Mayor Richard M. Daley. Open every day from 9:00 A.M. to 1:00 A.M. Phone (312) 226–4017. Inexpensive.

A block south—it's hard to miss—you'll find *St. Ignatius College Prep* (1076 West Roosevelt Road), not only home to a diverse city/suburban student body of students with some of the highest SAT scores in the area but also an architectural treasure. Designated a Chicago landmark by the Chicago Commission on Landmarks in 1987, it also has earned the National Honor Award from the National Trust for Historic Preservation for the quality of its ongoing restoration. Dedicated in 1870, the Jesuit institution was designed by Toussaint Menard, who used a Second Empire style with a combination of Italianate, Gothic, and Georgian detail. It is among the oldest buildings in Chicago, being one of only a few nonresidential structures to survive the 1871 fire.

With the facilities severely neglected in the mid-twentieth century, there were discussions whether to raze the building, fix it up, or build a new school. (At one point, there even was serious talk about closing it and joining the institutional exodus to the suburbs.) In 1981 the decision was made under then-president Donald F. Rowe, S.J., an architectural historian, to restore the building to its original style. Among the highlights are massive wooden doors leading into the vestibule and decorated with carved lions' heads; the Cuneo Chapel of the Jesuit Martyrs of North America, with its original cove ceiling and decorative stenciling; the Grand Gallery and student library (located in a space

Are There Stars Out Tonight?

*P*art of the original plans for what is now St. Ignatius College Prep called for a telescope to be installed in an observatory on the roof. However, by the time the building was completed in 1870, the surrounding area had become so densely populated and housed so much industry, that the increased level of pollution made the night sky a blur. The idea of the observatory was consequently scrapped. Not surprisingly, there has been no movement to bring it back.

that over the years was used as an auditorium and gymnasium and that housed World War I soldiers during their six-week training); and, particularly, the Brunswick Room, with its hand-carved oak panels, curved butternut wood staircase, and two-story bookcase units patterned after the great carved libraries of European monasteries. Formerly a natural history museum, the room now serves as a meeting and reception place, and has been described as "the most magnificent room in the school building." In recent years, new buildings have joined the old, including the Center for the Performing Arts and Sciences, new laboratories, and science classrooms. Originally an all-boys' school, St. Ignatius started admitting girls in 1979. Numerous quotes, incidentally, are enshrined above the school's doors, including words over a third-floor elevator from, appropriately, an architect. "The doctor can bury his mistakes," said Frank Lloyd Wright, "but an architect can only advise his client to plant vines." Tours are available by calling (312) 421–5900.

Right next door to the west of the school is **Holy Family Church** (1080 Roosevelt), also one of the few nonresidential buildings to survive the fire. Organized in 1857 by the Reverend Arnold J. Damen, a Jesuit priest, it quickly became known, in the words of historian James W. Sanders, as "the single great Irish workingman's parish." (Trivia alert: One site previously rejected was known as the Bull's Head property, named after a tavern.) The firm of Dillenburg & Zucher drew up plans for the church, and Chicago architect John Van Osdel designed the interior. When it was dedicated on August 26, 1860, it was reportedly the third largest church in the country. A *Chicago Tribune* story about the dedication noted that the exterior "from most points is huge and unattractive, and the structure looms above the humble erections in that suburb [*sic*] like a stately ox among so many sheep, but the front of the church is massive and handsome, in Milwaukee brick, with cut stone trimmings." Following concerted fund-raising efforts, restoration on the German Gothic structure has been going on since 1991. The church is open only Sunday for the 9:45 A.M. Mass. For tours at other times (groups only, please), phone (312) 226–4426.

Back to Taylor, where food, it should be evident, is king. You might try Francesca on Taylor (see "Places to Eat"), or go farther west to **Pompeii** (1531 West Taylor Street), which started out in 1909 strictly as a bakery and continues to sell all kinds of breads. For those not in the know, a sign over the counter explains: THE WAY ITALIANS USE A LOAF OF BREAD . . . FIRST DAY, "WITH PASTA"; SECOND DAY, "AS TOAST"; THIRD DAY, "MAKE MEAT BALLS." Most of Pompeii's business these days comes from its restaurant. People from the close by University of Illinois at Chicago Medical Center and other patrons—dressed in everything from suits to sweatshirts—cheerfully line up and place their orders for the tasty food at modest prices: pizza, Italian sandwiches (including Mama Marie's homemade meatballs), handmade ravioli, handcut pasta (try the spaghetti with portabella mushrooms), and desserts like Italian chocolate sheet cake and Taylor Street cheesecake. The place is lively, the service efficient, and the decor amusingly kitschy (fake "classical" columns, etc.). The establishment, by the way, was so named because it was located near Our Lady of Pompeii Church, and, as its menu notes, Pompeii has been serving families for three generations. Open Monday through Saturday from 10:30 A.M. to 10:00 P.M., Sunday from 11:00 A.M. to 9:00 P.M. Phone (312) 421–5179. Inexpensive.

Moving on to Pilsen, walk a couple blocks east of Ashland Avenue on 18th Street to locate *Cafe Jumping Bean* (1439 West 18th Street), a funky place in a funky building. One of those compact, friendly, laid-back, '60s-type coffeehouses, it features ceiling fans and artwork on the walls that is "interesting," as they say, along with tables with color-fully painted tops. Coffee specialties include something called Screaming Bean and, appropriately enough, Chocolate Mexico and Café Olé. The food lineup veers from bagels and scones to hot focaccia sandwiches, garden burgers, salads, and soups. And there's a *really* funky unisex washroom/storage closet. Open Monday through Friday from 7:00 A.M. to 10:00 P.M., Saturday from 8:00 A.M. to 8:00 P.M., Sunday from 10:00 A.M. to 6:00 P.M. Phone (312) 455–0019. Inexpensive.

A little west are two Mexican restaurants right across the street from

Best Place to Pig Out

*W*ant some chicken? Sorry, you're out of luck. Maybe beef? Not a chance. Nada. Actually, at **Carnitas Uruapan** (1725 West 18th Street) the only thing available to eat in or take out is pork. Take it or leave it. And delicious it is. The small space in this Pilsen restaurant is quite stark, with the decor, such as it is, consisting of cartoon drawings of—what else?—pigs. Some are mouthing things like, "Oh, Dios!" and "Ay, Mama!" as a butcher pursues them with a large knife. A sign on the wall translates as THERE IS NO LOVE MORE PURE AND SINCERE AS THAT OF A BUTCHER. As for the name of the place: Carnitas *means* pork, and Uruapan is the second largest city in Michoacán, the proprietors' home state in Mexico. Open Monday through Friday from 8:00 A.M. to 6:00 P.M., Saturday and Sunday from 7:00 A.M. to 6:00 P.M. Phone (312) 226–2654. Inexpensive.

each other. The ambience obviously isn't the drawing card at **Playa Azul,** a seafood restaurant at 1514 18th Street. The no-frills, peeling kind of decor consists of utilitarian tables, a representation of a mermaid, and the obligatory fishnets on the ceiling, seemingly put there as an afterthought. Several colorful murals, though, do give the place a touch of splash. Those who come for the seafood won't be disappointed. Try the crab soup (with generous hunks of crab), or choose from other items that include pulpo ranchero (octopus seasoned with hot peppers, tomato sauce, onions, and cilantro), seafood medley with rice, grilled red snapper, and grilled lobster in garlic sauce. Playa Azul affords a good chance for gringos to brush up on their Spanish, since a minimum of English is spoken. (Trying to find out the hours by phone was like a Marx Brothers routine.) Open Monday through Thursday from 8:00 A.M. to midnight, Friday through Sunday from 8:00 A.M. to 2:00 A.M. Phone (312) 421–2552. Inexpensive.

Established in 1962, family-owned **Restaurante Nuevo León** (1515 West 18th Street) consists of two contradictory main rooms—one plain and utilitarian with little charm, the other bright and appealing. Whichever you choose (the answer seems to be obvious, unless you have some kind of perverse aversion to cheerful surroundings), the food is abundant and tasty. There is whole red snapper, broiled catfish, grilled shrimp, pork stew, beef tongue, chicken in mole sauce, and menudo (tripe soup), along with Mexican standbys from tacos to flautas. Steadfastly popular with locals, it is the kind of no-nonsense place where decaffeinated coffee costs extra. Be sure to check out the perkily painted exterior. Open very long hours: Sunday through Thursday from 7:00 A.M. to midnight, Friday from 7:00 A.M. to 4:00 A.M., Saturday from 7:00 A.M. to 5:00 A.M. Phone (312) 421–1517. Cash only. Inexpensive.

Walk into **Artesanias D' Mexico** (1644 18th Street), and you'll be cheered up even on a depressingly gray day. Owner Efrain Loza makes trips to Mexico four times a year, dealing directly with local artists. Selling wholesale and retail Mexican items in his crammed quarters, Loza offers fountains, baskets, religious icons, toys, masks, mirrors, lamps, and chess sets—all of varying quality. There are also *historias,* or stories, painted on *papel amate* (made in the state of Guerrero from the bark of the amate tree), and the most popular seller, black clay pottery from Oaxaca. Open Monday through Saturday from 10:00 A.M. to 7:00 P.M., Sunday from 10:00 A.M. to 3:00 P.M. Phone (312) 563–9779.

A couple blocks west of Ashland and 1 block south of 18th you'll find the **Mexican Fine Arts Center Museum** (MFACM) at 1852 West 19th Street in Harrison Park, which opened in 1987 and houses over 1,500 works in its permanent collection. Among the artists are Mexican masters, such as Diego Rivera, José Orozco, David Siqueiros, and Ruffino Tamayo, and contemporary work by U.S.–Mexican artists, including Carmen Lomas Garza and Alejandro Romero. Not only is it the largest Mexican or Latino arts institution in the country, but it was the first and only to be accredited by the American Association of Museums and is a sister museum of the Museo del Templo Mayor (the Aztec Main Temple Museum) in Mexico City. The MFACM recently underwent a $7 million expansion project that tripled the size of the museum. Added facilities include more exhibition galleries, class rooms, and an improved performing arts space.

The museum has the largest collection outside Mexico of prints by Leopoldo Méndez, one of his country's finest printmakers. Also featured are special exhibits such as "Multiplicity," a superb collection of prints in four categories: lithography, serigraphy, relief, and intaglio. One noted annual exhibition in the fall focuses on the Dia de Muertos (Day of the Dead), the largest of its kind in the country. Other exhibitions include works of young and emerging artists and those of participants in the art classes, which involve children, families, and seniors. In addition, ten of the MFACM exhibitions have traveled to other museums around the United States, and four have been sent to Mexico. Exhibits have included such subjects as ancient Mexico, twenty U.S.-Mexican artists, and the first international retrospective of twentieth-century painter María Izquierdo. The museum also presents two annual performing arts festivals that were inaugurated in 1994. One, held in the spring, is the Del Corazón Performing Arts Festival, celebrating the artistry and diversity within the Mexican culture in both Mexico and the United States. The other, in autumn, is the Sor Juana Festival, paying tribute to the artistic achievements of Mexican women both in and outside Mexico. Participants in the festivals have included Octavio Paz, Carlos Fuentes, Ana Castillo, and—if you're ready for this—Dr. Loco's Rockin' Jalapeño Band.

There's also Tienda Tzintzuntzan, a fine gift shop offering traditional items from such regions as Michoacán, Guanajuato, Guerrero, and Oaxaca. Among them are kites, pottery, jewelry, masks, toys, mirrors, books (including children's), textiles, and, perhaps best of all, Day of the Dead T-shirts, mugs, and postcards. Open Tuesday through Sunday from 10:00 A.M. to 5:00 P.M. Closed Monday and major holidays. Admission is free, and free guided tours are available in English and Spanish. For general information, call (312) 738–1503.

**Holiday Inn Hotel
& Suites,**
506 West Harrison Street;
(312) 957–9100.
A late addition to the
Chicago scene, this establishment is located on the
Near West Side, relatively
close to the Loop. There are
145 rooms, including 27
suites, with data ports and
dryers, along with a fitness
center, business center,
rooftop pool, and restau-
rant/cocktail lounge.
Moderate.

**Quality Inn—Downtown
Chicago,**
Madison and Halsted
Streets;
(312) 829–5000.
Conveniently located near
Greektown, the University
of Illinois Chicago campus,
and the western part of the
Loop, Quality Inn offers
the usual standard chain-
motel rooms (406), some
with excellent views of the
city and all with balconies.
There are also a full-
service restaurant and
Matches Sports Bar & Grill,
and—a real plus—ample
parking. Inexpensive.

Al's #1 Italian Beef,
1079 West Taylor Street;
(312) 226–4017.
See page 34 for full
description.

Cafe Jumping Bean,
1439 West 18th Street;
(312) 455–0019.
See page 36 for full
description.

Carnitas Uruapan,
1725 West 18th Street;
(312) 226–2654.
See page 36 for full
description.

Francesca's on Taylor,
1400 West Taylor Street;
(312) 829–2828.
Heading out on Taylor west
of Racine Avenue, coming
across several blocks of
mostly boarded-up public
housing units (a sitting
duck for gentrification),
one is tempted to pack it
in. But suddenly, just east
of Loomis Street, the area
starts looking respectful
again, and Francesca's is a
big reason. The excellent
Italian restaurant serves
entrees from linguine in a
spicy marinara with
scampi, scallops, clams,
mussels, and calamari to
spinach-filled pasta in a
four-cheese sauce; roasted

mahi-mahi with red and
yellow peppers, pine nuts,
and green onions; sautéed
chicken breast topped with
mozzarella and prosciutto;
roasted pork chops; and
various kinds of thin-
crusted pizza. A handsome
dark-wood atmosphere
adds to the dining plea-
sure. Open for lunch Mon-
day through Friday from
11:30 A.M. to 2:00 P.M., dinner Sunday and Monday
from 5:00 to 9:00 P.M.,
Tuesday through Thursday
from 5:00 to 10:00 P.M., and
Friday and Saturday from
5:00 to 11:00 P.M.
Moderate.

Lou Mitchell's,
565 West Jackson
Boulevard;
(312) 939–3111.
A favorite of business
types during the week and
other locals on weekends,
this family-owned restau-
rant—a block west of
Union Station—has been
in the same place since
1923. Although open for
lunch, it is especially
known for its breakfasts—
fresh orange and grape-
fruit juice, waffles,
pancakes, French toast,
and, particularly, its "dou-
ble-yolk" eggs. For those
who want them, stewed
prunes are complimentary,
as are little packs of Milk
Duds (for some reason,
offered to women and children only). It's a belt-
buster kind of place,

specializing in its own baked goods: cakes, pies, apple fritters, pecan rolls, and "Uncle Lou's famous cookies." The staff is friendly, efficient, and direct. After my wife said she didn't want the smoking section, the hostess asked her, "So where did you get that [deep] voice?" Open Monday through Saturday from 5:30 A.M. to 3:00 P.M., Sunday from 7:00 A.M. to 3:00 P.M. Cash only. Inexpensive

Manny's Coffee Shop,
1141 South Jefferson Street; (312) 939–2855. See page 32 for full description.

Pegasus,
130 South Halsted Street; (312) 226–3377. See page 28 for full description.

Playa Azul,
1514 West 18th Street; (312) 421–2552. See page 37 for full description.

Pompeii,
1531 West Taylor Street; (312) 421–5179. See page 35 for full description.

Restaurante Nuevo León,
1515 West 18th Street; (312) 421–1517. See page 37 for full description.

Santorini,
800 West Adams Street; (312) 829–8820. What distinguishes Santorini from the other Greektown restaurants jammed into a 2-block area is its emphasis on seafood, from whole-roasted snapper and whole black sea bass to pan-fried squid.

For those who disdain what one of my Texas friends lumps together as "fish" (or, more accurately, "feesh"), there are also the traditional Greek dishes such as dolmades, lamb artichokes, and spinach pie. As a centerpiece for the ambience, there's an always welcoming fireplace. Open Sunday through Thursday from 11:00 A.M. to midnight, Friday and Saturday from 11:00 A.M. to 1:00 A.M. Moderate.

Tufano's Vernon Park Tap,
1073 West Vernon Park Place; (312) 773–3393. See page 33 for full description.

Tuscany,
1014 West Taylor Street; (312) 829–1990. See page 33 for full description.

Near North Side and Old Town

The Near North Side—which includes a distinctively separate area known as Old Town—is perhaps Chicago's most economically diverse area, spreading from the swank stores on North Michigan Avenue ("The Magnificent Mile") and luxury apartments on North Lake Shore Drive to the desperately poor Cabrini-Green housing project farther west. (Interestingly, children from both sections mingle together at Lincoln Park High School, a highly respected magnet institution.)

In the 1840s shipyards, iron foundries, and breweries located along the Chicago River on what is now known as the Near North Side, one of the city's oldest areas, and in 1847 the first railroad (the Galena and Chicago Union, later known as the Chicago and North Western) ran down the center of Kinzie Street. In the late 1850s several large industries, including the McCormick reaper works, also settled on the riverbanks. Many of the neighborhood residents were Irish immigrants, who mainly worked as laborers in the nearby factories and railroads. Farther north, German immigrants ran cabbage, potato, and dairy farms in an area known as "North Town," which, in 1851, was annexed by the city of Chicago.

The majority of housing consisted of wooden cottages built by a method called balloon framing. The fire of 1871 destroyed these structures, but families quickly rebuilt. By 1882 Potter Palmer, a major force behind the retail development of downtown's State Street and husband of top-dog socialite Bertha Palmer, bought land covered by frog ponds on what became ultra-fashionable North Lake Shore Drive and built a mansion there. Within a decade this "Gold Coast" (a name still used today) became the home of the city's elite "Four Hundred," many of whom had lived on the no-longer-fashionable South Side. In the early 1900s, several blocks west, light industry and commercial businesses moved onto Wells Street, North Town's main thoroughfare, and small apartment buildings were converted to densely populated rooming houses.

In the 1920s the Near North Side developed extravagantly, with retail shops, hotels, and office buildings established on North Michigan

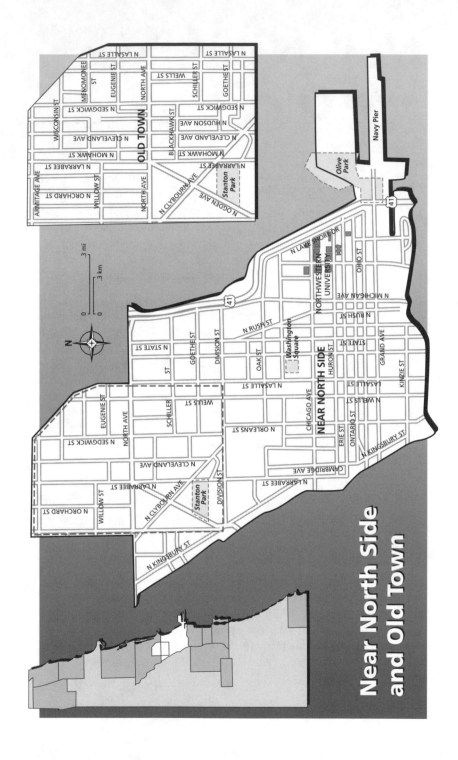

Near North Side and Old Town

NEAR NORTH SIDE AND OLD TOWN

TOP ATTRACTIONS ON THE NEAR NORTH SIDE AND IN OLD TOWN

Courthouse Place

Jazz Record Mart

Museum of Contemporary Art Store

The Abraham Lincoln Book Shop

St. James Chapel at Quigley Seminary

The International Museum of Surgical Science

Avenue, along with Tribune Tower and the Wrigley Building. Nearby, on the fashionable side streets, high-rise apartment buildings sprang up, along with Northwestern University's Chicago campus. And, back down along the river, the Merchandise Mart was finished in 1930.

After World War II, North Town became known as Old Town, and in the 1960s it was a well-known tourist area with its folk-singing clubs such as the Earl of Old Town and beer-and-banjo bars, where patrons were allowed to toss their peanut shells on the floor. Many of the compact houses are charming, as are the narrow side streets.

In 1959 an improvisational theater called The Second City (taken from a condescending *New Yorker* article about Chicago by A. J. Liebling) set up shop on Wells Street in what had been a Chinese laundry. In 1967 it moved a short ways into its present home at 1616 North Wells. But Wells became seedy and rundown, until it finally made a comeback in the 1980s. Today, it's booming again, the site of numerous restaurants and shops, many of them quite upscale, while the residential market commands outrageous prices. A short walk to the east is the Carl Sandburg complex, built during the 1960s and 1970s as an urban renewal project, but now attracting soaring prices for its condominiums.

In 1943 the Chicago Housing Authority built the Francis Cabrini Homes not that far west of Wells, then added the Green Homes in 1962. In recent years, as land has become increasingly valuable and gentrification has wildly spread, the projects are rapidly being demolished. As for where the displaced residents are ending up, no one seems to be exactly sure—or no one is saying.

Those wanting to visit North Michigan Avenue's shops and restaurants from the river to Oak Street should find it an easy stroll. For sections of the Near North Side farther north, take the #151 bus on Michigan, the #36 bus, which runs up State Street, then turns west on Division Street and north onto Clark Street, the #22 on Clark, and the #156 on LaSalle Street. The subway, boarded in the Loop on State Street, stops at Chicago Avenue and State Street, as well as Clark and Division.

A good place to start exploring this area might be just north of the Chicago River near the Merchandise Mart, which is hard to miss (although some taxi drivers, oddly, don't have a clue where it is).

"We've been here for years and years," says the staffer at the **Antiques Centre at Kinzie Square** (220 West Kinzie Street), one of several antiques places that are literally in the shadow of the Mart. "There's another antiques district up north on Belmont Avenue, but they get the collectibles while we get the higher-end things." A showroom for more than twenty dealers, the Center—sorry, *Centre*—offers eighteenth, nineteenth, and early-twentieth-century furniture, chandeliers, textiles, jewelry, Orientalia, rugs, and paintings, as well as not easily categorized items such as carousel horses and hats from the French Foreign Legion. Open Monday through Friday from 10:00 A.M. to 5:00 P.M., Saturday from noon to 4:00 P.M. Phone (312) 464–1946, or check out www. chicago-antiques.com/antique-centre.htm.

Now walk east over to **Courthouse Place** (54 West Hubbard Street), between Dearborn and Clark Streets, formerly used by Chicago's police, the board of health, and other city offices until it was beautifully restored in 1986. It is best known, however, as the former Cook County Criminal Courthouse, site of some of the most classic criminal trials in the city's history. Built in 1892, the building—an example of Romanesque Revival—now has a cleaned Bedford limestone facade and restored cast-iron and copper metalwork over the arched entrance, along with an attractive lobby.

Photos and sketches on the walls are reminders of those glamorous/notorious days. There's Carl Sandburg, who was an apprentice newspaper reporter in the building's press room, and Ben Hecht, who, with Charles MacArthur, wrote *The Front Page,* the blockbuster play (and subsequent movie versions) that was based largely on their coverage out of that ragtag press room. There's sausage king Adolph Luetgert, convicted of killing his wife after her wedding ring and a small fragment of bone were found in a vat in the sausage factory. It was also in this building that Clarence Darrow in 1924 defended Nathan Leopold and Richard Loeb, who kidnapped and murdered a 13-year-old boy just for the thrill of it; because of Darrow's impassioned plea against capital punishment, the killers were given life imprisonment. It was here, in a controversial 1886 trial, that five of the eight Haymarket Square "anarchists" were sentenced to death. And it was here that "Terribly Tommy" O'Connor, convicted for murdering a policeman, escaped. (The jail's gallows, built especially for him, were kept for his recapture—which never happened. The gallows were torn down in 1977.)

Walk east a couple blocks and you'll arrive at **Andy's** (11 East Hubbard), which has been around since 1951. The bar/restaurant really got going in the 1970s when it began offering live jazz Fridays at noon. Audiences sitting around the tables and that wonderful oval bar included newspaper people from the *Sun-Times* and *Tribune* and advertising types from the agencies (who were used to closing down the week early). Players included Barrett Deems, who billed himself as "the world's fastest drummer" and who had gained fame appearing with Louis Armstrong's band in the 1956 Hollywood musical *High Society*. Word quickly spread, despite the less-than-sparkling food, and Andy's gradually expanded its schedule. These days the joint is still jumpin', with jazz at noon blasting forth Monday through Friday, along with evening sessions every day of the week. In addition to Jazz at Five on Friday, there's also Blues at Nine. Jazz musicians in recent times have included Franz Jackson, Wayne Jones, the Chuck Hedges Swingtet, and Henry Johnson's Organ Express, Russ Phillips and the Windy City All Stars, and Men of Note. Among the blues folks have been Big Time Sarah and Peter Dames and the Rhythm Flames. Open Monday through Saturday from 11:00 A.M. to 2:00 A.M., Sunday from 6:00 P.M. to 1:00 A.M. Phone (312) 642–6805, or check out www.andysjazzclub.citysearch.com.

In the same mode, explore the wonders of the *Jazz Record Mart* (444 North Wabash Avenue), which is advertised as "the largest jazz and blues record store in the world," and who's to doubt it? The place has

Smoke 'Em If You've Got 'Em

*T*he Chicago Tribune *(built 1923–1925), at 435 North Michigan Avenue, is best known for the distinctive architecture of its tower (the building is irreverently characterized by its reporters as "the Gothic Silo"), the result of an international competition for design of what the* Trib *honchos proclaimed with typical modesty would be "the most beautiful office building in the world." This is the same paper that, for years, called itself "the World's Greatest Newspaper." (The company's radio station call letters are thus WGN.) The Tower is also known for being embedded with pieces of*

famous structures from around the world, such as the Alamo, Arc de Triomphe, and Fort Sumter. But visitors looking for a little local trivia should check out the front courtyard with a statue of Revolutionary War patriot Nathan ("I only regret that I have but one life to lose for my country") Hale. Formally known as the "Nathan Hale Court," it is now the place where resident cigarette smokers congregate, having been banished from the building at light-up time. Which has prompted those caustic staff members to come up with a revised name: "the Nathan Inhale *Court."*

such a large inventory that it can put out only one copy of a record at a time. Its best-selling items are designated "killers," and owner Bob Koester believes that Miles Davis's *Kind of Blue* (the store sells 1,000 a year) is the best-selling jazz record of all time. Some hard-core jazz buffs drop in every day, but for the casual folks, there are not only several rooms full of scores of CDs , tapes, and records (some selling for as low as 99 cents) but also in-store concerts and jazz book signings, T-shirts (from Cab Calloway to Gene Krupa, Charlie Parker, and Lightnin' Hopkins), posters, and jazz videos. There's also a well-used bulletin board with industry updates and, more and more often, news of departures ("We are sorry to inform you that Jack McVea—'Open the Door, Richard'—passed away on Dec. 27"). Open Monday through Saturday from 10:00 A.M. to 8:00 P.M., Sunday from noon to 5:00 P.M. Phone (312) 222–1467.

If you want to hear the music *live*, it's only a short walk over to the *Jazz Showcase* (59 West Grand Avenue), a relatively new location, although the jazz spot has been around in other locations for over fifty years. "Come to Where the Heavies Are!" its ad proclaims, and among its heavies in the new century have been the Mose Allison Trio, the Gerry Mulligan Tribute Band, Bill Russo and the Chicago Jazz Ensemble Big Band, and Larry Coryell, described by esteemed *Chicago Reader* jazz critic Neil Tesser as "one of the most gifted and fascinating guitarists in American music." For performers, show times, and cover prices (not exactly cheap), phone (312) 670–2473.

Walk farther east, pass by the famous Billy Goat's, and climb the stairs to North Michigan Avenue and the start of the Magnificent Mile. Right away, there are two restaurants worth noting. Now, the folks at *Bandera* (535 North Michigan Avenue) would like more passersby on the street to look up once in a while. Maybe then they would discover this appealing second-floor establishment with its welcoming bar, fine food, and great views of that same avenue. The nothing-fancy "American cooking" menu ranges from the highly touted spit-roasted chicken to sliced leg of lamb, barbecued back ribs, filet mignon, barbecued salmon, and "simple grilled fish." There's also live jazz, starting at 6:00 P.M. The main problem, it seems, is just letting people know it's there. And, no, one staff member says, they *won't* resort to dressing up a guy in a chicken or lobster costume to pass out handbills on the street. Open Monday through Thursday from 11:30 A.M. to 10:00 P.M., Friday and Saturday from 11:30 A.M. to 11:00 P.M., Sunday from 5:00 to 9:00 P.M. Phone (312) 644–3524. Moderate.

Tucked away just half a block east of Michigan, there's *Sayat-Nova* (157 East Ohio Street), a little, often overlooked gem. The cozy, romantic Armenian restaurant has been around for over thirty years and has drawn a loyal band of customers. No wonder; the place is charming, the food is tasty, and the prices (especially at lunch) are very reasonable. Among the entrees are char-broiled shish kebabs and shrimp kebabs, trout with herbs, lamb chops, sautéed scallops, and chicken couscous. A good initiation for lunch-goers is to order the kibbee, which is fresh ground lamb mixed with cracked wheat, stuffed with meat and spices, then baked.

The restaurant's decor is attractive, with handmade Middle Eastern items such as saddlebags hanging on the wall (and offered for sale). Sayat-Nova undoubtedly lost considerable business during construction in the area—a huge Gap store went in on the corner—but has managed to survive quite nicely as it rolls on its way to forty. Open for lunch Monday through Saturday from 11:30 A.M. to 4:00 P.M., dinner from 4:00 to 10:00 P.M. Monday through Saturday and Sunday from 3:00 to 9:00 P.M. Phone (312) 644–9159. Moderate.

If you're looking for simpler fare—*much* simpler—one place that has no trouble whatsoever drawing crowds is the *Garrett Popcorn Shop* (670 North Michigan). One of five stores in the Loop and Near North Side (Garrett has been around since 1949), it sells registered/trademarked goodies like Pecan CaramelCrisp, Cashew CaramelCrisp, Macadamia CaramelCrisp, and, yes, just plain popcorn. The biggest seller, according to one clerk, is the special combination of CaramelCrisp and Cheese Corn. A Garrett brochure states that the popcorn is "hot-air popped using no oils or fats" and then "gently folded into our secret family recipes which have been handed down through three generations." Whatever, it works. Store hours vary. ("It depends on the season, whether there's a convention in town, and employee availability," says one spokesperson.) Phone (312) 944–4730, or chew on www.garrettpopcorn.com.

A River Runs Backwards

*S*ince 1900, the Chicago River has flowed "backwards" down the Sanitary and Ship Canal, in order to divert the river away from Lake Michigan and keep sewage out of the city water supply.

Before 1900 the river flowed into the lake. Sewage dumped into the river polluted the lake—and drinking water—with bacteria, causing typhoid, cholera, and other deadly diseases.

Walk farther north on Michigan and cross the street at Chicago Avenue, then head east and you'll find the Museum of Contemporary Art—yes, that plug-ugly building over there at 220 East Chicago. Although it's not off the beaten track, it is worth noting, as a shopping stopover, the unique **MCA Store** on the main floor. Here you'll find an assortment of often-wacky items not carried (for better or worse) by the more traditional shops in the Michigan Avenue area. These include T-shirts and mugs that read FEAR NO ART, provocative posters by Hollis Sigler, and stationery by Roy Lichtenstein. There are books on film noir, sci-fi volumes *(It Came from Bob's Basement!)*, 3-D purses, magnetic poetry kits, and clocks shaped like books. Then there are the postcards you won't find in Marshall Field's or Bloomingdale's—everything from those featuring filmmaker Leni Riefenstahl (best known for *Triumph of the Will,* her controversial documentary on Hitler's 1934 Nuremberg rallies), to those of Hollywood "B" movies *(Reform School Girl),* and others with mock comic-book motifs *(Jetman Meets the Mad Madam).* Store hours are Tuesday from 10:00 A.M. to 8:00 P.M., Wednesday through Sunday from 10:00 A.M. to 6:00 P.M. Use the street-level entrance to avoid museum admission fees. (Entrance is free on Tuesday.) Phone (312) 280–2660, or artfully bring up www.mcachicago.org.

Another detour, perhaps, this time west on Chicago, is **The Paper Source** (232 West Chicago), which, as its name suggests, is a terrific source for papers from around the world that can be used for stationery, invitations, and so on. The three-floor store also handles delightful, eclectic merchandise such as note sets, travel journal books, photo albums, ribbons, paper lampshades, wedding and shower invitations, greeting cards, rubber stamps and ink, and an assortment of books from the rather expected *(Hand Papermaking, Japanese Stab Binding, The Mad, Mad, Mad World of Carving Rubber Stamps)* to the rather surprising *(White Trash Cooking, A Field Guide to Cows).* Open Monday through Friday from 10:00 A.M. to 7:00 P.M., Saturday from 10:00 A.M. to 5:00 P.M., Sunday from noon to 5:00 P.M. Phone (312) 337–7416.

A little farther west is **The Abraham Lincoln Book Shop** (357 West Chicago), attracting Civil War buffs from around the world. "We get orders from places like England, Australia, and even Sweden," says the proprietor. "There are Civil War nuts all over the place." The store, indeed, specializes in works dealing with what some call the War Between the States, and buffs may choose among volumes that deal with subjects like the battle of Shiloh, the Army of the Potomac, and General Jeb Stuart, although the biggest sellers are those dealing with military tactics at Gettysburg. There are also loads of Lincoln artifacts, as you might suspect, and all kinds of valuable (and expensive) auto-graphs—on books, prints, and photos—of such folks as Ben Franklin, Winston Churchill, Chicago attorney Clarence Darrow, *Gone with the Wind* author Margaret Mitchell, Harry Truman, and even Daniel Boone. There are also busts and bronzes, maps, and appropriate card games ("Famous Generals of the Civil War"). The shop has been in business since 1938 (at this location since 1990), and parked in the front of the place is Abraham Lincoln's family bed—on which one is admonished not to sit. Open Monday through Saturday from 9:00 A.M. to 5:00 P.M. Phone (312) 944–3085, or visit www.ALincolnBookShop.com.

A little south and a little west of here are two (cheap) places you might want to eat. "On this site in 1897, nothing happened," a plaque proudly proclaims on the front of the ***Green Door Tavern*** (678 North Orleans Street), but in 1921, something obviously *did*, as the restaurant/bar first opened its doors. The food—burgers, chili, ribs, fish and chips—is decent enough, but the clientele, from yuppies to blue-collar types, undoubtedly comes here for the atmosphere, along with the large assortment of beers (and hot buttered rum and hot toddy in the cold months). It's a battered-wood, funky kind of place that never seems to throw things away, and instead hangs them on the ceiling or slaps them up on the walls: model airplanes, baseballs and bats, a moosehead, all kinds of beer and whiskey promotional items, knocked-around signs that say things like WE SELL HORSESHOE TOBACCO. Another contrarian sign, behind the well-frequented bar, reads, SMOKE AND THE WORLD WILL SMOKE WITH YOU, and nearby is one of those "strength machines"—"Shake with Uncle Sam"—found at old-timey amusement parks. The Green Door's smoking section, as so often is the case, is the most colorful, and in the whole place, baseball-cap-wearing is de rigeur. Open Monday through Thursday from 11:30 A.M. to 11:00 P.M., Friday and Saturday from 11:30 A.M. to midnight. Phone (312) 664–5496. Inexpensive.

A favorite spot for local meat eaters, ***Mr. Beef on Orleans*** (666 North Orleans) came into national prominence when TV talk-show host Jay Leno originated his show from Chicago and gave it frequent, enviable plugs. Autographed photos adorn a large wall giving testament to other celebs who have tasted the fine Italian beef and Italian sausage—names like musicians Pete Fountain and George Benson, former Bears maverick quarterback Jim McMahon, and George Wendt (best known as bar anchor Norm on "Cheers"). Of course, there's also a note from Leno himself ("Yo! Men of beef, the best"). Either take out the beef or devour it at long tables in the facetiously named "Elegant Dining Room." Open Monday through Friday from 7:00 A.M. to 4:45 P.M., Satur-day from 10:30 A.M. to 2:00 P.M. Phone (312) 337–8500. Inexpensive.

If neither of these appeal to you, head back to Michigan Avenue and check out *Chicago Flat Sammies,* a quality fast-food place—next to the Visitors Center in the historic (1869) Chicago Avenue Pumping Station at 163 West Pearson Street—featuring a unique eating area. Some of its tables are lined up on a kind of walkway, where diners overlook the actual pipes (labeled with mysterious names like "Old DePaul" and "Old Pouliot") and other mechanical marvels of the still-operating station, which has a capacity of 250 million gallons per day, providing fresh water for a population of more than 390,000 persons in the city's central district. The menu is mostly soups, sporadically upscale sandwiches (grilled pesto chicken, but also tuna melt), and flat bread pizza. (The *flat* in the restaurant's name refers to the wheat bread.) Open every day from 7:30 A.M. to 7:00 P.M. Phone one of those cutesy numbers at (312) 664–BRED. Inexpensive.

Time for a time-out. Located a short walk west from the bustle and swank of North Michigan Avenue, Archbishop Quigley Seminary on Rush Street between Pearson and Chestnut Streets is a peaceful urban enclave—a limestone French Gothic complex that includes a school, courtyard, and *St. James Chapel,* in which the magnificent stained-glass windows have undergone a remarkable renovation. In 1994 a businessman named Neal Ball visited the chapel and—stunned by the condition of the windows—arranged to have Jean-Marie Bettembourg, an expert in stained-glass restoration from the French Ministry of Culture, examine the windows. Bettembourg determined they were in a serious state of disrepair due to lead deterioration, pollution, and extreme temperatures. The Friends of the Windows, a nondenominational group, was subsequently formed to raise funds for the multimillion-dollar restoration.

The Towering Non-Inferno

*M*ost Chicagoans probably know that the **Chicago Water Tower** at Michigan and Chicago Avenues, erected in 1869, was one of the few buildings to survive the Great Fire of 1871. What they may not know is that the structure is made out of Joliet limestone blocks quarried in Illinois (the fire didn't have a chance) and that it was designed by prominent architect William W. Boyington, who also designed the first University of Chicago, the entrance to Rosehill Cemetery, and, most impressive of all, the prison at Joliet. Another bit of Tower trivia: On its centennial in 1969, it was nationally recognized as the First American Water Landmark.

An example of Gothic Revival, the chapel is a replica inspired by Sainte-Chapelle in Paris, the mid-thirteenth-century Gothic structure built by King Louis IX to house his acquisition of what was believed to be Christ's crown of thorns. With initial financing for the chapel, including $20,000 collected by schoolchildren in the Roman Catholic diocese, the chapel was completed—except for the windows—in 1919. The English antique glass windows, finished in 1925, were designed and painted by Robert Giles and his wife in the studio of the John J. Kinsella Co. of Chicago. More than 700,000 pieces of glass—including antique pieces sent from England—were framed and installed. The windows depict events from the Old and New Testaments, and the huge rose window on the west wall is devoted to the life of Mary. Free docent tours of the chapel are available Tuesday, Thursday, Friday, and Saturday from noon to 2:00 P.M. For tour information, phone (312) 782–3532. Our guide, by the way, revealed that she was also a tax preparer. "Just like St. Matthew," she appropriately noted.

For those interested in international publications, **Europa Books** (832 North State Street), a short walk west of Quigley Seminary, is a don't-miss destination. Here are British newspapers (both the classy and tacky ones), French calendars and comic books, Italian cooking magazines, German travel publications and crossword puzzle books, Spanish fashion magazines, and English football and rugby magazines. There are also *Paris Match* posters and postcards from all over, along with novels, dictionaries, travel books, cookbooks, and children's books, including Maurice Sendak in German and, inevitably, the adventures of Harry Potter in Spanish, French, and German. Open Monday through Friday from 8:00 A.M. to 8:00 P.M., Saturday from 9:00 A.M. to 8:00 P.M., Sunday from 9:00 A.M. to 6:00 P.M. Phone (312) 335–9677.

Back on Michigan (at Chestnut), the **Fourth Presbyterian Church of Chicago** (126 East Chestnut) has long been known for serving one of the city's wealthiest congregations, but it is also widely known for its extensive volunteer outreach opportunities, including a program for tutoring children at the not-so-far-away Cabrini-Green public housing projects. For visitors, "Fourth Pres," as it is popularly known, also offers free concerts at 12:10 P.M. on Fridays, attended by everyone from local workers to peace-seeking Michigan Avenue shoppers to retirees, with the attendees wearing everything from three-piece suits to (as evident one Friday) a Harley-Davidson jacket. That same noontime, the excellent concert—no amateurs here—featured soloists, both instrumental (flute and oboe) and vocal (soprano), as well as a quintet (flute, clarinet, horn, bassoon, oboe), with compositions including songs by Ralph Vaughan Williams based on poems by William Blake. During the year, the church also sponsors evening and Sunday afternoon concerts (some free), which have featured such musicians as the Dave Brubeck Quartet, the Chicago Chamber Orchestra, and His Majestie's Clerkes, Chicago's premier a cappella chamber choir. On occasional Saturdays there's a children's concert series.

The church itself, opened in 1914, is the oldest surviving structure on Michigan north of the Chicago River, with the exception of the Water Tower 2 blocks south. The main sanctuary was designed by Ralph Adams Cram, America's leading neo-Gothic Revival architect, whose best known achievement is the Cathedral of St. John the Divine in New York. While enjoying the music at Fourth Presbyterian in its 1,200-seat sanctuary, take a look up at the lovely colorful, Scandinavian-influenced timber ceiling, characteristic of English churches and cathedrals. Also note the fourteen carved angels, slightly larger than life-size and each holding a different instrument; the large carved oak screen behind the altar; and the stained-glass windows, particularly those over the Michigan Avenue entrance depicting the four evangelists (Mark, Matthew, Luke, and John). Outside, there's a short cloister leading to the charming garth (courtyard), designed by Howard Van Doren Shaw, that serves as, at least, a partial sanctuary from the Michigan Avenue horn honkers. In the summer the church sponsors free concerts twice a week in the courtyard, which is also the location in the fall for exhibits at the Annual Arts Festival. The church is generally open from 9:00 A.M. to 5:00 P.M. weekdays, as well as for Sunday services. For specific information, call (312) 787–4570, or log onto www.fourthchurch.org.

Long situated on Rush and Oak Streets, the thirty-year-old-plus *Oak Tree* restaurant moved a while back to the sixth floor of a high-rise mall at 900 North Michigan Avenue also occupied by, among others, Bloomingdale's,

Best Near North Name: Material Possessions

*T*his store with the delicious in-your-face name at 54 East Chestnut Street in the heavily trafficked Rush Street area has been around for over twenty years. Items range from household accessories, glassware, and dinnerware to unique furniture from around the world, some of it antiques, some of it wonderfully individually hand-crafted. Open Monday through Saturday from 10:00 A.M. to 6:00 P.M., Sunday from noon to 5:00 P.M. Phone (312) 280–4885.

Williams-Sonoma, J. Crew, Coach, Mark Shale, and, yes, Glove Me Tender. It's a highly popular spot with both folks who live in nearby Gold Coast condos (especially for weekend breakfast) and Michigan Avenue shoppers at noontime. The atmosphere is pleasantly calming, with pastel, country French–like murals, and the menu is eclectic, if not somewhat peculiar. Sandwiches, for instance, range from upscale (duck breast with mango chutney, curry chicken salad) to the mundane (patty melt, pastrami). Whatever, the food is excellent. Also on hand are homemade soups to die for, ambitious salads (char-grilled asparagus and chicken, Canton chicken and noodle), and perhaps-to-die-because-of desserts such as hot fudge sundaes and a variety of cakes made by Sweet Mystery Bakery. Breakfast is served all day. Open Monday through Friday from 7:30 A.M. to 6:30 P.M., Saturday and Sunday from 7:30 A.M. to 5:30 P.M. Phone (312) 751–1988. Inexpensive.

One of the highest compliments some Chicagoans (not all) can make about a drinking establishment is that it's "like a New York bar." Such is the case of *Coq d'Or,* a lounge/restaurant on the ground level of the Drake Hotel (140 East Walton Street) that features a dark, woody, leathery ambience. In 1933, according to the menu, it was the second bar in town to serve drinks after the repeal of Prohibition. (The first, tellingly, is not mentioned.) With the countdown to 8:30 P.M.—the official start of a new wet era—the lines were so long, the story goes, that the bartenders only had time to "pour whiskey at 40 cents a glass." They're still pouring these days, although, not of course, at those prices, and that menu, said one of my friends, "looks like something out of the '50s." Indeed, there are things like spaghetti (not "pasta"), hot turkey breast with mashed potatoes, the house hamburger, and—when's the last time you saw this on a dinner menu?—corned beef hash with two fried eggs. For years late-night entertainment was handled by legendary piano bar man Buddy Charles, who, unfortunately (for us, not him, undoubtedly), retired a while back. He's been replaced at his familiar spot (the music starts at 9:30 P.M.), but whether he can *really* be replaced is debatable. On a personal note, this is the bar where our two sons had their first "official" drink when turning 21. Much to our surprise—and delight—they both independently made the same, most unlikely choice: a Tom Collins. Bar hours are daily from 11:00 A.M. to 1:15 A.M., with the kitchen open from 11:00 A.M. to midnight. Phone (312) 787–2200. Inexpensive.

Before heading north for Old Town, you should be aware of two distinctly diverse places that are worth a stop. It seems the *Zebra Lounge* (1220 North State Street) has been around forever, and, indeed, it opened in 1933, right at the smack end of Prohibition, becoming the third bar in the city to get a liquor license. A dark, romantic, late-night spot where many couples spent their courting days, the tiny space is decorated with, of course, a zebra motif (paintings, lampshades, a wall hanging) and alternating piano bar players who begin around 8:30. According to the knowing bartender, the Zebra draws locals during the week and a younger assortment that on the weekends wanders over from the bars on Division Street. Open Sunday through Friday from 4:30 P.M. to 2:00 A.M., Saturday from 4:30 P.M. to 3:00 A.M. Phone (312) 642–5140.

A few blocks north and 1 block east (toward the lake), *The International Museum of Surgical Science* (1524 North Lake Shore Drive) is a fascinating place where visitors can spend at least an hour roaming exhibits on four floors. One room contains paintings of such pioneers as Miguel Servetus, a sixteenth-century physician and surgeon who was the first to describe pulmonary circulation—and, for his "heresy," was burned at the stake. There's also Ignatz Phillip Semmelweis (1818–1865), who pushed for strict hospital hygiene in maternity wards, which dramatically reduced maternal mortality; he, too, was vilified and ended up dying in an insane asylum. In another room is a working iron lung, the respirator used to treat polio victims in prevaccine days. In another are statues of such greats as Hippocrates, "the father of medicine"; Joseph Lister, the developer of antiseptic surgery; William Harvey, who discovered the circulation of blood; and Marie Curie, who won the 1911 Nobel Prize for isolation of metallic radium. There are also displays of all kinds of vintage surgical instruments (which graphically make one appreciate modern medicine), old microscopes, a collapsible stethoscope designed to be transported in a top hat, and a model of an amphitheater at the University of Padua, where

He Did It His Way

*I*n 1886 Captain George Wellington Streeter, an adventurer who had run guns in the South, ran aground on a Lake Michigan sandbar near what is now Superior Street and subsequently convinced city contractors to dump hard fill in the section surrounding his boat. Later, he audaciously laid claim to this filled-in 185-acre tract and called it the "Free District of Lake Michigan." He sold lots to squatters in his "independent territory," and after numerous clashes with police, he was finally evicted in 1918. However, his name lives on. These days, the area roughly between Pearson and Oak Streets east of Michigan Avenue is a part of the Near North Side known as "Streeterville."

Harvey took part in dissections. Also check out replicas of an American doctor's office in 1875 as well as an early 1900s apothecary, with dozens of mysterious dusty bottles and patent medicine boxes boasting fantastic claims (such as Dr. Schiffmann's Cigarettes, guaranteed to relieve bronchial distress), and an exhibit devoted to radiology, complete with one of those fluoroscope X-ray machines that used to be the staple of every children's shoe store ("Look, there're the bones in my feet!"). A couple of my favorite pieces are an old X-ray transformer that looks like something out of a 1930s "mad scientist" movie and an aluminum chest brace, circa 1850, that resembles an unyielding girdle/implement of torture. Feminists probably will notice that an exhibit labeled "Nursing" gets precious little space of its own. Just to show that surgeons *do* have a sense of humor (you never knew?), the museum peddles T-shirts reading, "It's Not Rocket Science . . . It's Brain Surgery!" and scrub shirts with a cartoon showing folks in the operating room and the caption "All right, so we dropped the heart. The floor is clean." The museum is housed in an historic 1917 lakeside mansion designed by noted Chicago architect Howard Van Doren Shaw and patterned after Le Petit Trianon, a French chateau built at Versailles for Louis XVI and Marie Antoinette. The museum, a division of the International College of Surgeons, is open Tuesday through Saturday from 10:00 A.M. to 4:00 P.M. Admission is $5.00 for adults, $3.00 for students and seniors. Phone (312) 642–6502, or log onto www.imss.org.

The main corridor in Old Town is Wells Street from Division Street to a little ways north of North Avenue. A good place to start, just north of Division, is **Salpicón!** (1252 North Wells), an upscale Mexican restaurant that serves regional, traditional, and contemporary cuisine and is owned by chef Priscila Franco Satkoff, a native of Mexico City, and her husband, Vincent Satkoff, a Chicagoan. "I have fresh fish all the time, and have very different meats like venison," says Priscila, a former personal assistant to chef Rick Bayless of Chicago's famed Frontera Grill. "One of the dishes I love is the marinated, grilled quail. I also love the cured grasshoppers—which are traditional in Oaxaca. My philosophy is, I won't give my customers something *I* wouldn't eat."

Try the quail, in fact, and you won't be disappointed, or go for the grilled tiger shrimp in a sweet garlic sauce and olive oil with avocado chunks and guajillo chiles. Other entrees include grilled double-cut pork chop tenderloin, in a spicy roasted tomato-chipotle sauce with chorizo and potatoes, and grilled filet of Atlantic salmon glazed with ancho chile and served with a creamy tomatillo-serrano sauce. (A menu caveat: "Due to Mother Nature, spice levels may vary greatly from chile to chile, and She is responsible, not us!") Among the irresistible desserts are chocolate espresso cake with vanilla bean ice cream and fresh pear and mango cobbler with almonds topped with cajeta ice cream. Along with the fine wine assortment, there is another, quite unusual list: more than eighty different tequilas, including an 1800 number that sells for $150 a bang. Refreshingly, Salpicón! attracts a diverse clientele, not just youthful trendsetters. The colorful decor includes original art by Chicago's Alejandro Romero, and the name of the restaurant can mean "a typical dish from Mexico of shredded beef or chicken," "a *very* spicy salsa native to the Yucatán made with Habanero chiles," or "a splash." Open Sunday through Thursday from 5:00 to 10:00 P.M., Friday and Saturday from 5:00 to 11:00 P.M., and Sunday brunch from 11:00 A.M. to 2:30 P.M. Phone (312) 988–7811. Moderate.

Next along the way is *Barbara's Bookstore,* born in 1963 and for years ensconced in not-nearly-as-tony quarters on Broadway near Diversey. Now it is in residence in a retail-residential complex known as Cobbler Square, (1350 Wells Street), created from about twenty buildings that had been erected from 1880 to 1959. These included some belonging to a bicycle manufacturer, the Western Wheel Works, and Dr. Scholl, the company of foot-care fame. The bookstore features a pleasing, light-wood atmosphere, with a colorful kids' section. But—and this may be a strictly personal assessment—the staff itself doesn't seem nearly as friendly (or knowledgeably helpful) as it did in its Broadway incarnation. Besides a wide selection of books, with hand-written recommendations, Barbara's sponsors numerous authors' readings in the evenings. Open Monday through Saturday from 9:00 A.M. to 10:00 P.M., Sunday from 10:00 A.M. to 9:00 P.M. Phone (312) 466–0223.

Wonderful smells hit you as you enter *The Spice House* (1512 Wells Street), and even if you're just passing by, the smells will hit you as well if the store's outgoing fan is whirling away to entice customers. "We turn on the fan when we're grinding cinnamon," says Patty Erd, co-owner with her husband, Tom. "We *don't* have it on when we're grinding pepper." Spices and seasonings are ground by hand weekly—including over 100 pounds of cinnamon and 100 pounds of black pepper—and the dozens of jars contain such intriguing labels as Rocky Mountain seasoning, shrimp and crab boil, Singapore steak spice, Hungarian sweet paprika, and genuine Spanish saffron, "the most expensive of all spices" (at this writing, about $80 an ounce). There are also whimsical names reflecting local neighborhoods: Historic Pullman Pork Chop Seasoning, Bronzeville Rib Rub, Pilsen Latino Seasoning, Old Taylor Street Cheese Sprinkle. The family business was founded in 1957 in

Wisconsin by Erd's parents, and there's another store in suburban Evanston. "There are not many places you can walk in and have all kinds of tastes—other than '31 flavors,'" says Patty Erd. Incidentally, the name of the place really is The Spice House, even though the sign outside says Spice Merchants. "I did that because, in this neighborhood, I didn't want people to think we were another restaurant," says Tom Erd. "I wanted them to know exactly what we did." Open Monday through Saturday from 10:00 A.M. to 7:00 P.M., Sunday from 10:00 A.M. to 5:00 P.M. Phone (312) 274–0378 or visit www.thespicehouse.com.

To the delight of those craving a sugar fix, *The Fudge Pot* (1532 Wells Street) has been around since 1963, serving up "handmade chocolates, caramel apples, fudge, and personalized lollipops." There are also other treats such as chocolate strawberries and frozen bananas, and more unconventional goodies such as miniature chocolate tennis rackets, chocolate trucks, chocolate cows, chocolate turtles, chocolate guitars, and even—heaven help us all—chocolate cell phones. Open Monday through Thursday and Sunday from noon to 10:00 P.M., Friday and Saturday from noon to midnight. Phone (312) 943–1777.

An Old Town staple, *Zanies* comedy nightclub (1548 Wells Street) has featured stars or soon-to-be-stars like Jay Leno, Tim Allen, and Jerry Seinfeld, as well as many rising performers, some of whom have risen

The Bells of St. Michael's

*A*ccording to local legend, if you can hear the bells of St. Michael's, you are in Old Town. In 1871, *St. Michael's Roman Catholic Church* (447 West Eugenie Street), which had opened only two years before, survived the Great Fire—at least, its exterior walls survived. The roof and floor burned, but the mostly German parishioners didn't give up and started the rebuilding process. The church, the tenth oldest in the city, features a Romanesque architectural style, with an ornate Bavarian Baroque interior. Walk into it, and you could be in one of those Old World churches in Europe, with its four side altars, all kinds of polychromatic statues, and exquisite stained-glass windows. Way above the high altar is an 8-foot St. Michael, flanked by archangels Gabriel and Raphael and standing over a vanquished Lucifer. (To further clarify things, there's also a statue of St. Michael in front of the church.) The tower—an Old Town landmark that can be seen for miles away—was rebuilt in 1866. A more recent ($1.5 million) renovation was undertaken in the 1990s. Open daily from 8:00 A.M. to 7:00 P.M. Phone (312) 642–2498.

much faster and more visibly than others. Those taking the stage in recent times have included the veteran comedienne, and Chicago favorite, who calls herself Pudgy ("the Queen of Tease"); another long-time local choice, Larry "Uncle Lar" Reeb ("It's a sick world and I'm a happy guy!"); and lesser-knowns such as Owen Smith ("A young, hip Cosby!"), Dom Irrera ("Bada boom! Bada bing! He's been on everything from 'Letterman' to 'Dr. Katz'!"), and Chipps Cooney, who presumably has carved out his own niche as "a hilarious sadsack magician." Call (312) 337–4027 for schedules.

In business since 1963, *Up Down Tobacco* (1550 Wells Street) is per-haps best known for its annual pipe-smoking contest, a competition—over twenty years old—to see who can keep his or her pipe lit the longest. The way it works, each contestant is given a sample of tobacco and two matches, and the winner usually manages to stretch it out to about an hour and fifteen minutes. The store sells humidors, pipe racks, cigars, and, of course, pipes, including a handsome array of Meer-schaum models. At the front of the store, however politically incorrect, is—what else?—a cigar store Indian. Open Monday through Thursday from 10:00 A.M. to 11:00 P.M., Friday and Saturday from 10:00 A.M. to midnight, Sunday from 11:00 A.M. to 11:00 P.M. Phone (312) 337–8505 or check out www.updowncigar.com.

While you're in the area, take a short detour down West Burton Place in a cul-de-sac between Wells and LaSalle. Once known as Carl Street, it features intriguingly offbeat houses—using materials such as copper tubs, wooden doors, and hardware picked up in flea markets—that formed an artists' community. Of particular note are the *Carl Street Studios* (155 Burton Place), converted from an old Victorian house, starting in 1927, by entrepreneur/artist Sol Kogen and artist Edgar Miller. Displaying an art deco style, the mishmash building includes a front exterior wall pocked with tiles, along with a charming little court-yard (visible by peeking through a small opening). Instead of studios, there are now, not unexpectedly, condo units.

One more Old Town building may be seen when visiting St. Michael's Church. It's a short walk over to a strikingly different place of worship, the *Midwest Buddhist Temple* at 435 West Menomonee Street. Designed by Hideaki Arao and built in 1971, it features a Japanese shrinelike pagoda style. (About 80 percent of the congregation is Japanese-American.) To arrange a tour (it depends on the temple staff's schedule), phone (312) 943–7801.

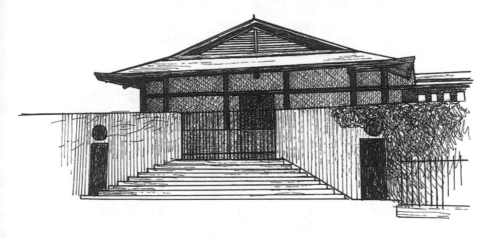

Midwest Buddhist Temple

PLACES TO STAY ON
THE NEAR NORTH SIDE
AND IN OLD TOWN

Best Western Inn of Chicago,
162 East Ohio Street;
(312) 573–3136.
Located just a block east of North Michigan Avenue's shops, this unassuming hotel attracts guests for its strategic location. There are 357 rooms, including 25 suites and 8 penthouse suites with sunken tubs; a fitness center; the outdoor Skyline Terrace; and a modestly priced ground-floor restaurant. For years, the facility was the Hotel St. Clair, which opened in 1928 and later housed the Chicago Press Club in its twenty-second-floor penthouse. After extensive renovations, it became the Inn of Chicago in 1982. Moderate.

Chicago Holiday Inn City Centre,
300 East Ohio Street;
(312) 787–6100.
Situated 2 blocks east of North Michigan Avenue and a short walk west of the lakefront, this twenty-six-floor high-rise contains 500 rooms and suites. There's also an outdoor pool/sundeck, two casual restaurants and a lounge on the lobby level, and the adjacent McClurg Court Sports Center, featuring an indoor swimming pool and other facilities, including (for a fee) racquetball and indoor tennis courts. Moderate.

The Drake Hotel,
140 East Walton Place;
(312) 787–2200.
Standing tall at the end of North Michigan Avenue across from Oak Street Beach, the Drake has proudly survived since the twelve-story Bedford limestone structure was formally opened as a summer resort on New Year's Eve, 1920, with a supper party of the city's biggest movers and shakers or whatever you called them then. Later open even in crummy weather, its visitors included other big shots, such as the emperor of Japan and Queen Elizabeth. There are a whopping 537 rooms, including 63 suites, and the hotel houses several shops, the Palm Court (impressive site of high tea), the well-known (and

overrated) Cape Cod Room, and the snug Coq d'Or restaurant/bar. (See page 53 for a full description.) The Drake even has its own coat of arms, containing a Latin phrase that translates as "An eagle does not catch flies"—however *that* fits into the overall picture. Expensive.

Omni Ambassador East, 1301 North State Parkway; (312) 787-7200. Located in a quiet residential location on the swanky "Gold Coast" a few blocks north of busy-busy Michigan Avenue, this used to be the hotel of choice for Hollywood royalty (who now seem to prefer the Four Seasons). It opened in 1926 and, after a $22 million renovation, now has 285 rooms, including 55 suites. The Ambassador is the home of the once-legendary Pump Room, where the waiters wore ridiculous plumed turbans and ostentatiously poured coffee from a height as high as they could reach. None of that nonsense goes on these days, and the restaurant seems to be surviving nicely without it. Walls of photos bring back memories of movie star diners—such as George Burns, Ginger Rogers, Joan Crawford, Doris Day, Abbott and Costello, and Tarzan himself, Johnny Weismuller—who, in those preflyover

days, would stop here between trains on the way to New York. The food fare is expensive, while the hotel rates are moderate.

The Whitehall Hotel, 105 East Delaware Place; (312) 944-6300. *Fortune* magazine has called it "one of eight great small hotels of the world." Originally an elegant apartment building (built in 1928), it was converted into a hotel with built-in kitchens in the mid-'50s, then upgraded in the early '70s with an opening gala at which Jack Benny entertained. Financial troubles caused its closing in the early '90s, but after a subsequent $25 million restoration completed in 1994, it's doing fine. There are 221 rooms, including 8 suites, with European furnishings and decor, a charming restaurant and lounge, and a fitness center. The hotel's luxury sedan is also available. Both the hotel (just off Michigan Avenue) and the restaurant are expensive.

PLACES TO EAT ON THE NEAR NORTH SIDE AND IN OLD TOWN

Bandera, 535 North Michigan Avenue; (312) 644-3524. See page 46 for full description.

Bistro 110, 110 East Pearson Street; (312) 266-3110. An attractive restaurant known for its lively Sunday jazz brunches, which always draw a crowd, Bistro 110 is conveniently located close to North Michigan Avenue. The menu offers such well-prepared dishes as steak au poivre, North Atlantic salmon, seared sea scallops, grilled rack of pork, and braised veal short ribs. Open Monday through Thursday from 11:30 A.M. to 10:00 P.M., Friday and Saturday from 11:30 A.M. to 11:00 P.M., Sunday from 11:00 A.M. to 10:00 P.M. Moderate.

Chicago Flat Sammies, 163 West Pearson Street; (312) 664-BRED. See page 50 for full description.

Coq d'Or, in the Drake Hotel, 140 East Walton Street; (312) 787-2200. See page 53 for full description.

Green Door Tavern, 678 North Orleans Street; (312) 664-5496. See page 49 for full description.

Mr. Beef on Orleans, 666 North Orleans Street; (312) 337-8500. See page 49 for full description.

The Oak Tree,
900 North Michigan
Avenue;
(312) 751–1988.
See page 52 for full
description.

Salpicón!,
1252 North Wells Street;
(312) 988–7811.
See page 55 for full
description.

Sayat-Nova,
157 East Ohio Street;
(312) 644–9159.
See page 47 for full
description.

Shaw's Crab House,
21 East Hubbard Street;
(312) 527–2722.
Walk into the swank, art
decoish bar area of this jus-
tifiably popular seafood
house, and you'd almost
expect Nick and Nora
Charles to be sitting at a
table, sipping dry martinis
and plotting their latest
"Thin Man" escapade.
Instead of moving on to the
main dining room—serv-
ing up the likes of splendid
sautéed Nantucket cape
scallops, grilled
Ecuadorean mahi-mahi,
and crab cakes, along with
the famed creamed
spinach—you might head
for the more chummy Blue
Crab Lounge, featuring an
"Oyster Hour" Monday
through Friday from 4:00
to 6:30 P.M. (The motto is
"Royster with the Oyster,"
which certainly sounds
snappy, although I don't
have the foggiest idea what

it means.) The dining room
is open Monday through
Thursday from 11:30 A.M.
to 2:00 P.M. and 5:30 to
10:00 P.M., Friday from
11:30 A.M. to 2:00 P.M. and
5:00 to 11:00 P.M., Saturday
from 5:00 to 11:00 P.M., and
Sunday from 5:00 to 10:00
P.M. Expensive.

Toast,
228 West Chicago Avenue;
(312) 944–7023.
Once you get inside this
compact space (there's usually a wait on weekends),
the experience is rewarding,
although you may not wish
to eavesdrop on your neighbors' conversation at the oh-
so-close next table,
especially if the party is on a
cell phone—which it often
seems to be. Just enjoy the
power tripping, and enjoy
the imaginative breakfast
("crabby eggs benedict,"
lemon poppy seed pan-
cakes, banana and chocolate
crepes) and lunch (seared
ahi tuna sandwiches) offerings. An interesting note:
Toast, which prides itself on
otherwise being a classy
operation, features over its
door a large, slowly turning,
lighted representation of,
well, a piece of toast. Open
Monday through Friday
from 8:00 A.M. to 3:00 P.M.,
Saturday and Sunday from
8:00 A.M. to 4:00 P.M.
Inexpensive.

Topo Gigio Ristorante,
1516 North Wells Street;
(312) 266–9355.
This warm place with fine
Italian food was a favorite of
now-deceased movie actor
Don Ameche. It's a favorite
of many others, judging by
the crowds it draws, especially on weekends. In the
warmer weather, it's often
hard to get a seat at the
bustling outdoor bar. The
name, as those of a certain
age will remember, comes
from that cute little mouse
puppet on "The Ed Sullivan
Show." It's hard to go wrong
with the menu items,
although, for old time's
sake, I always like to order
linguine alla Vic Damone.
And, no, I'm not going to
identify Vic Damone—or,
for that matter, Ed Sullivan.
Open for lunch Monday
through Saturday from
11:30 A.M. to 3:00 P.M., and
for dinner Monday through
Saturday from 4:00 to 11:00
P.M., Sunday from 4:00 to
10:00 P.M. Moderate.

Trattoria Dinotto,
163 West North Avenue;
(312) 787–3345;
Dinottoaol.com. "If you
can't pronounce it," the
waiter cracked to one
member of our party who
was placing an order, "I
can't serve it." He was kid-
ding, of course, because the
staff is extremely friendly
and helpful in this little
jewel of a storefront restaurant that's been around
since 1989. Intimate (that

is, the quarters are *close*) with tasteful, understated decor, the place is usually crowded, mostly, it seems, by locals who come for reasonably priced items like the penne pasta tossed with asparagus and mushrooms, linguine Genovese, roasted eggplant, goat cheese ravioli, fettucine with shrimp and broccoli, and veal marsala, enabled by a limited but decent wine list. Open Monday through Thursday from noon to 10:00 P.M., Friday and Saturday from noon to 11:00 P.M., Sunday from 5 to 9:00 P.M. Moderate.

Twin Anchors, 1655 North Sedgwick Street; (312) 266–1616. This steadfast restaurant has been around Old Town for more than sixty years, and it's *still* tough to get in there most nights without a wait. The reason most people come is for the house specialty—baby back ribs with "Zesty Sauce" or "Original Mild"—but there's also other no-nonsense fare like filet mignon, shrimp, and chicken. Open Monday through Thursday from 5:00 to 11:00 P.M., Friday from 5:00 P.M. to midnight, Saturday from noon to midnight, Sunday from noon to 10:30 P.M. Moderate.

Lincoln Park

O f all Chicago neighborhoods, Lincoln Park most exemplifies, for better or worse, the gentrification of the city. Once land occupied by working men and women, it has become exceedingly popular as the (highly congested) first stop for the postcollege crowd because of its location near Lake Michigan and Lincoln Park and proximity to downtown. Any semblance to a "real" American neighborhood may have ended in recent years when a longtime Woolworth's closed its doors.

The community contains refreshingly diverse architecture, from lakefront high-rises and modern town houses to frame and brick cottages, Victorian red-brick row houses, graystone three-flats, and plain old squatty, plug-ugly structures. Dubbed Yuppie Central, it is home to obscenely priced real estate (one huge single-family home—generically known as "starter castles" and "monster homes on steroids"—sold a while back for $4 million and change), latte-pouring coffee shops, trendy restaurants, highly respected theaters, pricey private schools, pocket-sized, upscale boutiques that seem to turn over faster than the merchandise, and plant-packed bars where, as someone once cracked, "You don't know whether to order a beer or a coleus."

Gone are the old-time characters, like the delightful lady who wouldn't think of wearing tennis socks with those little balls on the back, who cheerfully talked about her relative, the "cat" burglar, who would skip the houses on his own street out of neighborly courtesy.

Twenty years ago, the *Chicago Tribune*'s Sunday Magazine assigned two writers—one a Lincoln Parker, the other who lived in Hyde Park—to write about their neighborhoods and, not so incidentally, take playful swipes at the other one. The Hyde Parker (Jim Yuenger) proceeded to declare that Lincoln Park was the "land of the alfalfa sprout-and-avocado salad," where there are "300 different names for a hamburger," and where, "at any one time, there are 5,279 restaurants and 12 unoccupied parking spots."

In the 1830s the first wave of immigrants to Lincoln Park were Germans escaping religious persecution and political oppression in their

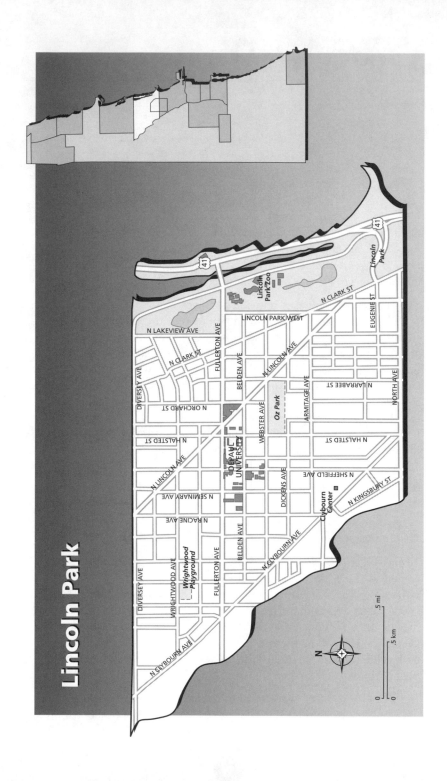

Lincoln Park

TOP ATTRACTIONS IN LINCOLN PARK

Farm in the Zoo

Peggy Notebaert Nature Museum

Elks Veterans Memorial Building

Oz Park

Victory Gardens Theater

Steppenwolf Studio Theatre and "Traffic"

homeland. Many became truck farmers. A small-pox hospital and the city cemetery were located in Lincoln Park until the 1860s because the area was still considered to be remote. In 1858 the first horsecar line ran along the central business district up Clark Street, and eventually it was extended to Wright's Grove, a popular German picnic grove and beer garden that became an Army camp during the Civil War.

In 1871 disaster struck with the Great Chicago Fire, which burned for three days and nights before being stopped at Fullerton Avenue and Clark Street. A building boom followed, with 60 percent of Lincoln Park's current structures built between 1880 and 1904—many of them workingmen's frame "Chicago cottages." Other architectural styles were Queen Anne, Italianate, Baroque, Georgian, and Prairie School.

By 1900 wealthy Germans were living in large houses near the lake, while middle-class and working-class Irish and Poles lived in flats farther west. Institutions attracted to the area included what are now Children's Memorial Hospital, DePaul University, and Lincoln Park Zoo (started with animals acquired from Barnum and Bailey Circus, and now one of the world's last free zoos). Lincoln Park continued to be an upscale residential district, but it tanked in the 1950s when families fled to the suburbs, as rundown rooming houses proliferated. Urban renewal took over in the 1960s, with members of neighborhood organizations (who called themselves "urban pioneers") determined to "turn back the bulldozers" and preserve the historic buildings, while poor families were forced out as gentrification pushed west beyond Halsted Street. Today, some sections of Lincoln Park are designated landmark areas in which facades of houses cannot be altered. (Theoretically, that is—this *is* Chicago.) Living side by side are persons in their twenties and thirties and middle-aged folks deserting their empty nests in the suburbs.

Lincoln Park is approximately 3 miles from downtown. Depending on traffic, taxi rides usually take from ten to fifteen minutes, while buses take twice that time. Lincoln Park is primarily served by the #151, which goes north along Lake Shore Drive and then wanders through the park; #156, which starts in the Loop financial district and also winds through the park; #22, which runs along Clark Street; and #36, which ends up on Clark. Chicago Transit Authority trains include the Red Line (Howard-Dan Ryan) to North Avenue and Fullerton, which you can board downtown along State Street or Grand or Chicago Avenues on the Near North Side, and the Brown Line (Ravenswood), which stops at Sedgwick, Armitage, Fullerton, and Diversey and which you can pick up at the Merchandise Mart. The three major streets for shopping and dining are Clark Street, Lincoln Avenue, and Halsted Street.

Both the park and the neighborhood begin at North Avenue near the Chicago Historical Society. It's a good place to start exploring the community. Walk along Clark Street north until you see the Days Inn Gold Coast, then take a right to North Cannon Drive and the *Farm in the Zoo.* Visitors rushing to check out high-profile tigers and seals at the main Lincoln Park Zoo may well miss this charming side attraction. The Farm is a great opportunity for city kids, especially, to learn the difference between the different animals—which isn't as far-fetched as it sounds. Reportedly, a petting zoo in the popular Wisconsin Dells resort area was forced to hang signs around the animals' necks because parents from Chicago would point out a "goat" to their children when it actually was a sheep. Apocryphal or not, the Farm in the Zoo makes it easy, dividing the animals into various barns, including Horse, Poultry, Dairy, and Livestock. Animals on display a while ago included a Shetland pony named Snickers, a Holstein calf named Rocket, and a huge mixed-breed sow named Minnie. There are also educational displays such as "Honeybee Trivia," an exhibit in which chicks "pip" (break open) their shells, and cow milking at 10:00 A.M., noon, and 2:00 P.M. Daily events include "Meet the Animals," "Horse Grooming," and "Butter Churning," and there's a farmer's market the fourth Sunday of the month from June through October. The Farm in the Zoo is open from 9:00 A.M. to 4:30 P.M. every day. Please, no inline skating or bike riding, and leave your pets at home. Phone (773) 742–2000, or visit www.lpzoo.com.

A Neighborhood and a Park

*T*he 1,212-acre **Lincoln Park,** Chicago's largest and busiest park, winds along 6 miles of Lake Michigan shoreline. Much of it was created from landfill, including the section from North Avenue to Webster Avenue, which originally was the municipal cemetery. As the population grew, there was pressure to relocate the bod-ies farther north for health reasons. Creation of Central Park in New York City inspired Chicago leaders—who had acquired 120 acres of swampland—to begin plans for Lake Park in 1864. Subsequently, Lake Park and its adjacent neighborhood were renamed Lincoln Park after the assassination of President Lincoln in 1865.

A place for a quick lunch near the Farm is the usual fast-food fare on the ground level of *Cafe Brauer,* located next to a lagoon where you can rent paddle boats. After being abandoned for years to pigeons and squirrels, Cafe Brauer (1908), a fine example of the Prairie School style, was gloriously restored in 1989. The Great Hall on the second floor rises 34 feet from the floor to the skylight and features two art-glass chandeliers. The cafe was highly popular until after the repeal of Prohibition, but the dining room hit the skids when state law forbade the sale of liquor in parks. No such law exists today, though, and at night the upstairs of the cafe is lit up brightly as the *Gatsby*-like scene of swanky fund-raisers and other events.

For a more ambitious lunch, you might want to try *R.J. Grunts* (2056 North Lincoln Park West), which proudly bills itself as having "the worst name for a restaurant in history" (no quarrel there) and was the first-established eatery (1971) in Lettuce Entertain You, the ubiquitous local empire. Outside, a list of '70s terms reflects that decade: "Hot Pants," "Peter Max," "Streaking," "Woodstock," "Spiro Agnew," "head shop," "Laugh In," "Lenny Bruce." Inside, over the front door, is a wood sculpture depicting heads of people stuffed into a sardine can, which is appropriate. The place uses every square inch of space, with some tables turning up in the most unlikely spots. On the walls are photos not of celebrities—a refreshing change—but waitresses who have worked there over the years. The menu, which is cutesy (sometimes too cutesy), announces that it is "Catering to the Neurotic Compensation of Eating," and that "these items meet no particular guidelines, but R.J. likes them and so does the Swedish Bikini team." On the back of the menu, a comiclike panel gives a whimsical history of the place. The food is satisfactory and aimed at its popular family trade. There is, of course, the "Gruntburger" (fortunately, tastier than it sounds), as well as ribs and chicken, and there's also a unique item called Temperature

Sorry, We Don't Serve Sea Lions Here

*I*n 1889, eighteen sea lions arrived at the Lincoln Park Zoo—but before their pool was completed. Two actually managed to get out and, so the story goes, waddled across the park and into a diner on Clark Street.

Soup ("We charge today's lakefront temperature")—which, naturally, is a real bargain in January and February. R. J. Grunts is open Monday through Thursday from 11:30 A.M. to 10:00 P.M., Friday and Saturday from 11:30 A.M. to 10:30 P.M., Sunday from 11:30 A.M. to 9:00 P.M. Sunday. Phone (773) 929–5363. Moderate.

Those feeling in a more sophisticated mood might wait for dinner and visit **Mon Ami Gabi,** located in the Belden-Stratford Hotel at 2300 North Lincoln Park West. Featuring a dark, romantic French bistro aura, the restaurant offers classics such as several sirloin steak frites options, bouillabaisse Marseilles, onion soup, boeuf bourguignon, Chilean sea bass, Coquilles Gabi, Mussels a la Claude, sautéed garlic potatoes, and terrific pommes frites. Desserts include crepes and chocolate mousse, and wine samples are available on a rolling cart. Dinner only. The restaurant is named after chef-owner Gabino Sotelino, who also runs the more pricey Ambria restaurant across the hotel lobby. Born in Spain, Sotelino worked his way up through top kitchens, has won many prestigious international awards, and is now a die-hard Chicagoan. "There's no city in this country I would change for it," he says. "Even in Europe, I say the same thing." Open Monday through Thursday from 5:30 to 10:00 P.M., Friday and Saturday from 5:30 to 11:00 P.M., Sunday from 5:00 to 9:00 P.M. Expensive. Phone (773) 348–8886.

Across the street, tucked away in a corner of the zoo, just east of the Lincoln Park Conservatory, is the wonderful **Zoo Rookery,** neglected by visitors and its keepers for years. Serving as an urban sanctuary for migrating and resident birds and ducks, it came about in 1937, when Alfred Caldwell redesigned a Victorian lily pool to make it look more like a Prairie School scheme. He put in layered stonework and native plants, but in recent years the zoo shamelessly let it run down. Now, as of this writing, it is finally getting the extensive renovation—including dredging of that pool—it deserves.

Right across Fullerton Avenue is the very spiffy, state-of-the-art **Peggy Notebaert Nature Museum** (2430 North Cannon Drive) on Lincoln

Slip Me Some Skin

*P*ark Cafe, now a popular restaurant in Lincoln Park Zoo, formerly was the home of snakes and crocodiles as the zoo's Reptile House. Originally, the building opened as the city's first aquarium.

Park land formerly occupied by a run-down maintenance building. Before it opened, the Chicago Academy of Sciences ran a museum a few blocks south in the park in a musty old building that featured equal parts charm and seediness. It was best known for its realistic-looking dioramas of plants and wildlife—wolves with just-caught prey in their mouths, that sort of thing. The new Nature Museum does contain dioramas of Midwest landscapes—dunes, a savanna, a prairie—but a lot more, including all kinds of interactive activities, buttons to push, and videos to start. One of the most original and interesting exhibits appears a short distance from the entrance: "Water Lab," where you can push buttons to create "rainstorms" and open and lower locks on a simulated Chicago River (yes, the one that flows "backwards"). In one setup, children (and adults) may create their own river features and experiment with the dynamics of water flow and river channels as they push around objects in a bed of sand on a large "stream" table. Another enjoyable exhibit is "Butterfly Haven," a 2,700-square-foot glass atrium that is home to some fifteen to twenty different species of butterflies and moths native to Illinois and North America. There are also signs warning: BUTTERFLIES MAY LAND ON YOU. CHECK FOR STOWAWAYS BEFORE YOU LEAVE. GENTLY BRUSH ANY HITCHHIKERS ONTO A PLANT. Other spots in the museum include a "Children's Gallery," with a walk-in model of a beaver lodge, and "Environmental Central," a computer-filled room (for ages 10 to adult) designed to sort out solutions to large-scale environmental problems. There are also snacks in the Butterfly Cafe and, in the Museum Shop, things for sale from a ladybug village to wind-up grasshoppers, a frog lamp and lampshade, and a leaf-collecting album. One complaint: For some reason, much of the museum is devoted to technology and industry, such as exhibits on how electricity and gas serve our homes, and displays of sewer lines. Fine, for the Museum of Science and Industry, but this is supposed to be a place about *nature*. And, blame it on the nostalgia of a parent with no-longer-young-and-wide-eyed kids, I still miss that funky old dark, mysterious building with the dioramas with wolves and things in their mouths. The Notebaert Nature Museum is open weekdays from 9:00 A.M. to 4:30 P.M. and weekends from 10:00 A.M. to 5:00 P.M. It's closed New Year's Day, Thanksgiving, and Christmas. Admission is $6.00 for adults, $4.00 for seniors, $3.00 for children, and $4.00 for students. Phone (773) 549–0606, or check out www.chias.org.

North Pond Cafe, which has been called "Chicago's Tavern on the Green" (there's that Second City thing again), lists itself as being at 2610 North Cannon Drive, but that really doesn't help much. Parking is horrendous. Just walk north on Clark Street and then 1 block east to Lakeview Avenue at Deming Place, cut over to the North Pond and you'll see the restaurant on the far shore. The building, a onetime ice skaters' shelter, of all things, has a Frank Lloyd Wright interior quality, with a sort of Midwest prairie/art deco motif. Even the banquettes have a stylish look with their representations of pond reeds. Inside and out (depending on the weather, naturally) there are lovely views of the park. Emphasizing regional Midwest dishes, the menu is excitingly ambitious—and sinfully rich. "If you're looking to watch your cholesterol," one waiter says with a knowing grin, "you've come to the wrong place." Appetizers may include roasted Wisconsin squash soup and sugar pumpkin gnocchi, while entrees may range from pan-roasted boneless Wisconsin pheasant to grilled Maine diver scallops, Prairie Grove frenched pork chop, roasted Illinois venison rack, and herb-crusted Maryland wild striped bass. Accompaniments, far from the ordinary, may include scarlet turnip and parsnip gratin, black trumpet and hedgehog mushroom ragout, sautéed Snug Haven spinach, and celeriac and Yukon gold potato puree. For dessert, try the Michigan bosc pear almond cream tart with cinnamon ice cream or the Washington state apple and lavender tart with pumpkin ice cream and vanilla custard. There's also a good list of California, Oregon, and Washington wines. Open Tuesday through Saturday from 5:30 to 10:00 P.M., Sunday from 11:00 A.M. to 2:00 P.M. (brunch) and 5:30 to 10:00 P.M. With the arrival of warm weather on April 1, lunch is also served Tuesday through Saturday from 11:30 A.M. to 2:00 P.M. Phone (773) 477–5845. Expensive.

Even many longtime residents of Lincoln Park, curiously, have never stepped foot inside a structure they often pass: the gargantuan *Elks Veterans Memorial Building* at 2750 North Lakeview Avenue, across from the park and just south of Diversey Avenue. So said our friendly guide on a tour one afternoon, as she led a group through an opulent—some might say gaudy—building that has an interior resembling the grandest of European castles. Passersby won't fail to notice the two life-size elk statues (by Laura Gardin Fraser) that flank the lengthy front steps. Inside, there are all kinds of statues and paintings and tons of marble (from six different countries), even marble radiator covers. Opened in 1926 and designed by New York architect Egerton Swarthout, it was dedicated to the memory of the Elks who died in World War I, and fallen veterans in subsequent wars have also been included. In recent times there was a five-year, $5 million restoration—twice the original cost of the building. The centerpiece is the 100-foot Memorial Rotunda, featuring colored marble and a dozen huge allegorical mural paintings, created by Eugene Savage. Close by is the Grand Reception Hall, which served as a location for *Richie Rich,* the 1994 movie adaptation of the comic strip about the world's wealthiest boy. Downstairs, a memorabilia room contains small

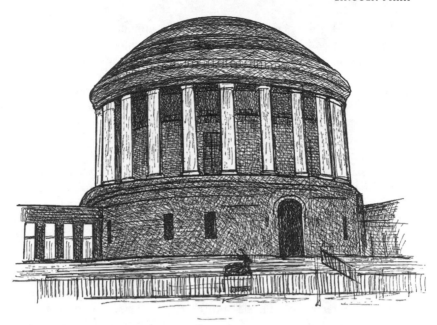

Elks Veterans Memorial Building

replicas of Elk Rose Bowl Parade floats. Along the tour, the guide also noted that even all the door knobs in the building feature Elk insignias, that the charity-oriented fraternity was founded in 1868 by fifteen actors and other theater types known as "the Original Jolly Corks," and that the membership roster has included Presidents Harry Truman and John F. Kennedy and actor Clint Eastwood. Looking at photographs in the Grand Exalted Rulers room, she pointed out that the Rulers in the late 1800s all had flowing mustaches that made them resemble a collection of Wyatt Earps. She added, with a smile, that late 1800s medals contained small replicas of moose heads. Seems one of the Elk founders was English and apparently didn't know the difference between a moose and an elk. The Memorial is open Monday through Friday from 9:00 A.M. to 5:00 P.M. year-round, and Saturday and Sunday from 10:00 A.M. to 5:00 P.M. from April 15 to November 15. Phone (773) 755–4700.

Walking west on Diversey, away from the park, brings you to Clark Street, where a mishmash of stores and fast-food places are located. Among those standing out is **2nd Hand Tunes** ("Buy-Sell-Trade"). There are now several locations, but this one at 2602–2604 North Clark is the flagship, having hung around in the same vicinity since 1976. Its wares are new and used compact discs and records—about 70 percent used, the rest new—and even the new stuff is deeply discounted. Also on sale are movie posters and videos. Unlike most of its counterparts, where the facilities are about as tidy as a 12-year-old boy's bedroom, the items are, surprisingly, neatly arranged. One space is mostly devoted to CDs, with categories that to persons of a certain age may seem befuddling: Trance and Ambient, Techno, Trip-Hop, Jungle/Electronica. Oh, yes, they also have Sinatra and Streisand. And opera, country, blues, reggae, comedy, movie sound tracks, and gospel. In the record space, there are new and used LPs from Beastie Boys to Bach to Brubeck. One afternoon I took a brief nostalgia trip, spotting albums by the likes of the Coasters, Bobby Darin, the McGuire Sisters, Julie London (be still my heart), and Mario Lanza. Plus, there were 7-inch records selling for, amazingly, a dime. Open Monday through Saturday from 11:00 A.M. to 8:00 P.M., Sunday from noon to 7:00 P.M. Phone (773) 281–6209 or 929–6027.

Reebie Storage & Moving Company (2325 North Clark) may be the only moving company in the country to feature a plaque listing it on the Department of Interior's National Register of Historic Sites. The reason? The colorful terra-cotta facade and interior of the seven-story warehouse, designed by Chicago architect George S. Kingsley and completed in 1923, displays an Ancient Egyptian Revival decor, which resurfaced nationally after the opening of King Tutankhamen's tomb in 1922. On the exterior of the building (now dubbed "King Tut on Clark Street") there are five ornate papyrus columns. Two 10-foot statues of Pharaoh Ramses II (said to represent founders William and John Reebie, although a company spokesman denies this) flank the bronze front door. The hieroglyphics at the base of the statues translate as "Forever, I work for all of your regions in daylight and darkness" and "I give protection to your furniture." The theme is also picked up inside in the marble and porcelain lobby, featuring lotus-blossomed pillars and thirty-one plaster plaques, some of which depict ancient Egyptians

Well, Which Was it?

*T*here is no dispute that the *Richard Bellinger Cottage (1869)* survived the Great Fire of 1871. Obviously, it did, because it's still standing at 2121 North Hudson Avenue, with a historic plaque and all. A good example of an 1860s Chicago cottage, it was located near the north end of the fire's reach, and legend has it that Bellinger, a Chicago policeman, soaked the roof with cider, although his wife claimed it was water and others have said it was iced tea. Whatever, it worked.

transporting and storing goods. (The building motto at the time of its opening, it should be noted, was "If old King Tut were alive today, he'd store his goods the Reebie way.") Just off the lobby is a bank-sized vault, where folks like the Vanderbilts and Rockefellers used to stash their jewels, and another space was once known as the "Piano Room," a storage area for the instruments before they were shipped to Orchestra Hall to be played by musicians like Artur Rubinstein. If all that weren't enough, Reebie—established in 1880 and now an Allied agent—also brags that it is the "Official Mover of the Chicago Cubs." Stop in or phone (800) 223–0120.

Tower Records (2301 North Clark) is best known for its extensive collection of CDs, especially classical and jazz, but it's also the place for those with different kinds of musical tastes. Young people gather here, mostly on weekends, for free performances by recording groups with not-so-classical names. (If you *do* know their names, you're probably not reading this book.) One afternoon, older customers may have been startled to see a notice on the door that opera star Leontyne Price—not exactly a favorite of Smashing Pumpkins fans—would be appearing at Tower. Was she unaware of the kind of venue in which she'd be performing? Possibly. A few days later, another notice stated that Miss Price's appearance had been canceled. No reason given. Lincoln Park historians may wish to note that Tower Records is located in a sprawling, unsightly building on a site that used to be a mini-mall. One of the establishments was the now-late, lamented, yes, legendary Belden Deli, where, on any given morning, one could observe men with huge cigars and bigger stomachs making deals over bagels and bialys. Tower is open every day from 9:00 A.M. to midnight. Phone (773) 477–5994.

Chicago pizza mavens often debate the merits of "deep dish" versus "thin crust," but at one longtime favorite restaurant, there is a third alternative. Packing crowds in most every night (be prepared to wait unless you're ready to become an early-bird diner) *Chicago Pizza & Oven Grinder Company* (2121 North Clark) offers up either a half-pound or one-pound Pizza Pot Pie. Sometimes described as "upside-down pizza," this concoction, which arrives in a bowl, resembles a pudgy, gooey mushroom. Perhaps the taste has to be acquired, but judging from those crowds, a lot of folks have acquired it. As for the ingredients, the menu reports that the individual servings feature "triple-raised Sicilian bread-type dough; a homemade sauce consisting of olive oil, fresh garlic, onions, green peppers, whole plum tomatoes, and a special blend of cheeses; sausage made from prime Boston butts [a notation which, judging from experience as a parent, is sure

Lincoln Park Trivia Part I

Question: *What actor played the Tin Woodman in the 1939 MGM version of* The Wizard of Oz?

Answer: *Jack Haley, who went on to make such forgettable films as* Scared Stiff *and* Vacation in Reno.

to draw guffaws from younger diners], and doorknob-size whole, fresh mushrooms." A vegetarian version is also available. The restaurant itself, opened in 1972, is located on the ground floor of a brownstone and is rather dark but charming in an old-fashioned sense, with low ceilings, booths, and pine paneling galore. Other items on the menu include those oven grinders (Italian sandwiches with choice of salami, ham, meatballs, or sausage) and salads, and there's an attractive bar. History buffs will want to note that the restaurant is almost directly across the street from the site of the infamous St. Valentine Day's Massacre. Rumor has it that the brownstone served as a lookout post for Al Capone's gunmen. Open Monday through Thursday from 4:00 to 11:00 P.M., Friday from 4:00 P.M. to midnight, Saturday from noon to midnight, and Sunday from noon to 11:00 P.M. Phone (773) 248–2570. Inexpensive. Cash only.

Farther south, Lincoln Avenue, which cuts diagonally through Lincoln Park up to Diversey Avenue, begins near the park and the Days Inn Hotel. Walk northwest for about ten minutes—or grab the #11 bus— and you'll come to *Oz Park,* which may be one of the most utilized public parks in the Chicago area per square foot. Once a jumbled parcel of vacant land with gnarled old trees that provided a haven for woodpeckers, it is now the site of all kinds of activities (too frantic for much birding, though). Bounded by Larrabee Street, Webster Avenue, Halsted Street, and Dickens Avenue, it is located next door to Lincoln Park High School, best known for its International Baccalaureate program. Depending on the season, someone strolling through Oz (named for the literary creation of onetime neighborhood resident, Frank L. Baum, who reportedly wrote his famous books from an office downtown in the Fine Arts Building) may see teenagers taking on each other in basketball, adults going at it in formal or informal touch football and softball games, local residents playing tennis, the high school football team preparing for its season in the broiling August sun, or pee-wee soccer players trying to figure out which goal is theirs. Along the Webster Avenue side, there's the wonderful "Dorothy's Playground," officially designed for ages 5 to 12 (although it's doubtful any self-respecting subteen would be caught dead there among the wooden play equipment) and constructed in the 1970s by neighbors who followed a plan drawn up by a national playground builder. Also along Webster is a lovely, grassy fenced-off garden area, where young mothers often watch their toddlers out of harm's way from the softball players, and where passersby—yes, even tourists—may rest on one of the benches. At the corner of Larrabee, Lincoln, and Webster is a 1995 sculpture by John Kearney, a local artist who specializes in working with old chrome car

The "Tin Man" at Oz Park

bumpers. This work, surrounded by yellow bricks, is, for some reason, entitled *Tin Man*. (The character in *The Wizard of Oz*—a little nit-picking here—is actually called the Tin *Woodman*.)

A short walk north of the park won't land you in Oz, but, perhaps, the 1960s. There sits *Sterch's* (2238 Lincoln Avenue), a no-nonsense saloon (not a fern in sight) where the clientele looks as if it might have just climbed out of a Jerry Garcia–style camper van after hugging a few trees. To make sure you get the point that present-day trendiness simply won't be tolerated, a well-worn sign in the window advises, NO CORONA. NO FOOLISH DRINKS. LIMITED DANCING. The bar is open every day from 3:30 P.M. to 2:00 A.M.—except, another sign notes, FOR BEAR GAMES, SOME CUB GAMES . . . WHEN HARLAN [the owner] IS LATE . . . AND WHEN WE FEEL LIKE DOING SOMETHING DIFFERENT. Phone (773) 281–2653.

As far as Europe, Chicago is known for its deep-dish pizza, or pizza-in-a-pan, consisting of tomatoes, cheese, sausage, and vegetables in a thick, doughy crust. Some, however, disdain it, such as the San Francisco visitor who snorted, "That's not pizza—that's pudding." Whatever, aficionados will find one of the best examples of the deep-dish at *Bacino's* (2204 North Lincoln Avenue), a bustling restaurant in the midst of the avenue's general bustle, that bills itself as serving "America's 1st Heart Healthy Pizza." I'm no cardiologist, but I know what we like, and my particular favorite is the Spinach Supreme, which not only is allegedly "heart healthy" but also comes with free mushrooms for those so inclined. Other choices include Bacino's Special (Italian sausage), Very Vegetarian, and Broccoli Bacino's. Open Monday through Thursday from 11:00 A.M. to 10:30 P.M., Friday and Saturday from 11:00 A.M. to 12:30 A.M., Sunday from noon to 10:00 P.M. Phone (773) 472–7400. Carryout and delivery also. Inexpensive.

Located essentially in a storefront at 2257 Lincoln Avenue, *Victory Gardens Theater* is one of the oldest of the city's Off-Loop theaters, founded in 1974 by a (still) married couple: Dennis Zacek, a Loyola University theater teacher, and Marcie McVay, a social worker. Nourishing local talent, it also has featured such performers as Julie Harris and William Petersen, and Sharon Gless (of television's popular female-cop show *Cagney and Lacey*). Victory Gardens has gone through some rough times in the always-competitive Chicago market, which seemingly has more theaters than pizza toppings. But its capacity a while back topped 91 percent, and it continues to earn multiple nominations for the prestigious local Joseph Jefferson Awards. Following renovations, there are now four small (200-person capacity each) performance spaces. Its mission statement reads that the theater is "dedicated to playwrights and their works," and over the years more than half of its 200-plus plays have been world premieres, many by the theater's own ensemble of twelve playwrights. The theater also is home to plays by the Irish Repertory of Chicago and operates a training center for actors, directors and playwrights. For information, call (773) 871–3000.

A few blocks later you'll come to the maddening intersection of Lincoln-Fullerton-Halsted, where every day is a shooting gallery for cars and buses taking aim at pedestrians. If you manage to figure out all the turn and "walk" indications and make it safely across, continue up Lincoln to the *Biograph Theater* (2433 Lincoln Avenue), where the marquee still pretty much looks like it did in the 1930s, except that there is no longer a banner that boasts COOLED BY REFRIGERATION. A plaque designates the theater a National Register of Historic Places by the Department of the Interior because it was on July 22, 1934, that "Public Enemy No. 1" hoodlum John Dillinger was gunned down by G-men in the nearby alley after he had caught a Biograph movie. The FBI agents had been tipped off by the bank robber's friend, Anna Sage, the infamous "Lady in Red." As of this writing, the theater had been sold to an independent company, which was presenting various "special event" film festivals, along with independent and art films and "alternative cinema." A spokesperson also promised to restore to its ticket booth photocopies of original *Chicago Daily News* stories with such headlines as "Desperado Dies with Revolver in Hand in Lincoln Avenue Trap," "Girl Tricks Dillinger," and "A Small Town Hick . . . and a Swelled Head." A notice stated that the theater would next become "the home of a variety of presentations including film, theater, music, dance, and special events."

If anything epitomizes the change in Lincoln Park over the years, it is *Uncle Dan's* (2440 Lincoln Avenue), which used to be one of those Army/Navy stores where you could buy things like rough-and-tough

Lincoln Park Trivia Part II

Question: *What movie was John Dillinger watching before he was gunned down by G-men at the Biograph Theater?*

Answer: Manhattan Melodrama, *with Clark Gable, William Powell, and Myrna Loy in a familiar 1930s Hollywood story of boyhood pals who remain adult friends even though one is a gangster and the other a district attorney.*

tank division patches from World War II. No longer. The sign hanging outside still reads ARMY, NAVY, CAMPING AND TRAVEL, but you might as well forget the Army/Navy bit. Decidedly, it's an upscale "Great Outdoor Store," as it also calls itself, with upscale clothing (all kinds of Polartec), costly backpacks, tents, and camping gear. Uncle Dan's these days also has, of all things, catchy marketing mottoes ("We've Been Outside for 29 Years and We're Not Coming In"). It's open Monday through Thursday from 10:00 A.M. to 8:00 P.M., Friday and Saturday from 10:00 A.M. to 7:00 P.M., Sunday from 11:00 A.M. to 5:00 P.M. Phone (773) 477–1918.

THE ONLY ENGLISH PUB FOR FOOD-DRINK proclaims the sign outside *The Red Lion* (2446 North Lincoln Avenue), started in 1984 by John Cordwell, a now-deceased Chicago architect and native Englishman who, as a downed RAF flyer, spent three and a half years as a prisoner of war in an infamous German camp, Stalag Luft III, the real-life site of the 1963 Steve McQueen movie *The Great Escape.* The pub decor includes a red London phone booth and map of that city's Underground. As for the pub food, it's good, nourishing, and authentically Brit: shepherd's pie (our family favorite), fish and chips, steak and kidney pie, bangers and mash, Cornish pasties, and for a sweet, an English trifle. (Unfortunately, the menu also panders to Americans with a "John Bull" burger and— God save the Queen!—*key lime pie.*) Bartender Colin Cordwell (John's son and now co-owner) cheerfully serves up pints of tasty beers and ales like Newcastle and Boddington's. Another bit of Red Lion history: It was there that director Barbara Gaines—head of the tremendously successful Chicago Shakespeare Theater on Navy Pier—first presented one of the Bard's plays, *Henry V,* on a shoestring budget on the roof of the pub in 1986. Gaines later recalled in an interview that it was pouring rain that night, but, miraculously, the drops never managed to hit the stage. The kitchen is open every day from 2:00 to 11:00 P.M. Phone (773) 348–2695. Inexpensive.

Serving the neighborhood since 1934, *Schmeissing Bakery* (2679 Lincoln Avenue) is an old-fashioned German establishment that features everything from custom-made birthday cakes for children to wonderful tortes and "artisan breads," including pecan raisin, cranberry walnut, and country French. Open Monday through Friday from 6:00 A.M. to 7:00 P.M., Saturday from 6:00 A.M. to 6:00 P.M. Phone (773) 525–3753.

The *Apollo Theater* (2540 Lincoln Avenue) was born in the 1970s, the brainchild of two young entrepreneurs who later departed for the movie business in California. Cleverly using the odd space—right next to the L tracks—the theater is stylish and comfortable, and incredibly soundproofed against those rumbling trains. The theater surely offers one of the most eclectic programming schedules in the city, with productions in recent years having included *The Buddy Holly Story, The Vagina Monologues,* and *Cinderella.* Phone (773) 935–6100 for show times and prices.

The **Lucky Strike** (2747 Lincoln Avenue) is not your father's bowling alley. (For starters, they call them bowling *lanes* these days.) Located on the former site of an Italian restaurant and a dinner theater, it is obviously geared toward the upscale locals and features a striking art deco marquee and decor, along with eight lanes, seven pool tables, and two bars. One night a while back, a beer company was giving a lecture about beer, including the history of brewing (who ever said bowling wasn't educational?), but a bartender says the place has discontinued the lectures as customers have become more savvy about, well, beer. Items from the menu—grilled portabella mushroom sandwich, Caesar salad—are decidedly not your standard Slim Jims-and-pretzels fare. "People like this place," says one 25-year-old patron, "because you don't have the top bowlers—you know, the guys in the leagues with those gloves." The Lucky Strike is open Monday through Friday from 5:00 P.M. to 2:00 A.M., Saturday from noon to 3:00 A.M., Sunday from noon to 1:00 A.M. Phone (773) 549–BOWL (2695).

When people walk into **Steve Starr Studios** (2779 Lincoln Avenue) and gawk at the wall filled with more than 800 original art deco photo frames filled with photos of movie stars, mostly from the '30s and '40s, they often spot one striking blonde and ask who she is. Starr tells them it is Veronica Lake, costar to Alan Ladd and other leading men and known for her famous "peek-a-boo bang" hairstyle obscuring one eye. The frames and photos are only some of the '30s/art deco items offered for sale by the proprietor, who has been in business since 1967. A sign in the middle of the store lists a bunch of no's, including NO UNSUPERVISED CHILDREN, NO BIKES, AND NO IDIOTS. (Starr says with a grin that he really doesn't attract many in the last category.) Collectors and browsers alike are captivated by the barware (especially the always-in-demand martini shakers and glasses), jewelry, cigarette lighters, ashtrays, lamps, hats, dresses, mirrors, and flasks. Like a good neighbor, Starr offers a guide listing other stores on Lincoln Avenue. Patrons over the years at his own place have included such *People* magazine types as Diana Ross, Bette Midler, and Harrison Ford—some of whom Starr says he recognized, unfortunately, only after they'd left. The store is open to the public from 2:00 to 6:00 P.M. Monday through Friday, 1:00 to 5:00 P.M. Saturday and Sunday. Phone (773) 525–6530.

Farther west is Halsted Street, an incredibly long street that runs through much of the city and which, in Lincoln Park, is the scene of varied attractions from North Avenue to Diversey Avenue. Starting at the south end (that is, North Avenue) is *Steppenwolf Theatre* (1650 North Halsted Street). The mainstage is the site of nationally known productions, some starring their celebrity members—such as John Malkovich, Gary Sinise, and Laurie Metcalf—who have gone on to film and television. For tickets to the hottest plays, theatergoers may line up for hours, as they did for the Sinise-starring *One Flew Over the Cuckoo's Nest*. But for those who want to experience good entertainment and don't want to put up with the hassle, Steppenwolf has two other options. The first is its Studio Theatre, accurately billed as "Big Drama in a Small Space." The upstairs space is dedicated to both the premiere of new works and the presentations of guest ensemble companies, such as European Repertory's production of Chekhov's *The Duel*. The second Steppenwolf choice is its "Traffic" series, presented on Monday nights when the mainstage is "dark." The lineup recently has ranged from '60s folk singer Ramblin' Jack Elliott to authors Frank McCourt and Kurt Vonnegut reading from their works. Phone (312) 335–1650 for information and ticket prices. The box office is open Monday from 11:00 A.M. to 5:00 P.M. and Tuesday through Sunday from 11:00 A.M. to 7:00 P.M.

Using the intersection of Halsted and Armitage Avenue as the hub, you can fan out for several blocks in either direction to find a number of diverse shops, from various chi-chi boutiques (many of which seem to come and go as frequently as this year's fashions) to a no-nonsense hardware store. Among the more interesting is *Expressly Wood* (825 Armitage Avenue), which sells items that are almost completely made out of you-know-what. Best-sellers, one clerk notes, are picture frames, jewelry boxes, and "kids' stuff," but there are also hat racks, clocks, chess and Chinese checker sets, clipboards, bookends, salad bowls, birdhouses, toy trains, and even fancy chopsticks. Open Monday through Thursday from 11:00 A.M. to 7:00 P.M., Friday from 11:00 A.M. to 6:00 P.M., Saturday from 10:00 A.M. to 6:00 P.M., Sunday from noon to 5:00 P.M.

A couple blocks to the west is the *Old Town School of Folk Music* (909 Armitage Avenue), housed in an 1896 Baroque building (restored in 1987), complete with cherubs and fancy corner bays. The Lincoln Park facility is home to a music store called the Little Strummer. (Performances at the legendary school, born in the 1950s, are now held at 4544 North Lincoln Avenue, where the school moved in 1998.) Items in the Little Strummer are aimed toward, as a staffer says, "age 6 months—maybe age *zero*—up to 10," although the store has been adding guitars for teenagers and adults. There are song books and CDs, tap and ballet shoes, small-fry guitars and ukuleles, tambourines, tom-toms, toy pianos, and even flageolets (a small woodwind instrument in the flute family, similar to a recorder). Next to the store, just off a funky lobby, is a snack bar called the Pick Stop. Classes for children and teens in music, art, dance, theater, and yoga are also offered at the Lincoln Park facility, including Wiggleworms music classes for ages 6 months to 3 years. Open Monday through Thursday from 10:00 A.M. to 9:00 P.M., Friday, Saturday, and Sunday from 10:00 A.M. to 5:00 P.M. Phone (773) 728–6000.

Across the street, next door to gourmet-heaven Charlie Trotter's restaurant, is **Lori's Discount Designer Shoes** (824 Armitage Avenue), which has expanded from its much smaller, nearby original location and calls itself, heh-heh, "The Sole of Chicago." Besides truly discounted footwear (including shoes for brides), there is a large assortment of purses. Open

Best Name in Lincoln Park: The Bourgeois Pig Cafe

*L*ocated a few blocks west of Lincoln Park, where tear-gassed demonstrators protested the 1968 Democratic Convention, this coffee house/restaurant at 738 West Fullerton Parkway is housed in a venerable building across the street from Children's Memorial Hospital. The name, besides being funny, is also meant to tweak those corporate coffee houses (most probably, the ones with the green and white awnings). Besides all kinds of coffee, some with cutesy names, the Pig serves up salads, soups, grilled panini, and sandwiches, also with cutesy names—including the "Henry VIII" (roast beef), "Merchant of Venice" (Genoa salami), and "Old Man and the Sea" (an excellent tuna salad, one of the best in the city).

The place is truly a throwback to the '60s, where you'd expect customers to be perusing The New York Times or lambasting the pols in Washington. The unisex bathroom has an old-fashioned bathtub, with a potted plant sitting in the middle of it. There's a well-worn oak floor, "lived in" (i.e., beat-up) chairs and tables and reading material (magazines, newspapers, used books), and a motley decor that encompassed, as of this writing, a vintage typewriter, fans, cigar boxes, a pear crate, a coffee grinder, and a potato chip can. The cafe, unusual for Lincoln Park, attracts a diversity of age groups, some of whom were even alive in the '60s, and is a favorite of police officers—who, of course, were once known in certain circles as . . . well, a certain farm animal. Open Monday through Thursday from 6:30 A.M. to 11:00 P.M., Friday from 6:30 A.M. to midnight, Saturday from 8:00 A.M. to midnight, Sunday from 8:00 A.M. to 11:00 P.M. Phone (773) 883–5282. Inexpensive.

Monday through Thursday from 11:00 A.M. to 7:00 P.M., Friday from 11:00 A.M. to 6:00 P.M., Saturday from 10:00 A.M. to 6:00 P.M., Sunday from noon to 5:00 P.M. Phone (773) 281–5655.

Many of the items at *Ancient Echoes* (1003 Armitage Avenue) are one-of-a-kind or reflect cultures from around the world. Among those offered for sale on a particular day may be Passover seder plates, steel wall mirrors, jewelry with historical motifs, such as an Egyptian scarab beetle, Tibetan hats, gold and platinum martini glasses, chandeliers, and washi boxes, which are used in Japan to store bulk tea. The store— "Fine Jewelry/Serious Art"—is open Monday through Friday from 11:00 A.M. to 7:00 P.M., Saturday from 10:00 A.M. to 6:00 P.M., Sunday from noon to 5:00 P.M. Phone (773) 880–1003.

Now go back to Halsted and walk a little way north to *Saturday's Child* (2146 Halsted Street). Look around carefully, and it's hard to find a battery in sight in this long-established local favorite that specializes in toys for kids, mostly from preschool age but up to 14. Noting the lack of high-tech bells and whistles and whatever, one member of the always-knowledgeable staff remarked, "We encourage creative play, with more classic items." Among those items available on one, well, Saturday were "Buried Treasure Mayan Dig!" "Anatomics Master Bug Kit," kites, blocks, and, naturally, Harry Potter products. There's also a well-stocked book section, mostly for young readers. The store is open Monday, Tuesday, Wednesday, Friday, and Saturday from 10:00 A.M. to 6:00 P.M., Thursday from 10:00 A.M. to 7:00 P.M., Sunday from 11:00 A.M. to 5:00 P.M. Phone (773) 525–8697.

Near the intersection of Halsted and Webster are an assortment of restaurants, two of which are venerable neighborhood choices. *O'Famé* (750 West Webster Avenue) has been run by the same Italian family since its opening in 1983, and according to a brief history on the menu, the owner's father still occasionally comes in to make his signature soups. The place is cheery and bright, and the decor is characteristic of this upscale neighborhood in an understated way. "The minute I walked in, I knew we were in Lincoln Park," one of my friends cracked, noting all the light wood and exposed brick. The menu includes wonderfully subtle thin-crust pizza. There are also tasty homemade pasta, such as pasta aglio de olio (olive oil, garlic, herbs, and parmesan), pasta zucca (zucchini sautéed with garlic, olive oil, and red peppers), and baked manicotti. Other specialties of the house include Steak O'Famé, lemon chicken, and eggplant parmigiana, and there are numerous soups, sandwiches, and salads. The wine list features good selections (mostly Italian, of course). Open Monday through Saturday from 11:00 A.M. to 11:00

P.M. (or thereabouts), Sunday from 5:00 to approximately 11:00 P.M. Delivery and carryout also. Phone (773) 929–5111. Inexpensive.

Area residents in the know undoubtedly had a smile on their faces when the **Athenian Room** (807 Webster Avenue) first joined the neighborhood trend by putting up signs offering valet parking. The parking, it turns out, costs $7.00, which is more than many of the Greek restaurant's entrees, which include tasty gyro dinners, chicken breast, and Greek feta charburgers on pita bread. The always-reliable Athenian Room, opened in 1972, doesn't serve alcoholic beverages, but that's no problem. Just walk through the door into the adjacent crowded, noisy Glascott's bar and bring the drinks back to your table. Open every day from 11:00 A.M. to 10:00 P.M. Phone (773) 348–5155. Inexpensive.

Farther west, about a ten minutes' hike, is another good one, *John's Place* (1202 West Webster Avenue), a charming neighborhood winner, especially in warmer weather when outdoor tables attract the most demand. There's the standard soup-salad-sandwich fare, but also items such as sesame-crusted ahi tuna, salmon bow-tie pasta, vegetable lasagna, turkey meatloaf, mango-glazed pork tenderloin, and grilled spice-rubbed catfish. Open Tuesday through Thursday from 11:00 A.M. to 10:00 P.M., Friday from 11:00 A.M. to 11:00 P.M., Saturday from 8:00 A.M. to 11:00 P.M., Sunday from 8:00 A.M. to 9:00 P.M. Be prepared to wait, especially on weekends. Phone (773) 525–6670. Inexpensive.

Other Lincoln Park treasures are even farther west. (It probably helps to have a car, although for the adventurous, buses are an option.)

Many shoppers determinedly roaming the aisles at oh-so-healthy, oh-so-trendy Whole Foods Market (in the mall at 1000 West North Avenue) may not even be aware that there's a fine restaurant up on the second floor. It's called **Eden, the Whole Foods Bistro,** and it serves delicious food in a pleasant atmosphere. But, hey, leave your groceries on the main floor. As a sign halfway up the staircase orders: PLEASE NO CARTS, BASKETS OR UNPAID MERCHANDISE ON THE 2ND FLOOR. So drag that cart back down the stairs. There are hearty soups like bean, corn chowder, and tomato basil, imaginative sandwiches such as curried chicken and a veggie BLT, and filling salads like grilled portobella mushroom. Specials include paella, whitefish, and tricolored pasta, and there's a good wine list. Since it is run by Whole Foods, there is also, not unexpectedly, "free-roam" chicken stir-fry and organic lemonade. Open for lunch and dinner Monday through Friday from 11:30 A.M. to 9:00 P.M., Saturday from 11:00 A.M. to 9:00 P.M., Sunday brunch from 10:00 A.M. to 4:00 P.M. Phone (312) 587–3060. Inexpensive.

Farther west, near the Kennedy Expressway at the fractional address of 1826½ North Elston Avenue, is the *Wine Discount Center,* located in a nondescript cinderblock building in an industrial area. Lovers of distinctive reds and whites couldn't care less, attracted by the fine selection at good prices and a friendly and knowledgeable staff. There are always great bargains available near the front of the store, including underrated reds from Chile, Argentina, and Italy. The monthly store brochure notes that every month the staff samples over 300 wines to find about 50 new ones, then adds, "If you find a lower current advertised price, bring in a copy of the ad and that price is yours." Open Monday through Friday from 10:00 A.M. to 7:00 P.M., Saturday from 9:00 A.M. to 5:00 P.M., Sunday from noon to 5:00 P.M. Phone (773) 489–3454.

If movie buffs have trouble finding a movie for rental at Blockbuster and the other usual suspects, they always know they have an excellent chance of locating it at *Facets Multi-Media* (1517 West Fullerton Avenue). In the lobby, along with motion picture publications, there are fat catalogues listing films to rent or buy—from silent films to animation, documentaries, and classic American films to "Campy Classics, Midnight Movies & the Just Plain Weird." Facets' Cinémathèque—a nononsense screening room that is about as far from a multiplex as one can get—constantly offers "Not Your Typical Movies." During one fall period, for example, the Cinémathèque showed, among others, a satire from Belgium, a comedy set in a late-night radio station, and, if you're ready, "a poolroom family drama." ("The hustlers of the inner city!") There are also all kinds of events, such as the "Festival of New French Cinema," and Facets offers its own series of film classes. To find out everything that's going on—and it may be more than you care to know—phone (773) 281–4114.

The Belden-Stratford Hotel,

2300 Lincoln Park West;
(773) 281–2900 or
(800) 800–8301.
With a choice location,
1 block south of Fullerton
Parkway and across from
Lincoln Park Zoo and Con-
servatory, this refurbished
hotel is a historical landmark (built in 1922),
notable for its mansard
roof and limestone facade.
Tasteful rooms range from
studio to two-bedroom
suites, many featuring formal dining rooms, fully
equipped kitchens, and
whirlpool baths. Hotel
amenities include two-line
phone service with voice
mail and data ports and, in
the arcade, a fitness center,
beauty salon, and dry
cleaner. The hotel also
houses two excellent
restaurants, Ambria and
Mon Ami Gabi. Moderate.

Comfort Inn,

601 West Diversey
Parkway;
(773) 348–2810.
Housed in a half-timbered
Tudor building, this hotel
in a very congested area
offers, of all things, parking. Granted, it's a small lot
and there's a fee and it's
first-come-first-served,
but, still, it's parking. The

seventy-four rooms (a few
suites come with whirlpool
or sauna) are adequately
furnished, and free continental breakfast is pro-
vided in an attractive room
off the lobby. It's within
easy walking to shops, the
park, and the lakefront.
Inexpensive.

Days Inn Gold Coast,

1816 North Clark Street;
(312) 664–3040.
This was formerly known
as the Hotel Lincoln—
there's still a faded sign
at the top that says as
much—a place of choice
for local actors as their
more or less permanent
digs. These days the rooms
have been renovated and
the name changed, however
geographically incorrect.
(It's not on the Gold Coast,
but on the boundary
between Lincoln Park and
Old Town.) The lobby is
pleasant, and so are the 231
rooms. Although rather
small, they're comfortable
enough, and some have a
terrific view of Lake
Michigan and Lincoln Park.
There's a complimentary
continental breakfast, a
courtesy shuttle bus, and a
restaurant, Louie on the
Park, located in the building. Inexpensive.

The Athenian Room,

807 West Webster Avenue;
(773) 348–5155.
See page 83 for full
description.

Bacino's,

2204 North Lincoln
Avenue;
(773) 472–7400.
See page 76 for full
description.

The Basil Leaf Cafe,

2460 North Clark Street;
(773) 935–3388.
This fine neighborhood
restaurant, specializing in
northern Italian food, had
its antecedents going back
to the mid-'80s in similar
restaurants owned by the
same folks on New York's
Long Island and in California before it opened in
Chicago in the '90s. The
place is cozy—that is, it's
small—so be prepared to
wait. The effort is decidedly
worthwhile, and the prices
are quite reasonable, especially for Lincoln Park.
Pasta dishes include
linguine marinara with
herbed tomato and basil
(Milano), penne broccoli
with roasted garlic or
walnuts (Sicily), jumbo
cheese ravioli with mari-
nara sauce (San Romano),
and, as a change of geo-
graphical pace, penne a
la vodka with poached

salmon and pencil asparagus (from, of all places, Sweden). Open every day from 11:30 A.M. to 10:30 P.M. Moderate.

The Bourgeois Pig Cafe,
738 West Fullerton Parkway;
(773) 883–5282.
See page 81 for full description.

Chicago Pizza & Oven Grinder,
2121 North Clark Street;
(773) 248–2570.
See page 73 for full description.

Eden,
1000 West North Avenue;
(312) 587–3060.
See page 83 for full description.

Four Farthings,
2060 North Cleveland Avenue;
(773) 935–2060.
This place is a study in contradiction. Its bar is loud and crowded, while its restaurant, located through swinging doors in a separate room that is pretty much sheltered from all the noise, is classy and understated. Those who've only been in the bar part would be shocked to know that the restaurant—with an open kitchen that gives the illusion of space—serves up appetizers like blackened squid over spinach salad and sautéed Andouille sausage over gnocchi, as well as entrees like roasted pork loin with

bourbon rosemary sauce, grilled mahi-mahi with a pesto cream sauce, and broiled tilapia with lemon capers. Open Monday through Thursday from 11:30 A.M. to 10:00 P.M., Friday and Saturday from 11:30 A.M. to 11:00 P.M., Sunday from 10:00 A.M. to 10:00 P.M. (featuring a nice brunch from 10:00 A.M. to 3:00 P.M.). Moderate.

Geja's Cafe,
340 West Armitage Avenue;
(773) 281–9101.
Whatever happened to fondue? It was all the rage in the '60s and '70s, when every house seemed to have at least one fondue pot (probably avocado-colored) and fondue restaurants were springing up all over the place. Well, at Geja's, which opened in 1965, fondue has never been out, and it is still one of the few places to serve the dip-your-own stuff. With its dark, woody, subterranean atmosphere and live flamenco music, Geja's is one of the most romantic restaurants in the city. Not that romance comes especially cheap, but many say you're paying for the ambience. Fondue dishes include beef tenderloin, lobster tail, jumbo shrimp, sea scallops, and chicken breast; and there's the Prince Geja Combo, which features all of the above. All the fondues include eight dipping sauces, and for dessert there's—what

else?—flaming chocolate fondue. Open Monday through Thursday from 5:00 to 10:30 P.M., Friday and Saturday from 5:00 P.M. to midnight, Sunday from 4:30 to 10:00 P.M. Expensive.

Jia's,
2545 North Halsted Street;
(773) 477–6256.
Classic Chinese dishes are presented in this intimate restaurant that's long been a local favorite. Try the eggplant in garlic sauce, the chicken broccoli, or the Szechuan pork. Cognizant of trends in a trendy neighborhood, Jia's also has gone beyond the China borders by adding a sushi menu. Open Monday through Thursday from 11:30 A.M. to 10:30 P.M., Friday from 11:30 A.M. to 11:00 P.M., Saturday from 4:30 to 11:00 P.M., Sunday from 4:30 to 10:00 P.M. Inexpensive.

John's Place,
1202 West Webster Avenue;
(773) 525–6670.
See page 83 for full description.

Mon Ami Gabi,
2300 North Lincoln Park West;
(773) 348–8886.
See page 68 for full description.

North Pond Cafe,
2610 North Cannon Drive;
(773) 477–5845.
See page 69 for full description.

O'Famé,
750 West Webster Avenue;
(773) 929–5111.
See page 82 for full
description.

R.J. Grunts,
2056 North Lincoln Park
West;
(773) 929–5363.
See page 67 for full
description.

The Red Lion,
2446 North Lincoln
Avenue;
(773) 348–2695.
See page 78 for full
description.

Trattoria Gianni,
1711 North Halsted Street;
(312) 266–1976.
The best thing about this
charming, intimate place,
besides the fine Italian
food, is its proximity to two
theaters: Steppenwolf and
the Royal George. Its
friendly staff is aware of
this, of course, and works
to accommodate ticket
holders so they'll make the
curtain on time. Antipasto
ranges from fried calamari
to mussels in a marinara
sauce, with main course
items including fettucine al
limon, tortellini baronessa,
linguine portofino, veal
scallopini and grilled
chicken breast. Open Tuesday through Thursday from
5:00 to 10:00 P.M., Friday
and Saturday from 5:00 to
11:30 P.M., Sunday brunch
from 11:30 A.M. to 3:00 P.M.,
Sunday dinner from 4:00 to
9:30 P.M. Moderate.

Lakeview

For years, it was two words—Lake View—but in recent times, for some reason, it has been smushed together. Whatever, the neighborhood of Lakeview seems to be home to more restaurants and entertainment spots per square foot than most communities in the city. The main commercial thoroughfares are Broadway, Clark Street, and Diversey, Belmont, Southport, Ashland, and Lincoln Avenues. (The big intersection is at Belmont-Lincoln-Ashland.)

The first European settler was Conrad Sulzer, of Switzerland, who arrived in Chicago in 1836 and subsequently erected a farmhouse and farm buildings on a site that is now Graceland Cemetery. In the 1840s other early settlers were from Germany, Sweden, and Luxembourg. Most were farmers, but some newcomers built elegant houses along the lake. In 1854 developers James Rees and Elisha H. Hundley opened a posh lakefront hotel, the Lake View House, at the corner of Byron Avenue and Sheridan Road or perhaps Grace Street. (It was demolished in 1890.)

In 1857 the Township of Lake View was organized, and eight years later the township was incorporated as the Town of Lake View. In 1887 it was incorporated as a city, and two years later Lake View was annexed to the city of Chicago. It was basically a truck farming area, particularly known as a celery-growing region. In 1885 a directory published by the R. R. Donnelley Company listed among the advantages of living in Lake View the fact that it was "accessible by no [fewer] than ten trains each way daily over the Chicago and North Western Railway and an equal number by the Chicago and Evanston Railway." Between 1900 and 1920 industry grew rapidly in the area. In 1908 Riverview Park, an amusement park at Belmont and Western Avenues, was incorporated, providing hours of entertainment in a charmingly tacky, decidedly nonantiseptic "theme park" sort of way until it outlived its usefulness and was finally shut down in 1967.

Lakeview is the location of Graceland Cemetery, a lovely, rolling oasis in the midst of urban noise and traffic, and, nearby at Clark and Addison Streets, Wrigley Field, the fabled "Friendly Confines" built in 1914 for

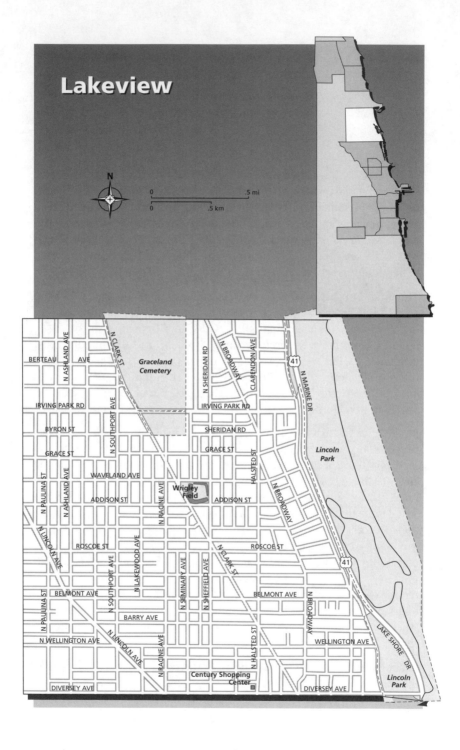

LAKEVIEW

TOP ATTRACTIONS IN LAKEVIEW

Alta Vista Terrace
Graceland Cemetery
Erwin
Pops for Champagne

the Chicago Whales of the Federal League and two years later occupied by the Chicago Cubs, who moved in from their old West Side park. These days "Cubs Park," as it is sometimes called, is where the team undergoes its annual exercise in futility. Not that it matters. "People come to see the ballpark itself more than the team," explains one resident. "It's a lovely, old-fashioned park, with the ivy-covered walls and a minimum of advertising, and on a warm summer afternoon, there's no place better." Others have suggested, a bit more unkindly, that Wrigley is "the world's biggest beer garden." The area surrounding the park is now known, unsurprisingly, as "Wrigleyville," where many of the residents protested the imposition of even-more-beery night baseball (it had been daytime only), which arrived in 1988.

Since the 1980s, Lakeview has become a popular residential spot for the much-derided yuppies, and there is a sizable gay population, which particularly frequents shops and restaurants in the Halsted area north of Belmont.

To get to the attractions on Lincoln Avenue, board the Red Line downtown, get off at Fullerton Avenue, and transfer to the #11 Lincoln bus going north. For those on Clark Street, take the #22 Clark bus, and for those on Broadway the #36 Broadway bus. To get to those on Belmont Avenue and those on Southport, take the #22 or #36 north to Belmont, and transfer to the #77 Belmont bus heading west. Another way to get to Southport is to take the Brown Line from the Loop to the Southport station.

A good place to start your visit of Lakeview—a made-for-walking community—would be to head up Clark north of Diversey. *La Crêperie* (2845 North Clark Street) was established in 1972, about the time that Americans were having a love affair with that French creation, *la crêpe*. A while later, of course, tastes and trends changed and diners moved on to fondue or something else. Despite ficklemindedness, this restaurant has stayed the course and remains a local favorite. "After my customers saw the movie *Chocolat*, they came running over here to have one of our chocolate crepes," says the proprietress-waitress Sara Roignant. For those who presumably don't "get it," La Crêperie offers orange roughy and steak frites, but why bother? Dinner includes a cup of soup du jour or house salad, plus two (one entree and one dessert) crepes. Among the former choices are broccoli/cheese, spinach crème, chicken/mushroom, coq au vin, chicken curry and rice, and boeuf bourguignon, while the dessert crepes range from fresh lemon to crème Anglaise, Grand

Put 'Em Up, Put 'Em Up . . . !

"Chicago ain't no sissy town!"

— *"Hinky Dink" McKenna, 1st Ward alderman, 1897–1923*

Marnier, banana, and Suzette a la Germain. The ambience is cozy and bistrolike, the service is friendly, and the food is quite good. Decor includes well-aged French posters and an Air France model of the Eiffel Tower, which may be a bit too much. In the warm months, there's an outdoor area in back. Open Tuesday through Friday from 11:30 A.M. to 3:30 P.M. and 5:00 to 11:00 P.M., Saturday from 11:00 A.M. to 11:00 P.M., Sunday from 11:00 A.M. to 9:30 P.M. Phone (773) 528–9050. Moderate.

At times, the shoppers at *Chicago Comics* (3244 North Clark Street) may be just as interesting as the merchandise itself. Promising "New Comics Every Wednesday," the impressively large store carries an incredible assortment of offerings from familiar superheroes (Batman, Spiderman, the Fantastic Four) to "Astounding Space Thrills," "Tales of the Bizarro World," and presumable send-ups like "The 3 Geeks" and "Knights of the Dinner Table." Chicago Comics also sells book collections of classic pioneering comics such as "Little Nemo" (1905–1914), foreign imports, action figures (from the Road Warrior to Scooby-Do), "The Andy Griffith Show" lunch boxes, "Hulk" wastebaskets, "Little Lulu" note paper, "Rocky & Bullwinkle" paperweights, and comic-appropriate posters, refrigerator magnets, T-shirts, and Zippo lighters. (One afternoon there was also, for some unfathomable reason, a "Portrait of Christ" oil paint-by-the-numbers set.) Open Monday through Friday from noon to 8:00 P.M., Saturday from 11:00 A.M. to 8:00 P.M., Sunday from noon to 6:00 P.M. Phone (773) 528–1983.

Before many Chicago boys seriously discover girls, chances are they already have seriously discovered *Windward Sports* (3317 North Clark Street). But it's also for adults, both men and women, and more and more apparel has been added to the merchandise mix. The top-selling items, according to one salesperson, are "skateboards, wind-surfing boards, snowboards—and bikinis." There are also in-line skates, T-shirts and shorts, and, in the basement, a "half-pipe" ramp available to skateboarders (for a small fee), which caught the eye of a subteenish customer, who lamented that he couldn't use it at the moment because he had recently broken his leg—while skateboarding, of course. Store hours are Monday from 11:00 A.M. to 5:00 P.M., Wednesday through Friday from 11:00 A.M. to 8:00 P.M., Saturday and Sunday from 11:00 A.M. to 5:00 P.M. Ramp hours are Wednesday through Friday 4:00 to 8:00 P.M., Saturday and Sunday from 11:00 A.M. to 5:00 P.M. Minimal fee. Phone (773) 472–6868.

LAKEVIEW

AUTHOR'S FAVORITES IN LAKEVIEW

La Crêperie

Music Box Theatre

Uncle Fun

P.O.S.H.

In business since the mid-1950s, over twelve years at 3347 North Clark Street, *Aiko's Art Materials* specializes in washi, handmade Japanese paper, carrying over 500 different types, both plain and decorated and in a variety of colors, textures, and designs. The lovely store serves paper and book artists, bookbinders, painters, and those in book restoration and conservation. Its inventory includes some one hundred different brushes—some quite expensive—made of materials from badger and horsehair to sheep and cat hair; shapes and sizes are formulated for calligraphy, brush painting, stencil dyeing, and painting. Books include titles like *Painting Techniques of China and Japan, Japanese Book-Binding,* and *Inspired Flower Arrangements,* and other items range from woodcut prints to bamboo teapot handles, incense boxes, ironware paperweights, and gourd sake sets. The store was founded by Aiko Nakane, who was born in Seattle, and attended high school in Japan, where she was exposed to such traditional crafts as calligraphy and ikebana (flower arranging). Later, she studied at the Chicago Institute of Art. Aiko's also ships to such destinations as Mexico, England, Switzerland, and South Africa. Open Tuesday through Saturday from 10:00 A.M. to 5:00 P.M. Phone (773) 404–5600.

Despite lame jokes about its name referring to Chicago Cub loyalists, *"Nuts on Clark"* (quotes and all) has been selling, well, nuts for more than twenty years at 3830 North Clark Street, 2 blocks north of Wrigley Field. The family-run business is packed with buckets and bags filled with all kinds of nuts: cashews, chocolate-dip peanuts, honey-roasted peanuts, Spanish peanuts, redskins peanuts, blanched peanuts, filberts, hazelnuts, walnut halves, macadamia, almonds, Brazil, "jumbo" cashews, "mammoth" pecans, and "giant colossal" pistachios. "Nuts" also offers candy, dried fruit, cheese corn, and caramel corn. Asked to name the best sellers, one salesperson tersely remarked, "*Everything* sells. Otherwise, we wouldn't have it." Open Monday through Saturday from 9:00 A.M. to 4:00 P.M. Phone (773) 549–6622, or bite onto www. nutsonclark.com.

It's difficult to find, but *Alta Vista Terrace* in the 3800 block of North Alta Vista Terrace is worth a look. Located a couple of blocks north of Wrigley and 2 blocks east of Clark, it became, in 1971, Chicago's first designated historic district. The narrow, 1-block-long street is composed of twenty small, London-like row houses designed by Joseph C. Brompton and built from 1900 to 1904 by real estate mogul Samuel Eberly Gross. The mostly two-story houses vary in design and color, but

Alta Vista Terrace

each is duplicated with only minor variations at the diagonally opposite end of the block. All are made of Roman brick, except for four three-story graystones in the middle.

Besides housing the grave of William Hulbert, founder of the National League—his monument in the shape of, appropriately enough, a large baseball—*Graceland Cemetery,* headquartered at 4001 North Clark Street, is the patrician resting place of other heavy hitters: business tycoons, politicians, and socialites. Among those buried here are boxing champion Jack Johnson; Allan Pinkerton, founder of the legendary detective agency; meatpacking mogul Philip Armour; Potter Palmer, of the luxurious Palmer House hotel; architects Louis Sullivan and Ludwig Mies van der Rohe; and John Peter Altgeld, the Illinois governor who pardoned the anarchists protesting police brutality in the Haymarket Riot of 1886.

With its eclectic architectural treasures, it's a lovely urban sanctuary that was founded in 1860. Assuredly, there are no replicas of blue suede shoes or hound dogs in *this* Graceland, but its 121 acres do contain such resting places as the Louis Sullivan–designed tomb of lumber merchant Henry Harrison Getty, which Frank Lloyd Wright proclaimed to be the gem of American architecture; the George Pullman Monument, in which the coffin of the inventor of the sleeping car is sunk in a room-sized concrete block overlaid with railroad ties to protect his body from angry workers after the bitter 1894 strike against Pullman; the memorial for Daniel Burnham (the architect who created the blueprint for the city's lakefront), which lies in lovely, simple isolation on a wooded island in the lake; and "Memory," the statue of a sad-faced, seated female figure, a memorial for department store founder Marshall Field designed by sculptor Daniel Chester French and architect Henry Bacon and the prototype for their Lincoln Memorial in Washington. There is also one decidedly atypical Graceland gravestone. Close by the maintenance area, it belongs to Henry R. Schefe (1939–1979) and Carol L. Schefe (1939–). They are self-proclaimed "Outlaws Chicago"—motorcycle folks, apparently—better known to one and all as "Papa Snake" and "Mama Snake." Visitors can take a self-guided walking tour with the help of a guide book sold at the entrance office. The Chicago Architecture Foundation also offers inexpensive two-hour tours on Sundays. Phone (312) 922–TOUR.

Now walk a few blocks east to Halsted Street, then head back south. As befits its name, and proud of it, **Flashy Trash** (3524 North Halsted Street) is into far-out, colorful merchandise—lots of flowery things and leopard skin, felt and straw hats and boas and long gloves. And pop art-type jewelry and vintage Canadian ice hockey jackets and light-up rings and what-have-you. To use a favorite Midwestern adjective, the store is, simply, a "hoot." "What we carry depends on what's in fashion, which, of course, changes often," says a staff member. "We're especially popular for providing things for '70s theme parties. And, naturally, it depends on the season. This is, after all, Chicago, so we sell *tons* of sweaters." Flashy Trash, which has been in business for more than two decades, is open Monday through Saturday from 11:00 A.M. to 8:00 P.M., Sunday from noon to 6:00 P.M. Phone (773) 327–6900.

Water, Water Everywhere . . .

*R*iding on Chicago buses sometimes is quite an adventure in people watching. Local riders debate which bus line has the most "characters," the #36 or the #22, both of which roll through the Lakeview neighborhood. Maybe it depends how full the moon is on a particular day. Example: One Saturday a man was spotted boarding the 36, carrying, nursery rhyme–like, a pail of water. "No water on this bus," commanded the driver. "What you mean, no water?" the offended passenger replied. "Is there a sign that says, 'No water'?" A pregnant pause, sputtering, and muttering. "Well, no, there's no sign. But . . . " Then a resigned shrug. Not unexpectedly, as the bus jostled its way south, no one took the seat next to the water bearer, who calmly exited three or four stops later.

As in quite a few restaurants, the best seats at **Erwin,** "An American Cafe and Bar" at 2925 North Halsted Street, are in the smoking area. In this case, they are the several booths lined up along the front windows, and quite close to the intimate bar (hence, one presumes, the smoking designation). But there really are no bad seats in this cozy, charming place that specializes in New American cuisine. Try the Alaskan halibut with grilled eggplant and escarole, or the wild striped sea bass with mushroom pancake and spinach. Other main dishes include sautéed calf's liver with mashed potatoes, pork chop and basil sausage with sweet potato hash, and homemade pasta with asparagus. Among the starters are smoked trout with cilantro pancake, caramelized onion tart, and Yukon gold potato pirogi, while dessert offerings run from peanut butter mousse cake to walnut brownie sundae and Granny Smith apple pie. And there's an extensive wine list. Open Tuesday through Thursday from 5:30 to 10:00 P.M., Friday and Saturday from 5:30 to 11:00 P.M., Sunday brunch from 10:30 A.M. to 2:30 P.M., Sunday dinner from 5:00 to 9:30 P.M. Phone (773) 528–7200. Moderate.

Lakeview attractions are scattered all over the place and at times, frankly, it would be helpful to have a car. Entertainment possibilities abound and are too numerous to include here. A short stroll from Wrigley Field, **Metro** (3730 North Clark Street) is a popular entertainment spot serving up all kinds of performances, mostly rock, on its stage. This is where the well-known, now-disbanded Chicago group Smashing Pumpkins got its big break by playing there a lot, and also where they gave one of their last concerts. Post-Pumpkins groups— some of which have names that sound like racehorses—have included bands such as Hey Mercedes (composed, as if you didn't know, of former members of Braid), Sweep the Leg Johnny, Hot Stove Jimmy, Soft Boys, the rockabilly Rock*a*Teens, Slaves on Dope, Drowning Fool, Apocalypse Hoboken, Mustard Plug, Monkey Paw, and the ever-popular Oh My God. Metro is located in the Northside Auditorium Building, a 1928 Spanish Baroque Revival structure, the kind that housed many Roaring '20s entertainment palaces, and the music on any day may start as early as 6:30 P.M. Downstairs, there's a dance club called Smart Bar, open Sunday through Friday from 10:00 P.M. to 4:00 A.M., Saturday from 10:00 P.M. to 5:00 A.M. Phone (773) 549–0203, or check out www.metrochicago.com.

The vintage Vic Theatre at 3145 North Sheffield Avenue hasn't been holding many rock concerts in recent times, so many nights the theater is given over to its **Brew & View at the Vic,** whereby patrons sit at small tables, sipping beer and munching pizza (you can also smoke 'em if you've got 'em) while watching second-run films. "The really bad movies usually draw bigger crowds than the good ones," notes one young B&V attendee. "People boo and yell smart-mouth remarks at the screen." Phone (773) 929–6713.

Opened in 1977 in a longtime abandoned chocolate warehouse, *The Theatre Building* (1225 West Belmont Avenue) rents out its three, differently configured performance spaces—all seating 148—to between twelve and fifteen theater companies a year, attracting 45,000 to 50,000 ticket buyers. The different companies put on adult and children shows, from European Repertory Theatre's *Princess Turandot* (based on an ancient Chinese fable) to Famous Door Theatre Company's *Hellcab* (a collection of scenes from a day in the life of a Chicago cab driver) to Runamuk Productions' *Bud & Lou* (a vaudeville show recounting some of Abbott and Costello's most famous comedy routines). The Theatre Building offers acting classes and workshops and even rents out space for weddings. For show times and ticket prices, phone (773) 327–5252.

Opened in 1982, *Pops for Champagne* (2934 North Sheffield Avenue) is an intimate club known for its wide variety of jazz offerings, from traditional to Latin American, and an extensive wine list. Small groups of musicians such as Chicago favorites Judy Roberts, Franz Jackson, Alejo Povedo, and Jackie Allen play on the compact stage that sits above the semicircular bar, while customers pour through the listings of more than one hundred champagnes (some sold by the glass) as well as other offerings such as Cognac, Armagnac, Calvados, red and white wines, and port. There are also specialty drinks like the Bellini (a French classic combining peach nectar and champagne) and the Parisian martini (a vodka martini with a touch of Grand Marnier and a splash of cranberry, topped with champagne). You may also choose from a limited assortment of

Lakeview Celebs

*L*akeview *residents over the years have included silent film stars Gloria Swanson, Wallace Beery, and Ben Turpin, who all got their start at the old Essanay Studio on Argyle Street; ventriloquist Edgar Bergen, who attended Lake View High School; Broadway director-choreographer Bob Fosse; comedian George Gobel; singer Frankie Lane; radio stars Fibber McGee and Molly; Abe Saperstein, founder of the Harlem Globetrotters; basketball legend George Mikan; onetime Chicago mayor William Hale "Big Bill" Thompson; onetime U.S. Senator Charles Percy; and Iva Toguri D'Aquino, better known during World War II as the notorious propaganda broadcaster "Tokyo Rose."*

appetizers (caviar, smoked salmon, vegetarian pizza), cheese selections, and desserts (almond cake, chocolate chip cheesecake, chocolate roulade). Pops for Champagne's decor seems to be an odd blend of art deco and French provincial, and there's a pleasant outdoor area in back. Open Monday through Friday from 5:00 P.M. to 2:00 A.M., Saturday from 5:00 P.M. to 3:00 A.M.; the music starts weekends at 9:00 P.M., weeknights at 8:30 P.M. The modest cover varies depending on the night. Phone (773) 472–1000, or swing into www.popschampagne.com.

Paul Gapp, the *Chicago Tribune*'s late, great architectural critic, once wrote of the **Music Box Theatre** (3733 North Southport Avenue) that "the architectural style is an eclectic melange of Italian, Spanish, and Pardon-My-Fantasy put together with passion." The dark blue ceiling of the theater is filled with "twinkling stars" and "moving cloud formations," suggesting, as the theater folks themselves would have it, "a night sky," with the interior sides "reminiscent of the walls surrounding an Italian courtyard." Whatever, the Music Box originally opened in 1929 as an elaborate film palace—quite ready for the "talkies"—that was designed by Louis A. Simon, best known for his Depression-era post offices. Star comedy actor Jack Oakie once made a personal appearance there. Over the years, though, it declined to the point where it became a sleaze palace, even showing porno pictures. However, it was vigorously restored and opened as a class act once again in 1983. The Music Box now consists of two theaters (750 and 100 seats)—the second was built in an adjacent storefront in 1991—and presents first-run domestic and foreign and independent features and midnight cult films, as well as the popular *Sound of Music* sing-a-long. Phone (773) 871–6604.

Back in the daytime, there are other geographically diverse places to discover. On another day, you might want to walk north on Clark again, this time going west on Belmont. **Uncle Fun** (1338 West Belmont Avenue) is full of stuff that your mother might have called "cheap and tawdry junk." In other words, it's wonderful. And so are the cheap prices. Plus, the fully engaged staff is just bubbling with enthusiasm. The store is crammed full of large things and hundreds of the sort of small items that are found in kids' birthday party goodie bags. Among the merchandise are all kinds of refrigerator magnets, rubber snakes, plastic handcuffs and necklaces, a Dilbert "Boss Voodoo" doll, rearview spy glasses, a Dr. Seuss watch, yo-yos, smiley-face keychains, plastic spiders, plastic Martians, cheesy looking toy buses, monster teeth, light-bulb key rings, a plastic orange "Simpsons" sofa, and a battery-operated chimp ("He screeches, his eyes bulge in and out"). Uncle Fun has been in business well over twenty years, over eleven at this location. May it

Music Box Theatre

last many more. And so may its merchandise. Open Wednesday through Friday from noon to 7:00 P.M., Saturday from 11:00 A.M. to 7:00 P.M., Sunday from noon to 5:00 P.M. Phone (773) 477–8223.

Schubas Tavern (3159 North Southport Avenue at Belmont) is located in a 1903 building designed by the prolific architectural firm of Frommann & Jebsen that was one of dozens built by the Joseph Schlitz Brewing Company to house its saloons. Two Schlitz "world globe" logos are still prominently displayed on the exterior. Schubas is a restaurant/bar known for the eclectic entertainment offerings in its back room, especially rock bands with a folk or country flavor, although sometimes those with a gospel influence show up, as do singer-songwriters and acoustic guitarists and even an occasional cellist. The decent-enough menu in Schubas's Harmony Grill includes everything from the fairly exotic (char-grilled tuna steak, chicken and roasted red pepper quesadilla, portabella ravioli) to the decidedly mundane (patty melt, macaroni and cheese). The kitchen is open Monday through Friday from 11:00 A.M. to 11:00 P.M., Saturday and Sunday from 10:00 A.M. to 11:00 P.M., with brunch from 10:00 A.M. to 2:00 P.M. The music can start as early as 6:30 P.M., but make sure by calling (773) 525–2508. Inexpensive.

Quite a ways farther north on Southport you'll find *P.O.S.H.* (3729 North Southport Avenue), harboring a wonderful assortment of merchandise, much of which was once used by American and European hotels, restaurants, bistros, cafes, and steamship lines. On any day you can find items such as china produced for the now-defunct Dolphin Cruise Line; vintage china mustards pots, sugar bowls, and chunky creamers from the '40s and '50s; French cheese platters and place-card holders; silverplate covered dishes from the Grand Hôtel in the Belgian Congo; silverplate wine bottle coasters (1948) from the Waldorf Astoria in Manhattan; knives, forks, and spoons from the former Stevens Hotel (now the Hilton) in Chicago; and vintage folding wooden rulers from the 1920s and French irons from the early 1900s (suitable for use today as doorstops or paperweights). There also might be such miscellaneous items as classic French commercial postcards, Babar the Elephant plates and bowls, and Camp Fire Girl mugs. Open Monday through Friday from noon to 7:00 P.M., Saturday from 11:00 A.M. to 7:00 P.M., Sunday from noon to 5:00 P.M. Phone (773) 529–7674, or log onto www.poshchicago.com.

Sometime you might want to move on over farther west to Lincoln Avenue. Opened in 1922 in a then heavily populated German neighborhood, *Dinkel's Bakery* (3329 North Lincoln Avenue) is full of wonderful smells. In addition to various kinds of breads, products include inventively decorated birthday cakes, wedding cakes, coffeecakes, Black Forest cakes, Boston cream cakes, and "smash" cakes, along with a tempting assortment of scones, brownies, and cookies. There's also a section that sells coffee and shakes and smoothies, as well as several tables for in-house noshing. Open Monday through Friday from 6:00 A.M. to 7:00 P.M., Saturday from 6:00 A.M. to 6:00 P.M., Sunday from 9:00 A.M. to 5:00 P.M. Phone (773) 281–7300.

Finally, there are two special places that are worth a visit but happen to fall outside the official boundaries of Lakeview. If you have access to a car, you might check them out, or take a cab.

Founded in the late 1950s, the *Old Town School of Folk Music* for years was located in Old Town, on Armitage Avenue, and moved in 1998 to its present location at 4544 North Lincoln Avenue in the Ravenswood neighborhood. (The facility on Armitage, primarily offering classes for children and teens, still exists. See the Lincoln Park chapter.) In order to attract audiences who don't go into a nostalgic swoon over hearing "Tom Dooley" and "If I Had a Hammer," Old Town honchos hope to attract younger customers by expanding the school's lineup of Latin, Asian, and other ethnic music. But it's also sticking to its legendary roots, and on any night you can listen to labor union anthems, Hawaiian guitar melodies, Hungarian and Gypsy music, and "Canadian prairie" songs. Or perhaps a bluegrass fiddler, mandolin strummer, "mountain soul" singer, blues guitarist-vocalist, Afro-Cuban flutist, or Irishman on uilleann pipes. Not to mention good old, straightforward folk lyrics like "I have changed the locks on my heart since you were here. . . ." The school also offers all kinds of music classes, from banjo to songwriting and jazz singing. Phone (773) 728–6000, or visit www. oldtownschool.org.

And then there is *Metro Golden Memories* (5425 West Addison Street) in the Portage Park neighborhood. A nostalgia nut's nirvana, its founders include Chuck Schaden, the host of a popular radio program focusing on old-time shows. No surprise, then, that the deliciously cluttered store offers all kinds of tapes of oldie programs—from "Fibber McGee and Molly" to "The Great Gildersleeve" to "Inner Sanctum." But there's more, much more. Look around and you'll find such items as June Allyson and Marilyn Monroe paper dolls, Popeye T-shirts, a Lucy and Ethel "Million Dollar Idea" plate, a Betty Boop wastebasket, a "Wizard of Oz" lunch box, and, of course, all kinds of Elvis collectibles. There are also hundreds of new and old film and TV books; old movie posters and black-and-white photos, including a French poster for Audrey Hepburn in *Funny Face;* vintage radios; and hundreds of videos of long-ago movies, including rip-roaring '30s and '40s serials (Flash Gordon, Zorro, Dick Tracy). And talk about being specialized, there's even a whole section devoted to westerns starring Tex Ritter. Open Monday through Saturday from 10:00 A.M. to 6:00 P.M., Sunday from noon to 5:00 P.M. Phone (773) 736–4133.

PLACES TO STAY IN LAKEVIEW

Best Western Hawthorne Terrace,

3434 North Broadway; (773) 244–3434 or (888) 675–BEST. Located within easy distance from the lakefront and Wrigley Field, this hotel in a handsome old building obviously attracts Chicago Cubs' fans, who reserve well in advance, as do those attending the neighborhood's special events such as the Gay Pride Parade and Memorial Day festivities. The nicely renovated 59 rooms range in size from standard to junior suites with sofabed, and the deluxe rooms feature whirlpool tubs. Most rooms have refrigerators and microwaves, and there's a pleasant lobby with a fireplace, outdoor patio terrace, and cardio-vascular and weight training equipment. Moderate.

Days Inn Lincoln Park North,

644 West Diversey Avenue; (773) 525–7010 or (888) 576–3297 (reservations only). Despite its name, this remodeled Days Inn is technically located in Lakeview, on the north side of the two neighborhoods'

dividing line. The 133 rooms can be quite small and the views uninspiring, but it's close to numerous North Side restaurants and other attractions, including the Lincoln Park Zoo and Wrigley Field. During the Chicago Cubs' season, in fact, reservations may be difficult to come by, especially on the weekends. Some repeat customers even book rooms as far as a year ahead. The lobby is pleasant and a quiet diversion from bustling Diversey Avenue, and there's a restaurant/lounge, along with valet parking, complimentary continental breakfast, and complimentary passes to Bally's Total Fitness. Near the front entrance is one of the famous, droll "Chicago Cows on Parade," this one covered with maps of the world and entitled *Chicowgo*. Inexpensive.

Majestic Hotel,

528 West Brompton Avenue; (773) 404–3499 or (800) 727–5108. A charming "boutique" hotel with understated Old English decor, the Majestic is located a short stroll from Lincoln Park and Belmont Harbor. The lobby features furnishings upholstered in chenille and tapestry fabrics, and the inviting, woody library with fireplace is the setting for the continental

breakfast. Many of the 52 attractive rooms have two color schemes—violet and honey-gold with green accents, the other green and honey-gold with rust accents. For business travelers, there are workstations with data ports. A member of the Neighborhood Inns of Chicago. Moderate.

PLACES TO EAT IN LAKEVIEW

Bistro Zinc,

3443 North Southport Avenue; (773) 281–3443. Set amid a charming Gallic atmosphere, complete with zinc-topped bar, this popular place offers classic bistro fare in its cafe in front and more formal bistro (for dinner) in back. There's also a small outdoor area when the weather turns nice. For lunch, the quiche du jour is always a good bet, and one nearby diner claimed the lentil soup was "out of this world." Appetizers for dinner include a variety of homemade pâtés and mussels stewed with white wine, shallots, cream, and parsley. Main dishes range from steak frites to sautéed skate, seared medium-rare tuna, and grilled pork chop, and there's a nice assortment of wines— French, *mais oui*. All this, and service that is actually friendly. Open for lunch Tuesday through Friday from 11:30 A.M. to 3:00 P.M., for dinner Tuesday through Thursday from 5:00 to 10:00 P.M., Friday and Saturday from 5:30 to 11:00 P.M., Sunday from 5:00 to 9:00 P.M., and for brunch Saturday and Sunday from 10:00 A.M. to 3:00 P.M. Moderate.

Erwin,
2925 North Halsted Street; (773) 528-7200.
See page 96 for full description.

Half Shell,
676 West Diversey Avenue; (773) 549-1773.
People who don't mind noise, smoke, and subterranean semidarkness (there are two fireplaces) but enjoy good seafood should head for this extremely unpretentious restaurant/bar, a neighborhood favorite since its inaugural in 1968. The stars of the menu are the excellent steamed king crab legs, with other choices including broiled jumbo shrimp, fried smelts (a Chicago favorite), salmon, red snapper, soft shell crabs, and tuna steak. Among the appetizers are crab cakes, mussels, and squid. Open daily from 11:30 A.M. to midnight or

12:30 A.M. Moderate. Be warned: Cash only.

La Crêperie,
2845 North Clark Street; (773) 528-9050.
See page 91 for full description.

Matsuya,
3460 North Clark Street; (773) 248-2677.
According to one young Chicagoan who taught school in Tokyo for a while and is now a Lakeview resident, this is one of the top Japanese restaurants in Chicago. Featuring attractive, light-wood decor, the always-busy Matsuya is known for the quality of its sushi (the most expensive, you might want to know, is the broiled eel served over rice). Also on the always-changing menu are the usual tempura, sukiyaki, and teriyaki (portions are generous), with tempura ice cream for dessert. There often are waits for tables, but it's worth it. Open Monday through Friday from 5:00 to 11:30 P.M., Saturday and Sunday from noon to 11:30 P.M. Inexpensive.

P.S. Bangkok,
3345 North Clark Street; (773) 871-7777.
With its gracious, oak-paneled decor and dependable cuisine, this popular Thai place (born 1983) near Wrigley Field attracts locals and suburbanites alike, and maybe even discriminating Cub fans

(unless—cheap shot here—that's an oxymoron). For starters, there are items such as shrimp rolls and crab rolls, curried fish cakes, and chive dumplings, with "the House of Specialties" including "Golden Coconut Chicken," "Love Me Tender Duck," "Stir-Fried Seafood Curry," "Eight Angels" (fresh shrimp, squid, chicken, and cellophane noodles stir-fried with black mushrooms, carrots, bamboo shoots, and scallions), and "Fire Spinach" (self-explanatory). P.S. Bangkok also offers its "Grand Gourmet Buffet"—claimed to be the largest in the area—on Sundays from 11:30 A.M. to 4:00 P.M. Open Sunday through Thursday from 11:30 A.M. to 10:00 P.M., Friday and Saturday from 11:30 A.M. to 11:30 P.M. Inexpensive.

Samuel's Old Fashioned Delicatessen,
3463 North Broadway; (773) 525-7018.
With delis in Chicago seeming to disappear year by year, it's nice to come across family-owned Samuel's, with its no-nonsense eating area (a dozen or so tables) and take-out counter and old-timey outside sign that reads IF YOU CAN'T STOP, SMILE AS YOU GO BY. The food is solid and unsurprising. Sandwiches feature corned beef and pastrami, roast

brisket, and hard salami. You can also get lox and smoked trout, chopped herring, coleslaw and potato salad, as well as a "homemade" lineup (soup, noodle kugel, blintzes, meat and potato knishes). Open Monday through Friday from 8:00 A.M. to 8:00 P.M., Saturday from 8:00 A.M. to 6:00 P.M., Sunday from 8:00 A.M. to 4:00 P.M. Inexpensive.

Schubas Tavern, 3159 North Southport Avenue; (773) 525–2508. See page 99 for full description.

Edgewater and Rogers Park/West Ridge

Edgewater and Rogers Park/West Ridge, which are divided by an avenue named Devon—pronounced, in typical Chicago fashion, as "Da-VON"—started as farming communities. One of the first settlers in the Edgewater area was a man from Luxembourg named Nicholas Krantz, who in 1848 constructed a frame structure, on the corner of what today is Clark Street and Ridge Avenue, which served as a tavern, inn, and local meeting place. In the late 1800s Edgewater was known as "the celery-growing capital of the Middle West," but it remained sparsely populated until around 1900. Settlers were basically German, Scandinavian, and Irish. In 1889 Edgewater was annexed by the city of Chicago.

Prior to and after World War I, large mansions were built along the lakefront. Rapidly becoming a top-drawer neighborhood, Edgewater gained added prestige with the opening of the posh Edgewater Beach Hotel on Sheridan in 1916. But the area declined during the 1930s and 1940s, and starting in the 1950s those lovely mansions were mostly replaced by often ugly high-rise apartments, giving Sheridan an unfortunate high-density look.

Most Edgewater attractions these days are located in Andersonville, a community of Swedish heritage, and are found in a tightly packed few blocks along Clark Street north of Foster. After the Great Fire of 1871, "Swedetown" on the Near North Side lost its importance, and many of the residents moved to the Clark–Foster area. By 1930, first-generation Swedish immigrants accounted for 20 to 24 percent of the local population. Andersonville declined in the 1930s through the 1950s but started to come back in the 1960s and now is increasingly becoming gentrified, to many locals' disgust. "Obviously, the neighborhood's changed," says one shopkeeper. "In the '80s, we got hit by all the yuppies moving in." Adds another: "As you may have noticed, we have a Starbucks now. It's not the same old Swedish neighborhood." New

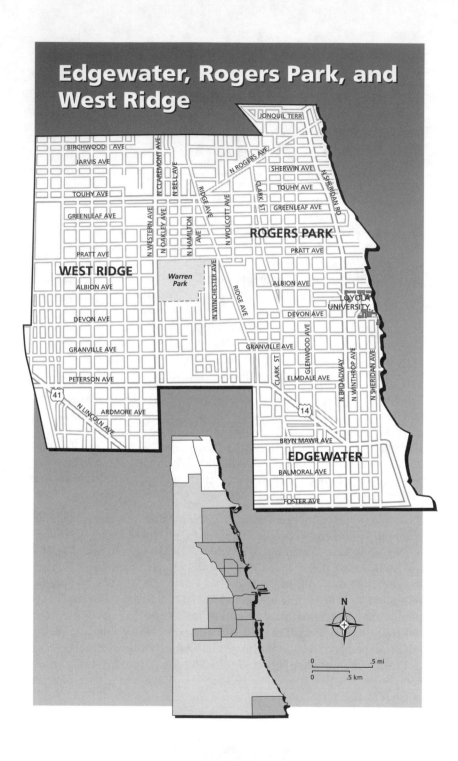

Edgewater, Rogers Park, and West Ridge

JONQUIL TERR

BIRCHWOOD AVE

JARVIS AVE

N CLAREMONT AVE

N BELL AVE

N ROGERS AVE

SHERWIN AVE

N SHERIDAN RD

TOUHY AVE

TOUHY AVE

CLARK ST

GREENLEAF AVE

RIDGE AVE

GREENLEAF AVE

N WESTERN AVE

N OAKLEY AVE

N HAMILTON AVE

N WOLCOTT AVE

ROGERS PARK

PRATT AVE

PRATT AVE

WEST RIDGE

Warren Park

ALBION AVE

N WINCHESTER AVE

RIDGE AVE

ALBION AVE

DEVON AVE

DEVON AVE

LOYOLA UNIVERSITY

GRANVILLE AVE

GRANVILLE AVE

CLARK ST

GLENWOOD AVE

PETERSON AVE

ELMDALE AVE

N BROADWAY

N WINTHROP AVE

N SHERIDAN AVE

41

N LINCOLN AVE

ARDMORE AVE

14

BRYN MAWR AVE

EDGEWATER

BALMORAL AVE

FOSTER AVE

N

0   .5 mi
0   .5 km

EDGEWATER AND ROGERS PARK/WEST RIDGE

TOP ATTRACTIONS IN EDGEWATER AND
ROGERS PARK/WEST RIDGE

Swedish American
Museum Center

Women & Children First

The Swedish Bakery

Broadway Antique Market

Rogers Park/West Ridge
Historical Society

nationalities have settled in, too. There are now more Middle Eastern restaurants along Clark than Swedish.

Full disclosure: As it happens, I grew up in Rogers Park, when its parts were known as East Rogers Park and West Rogers Park (my turf), with Ridge Avenue the dividing line. Today, East Rogers Park is called "Rogers Park," and West Rogers Park is "West Ridge." Whatever, they're the last northernmost neighborhoods before you hit suburban Evanston.

In the beginning were the Chippewa, Ottawa, and Pottawatomie Indians, with the first mark left by Europeans being a tavern built around 1809 on what is now Ridge and Pratt Avenues and which served as a stop along the stagecoach line. One of the earliest to homestead, in the 1830s, was Philip Rogers, a truck farmer who passed his land on to his daughter, Catherine, and her husband, Captain Patrick L. Touhy, who became the chief developer of Rogers Park. Many early settlers— Irish, English, Germans, Luxembourgers—were vegetable farmers and, later, flower growers. Meanwhile, the Native Americans were pushed farther west. In 1878 the village of Rogers Park was incorporated, and the village of West Ridge was formed in 1890; both were annexed to the city of Chicago in 1893. In 1906 the Jesuits started building Loyola University, which remains on the lakefront near Devon as the area's major institution.

The irony these days is the eastern portion, along the usually coveted lakefront, has become the less desirable area because of the blight and crime that started to take hold in the 1970s, especially near Howard Street, which borders on Evanston and was long known for its seedy bars. (Its image is gradually improving.) Family-oriented and stable (some would say dull), mostly residential West Ridge is still made up of tidy bungalows, many with exterior stucco, and well-maintained two- and three-flat apartment buildings. Once heavily Jewish and Roman Catholic, it now encompasses many diverse religions and nationalities. This can be seen on Devon Avenue. The stretch between Western and California Avenues is predominantly Indian, with stores with names like Gandhi Appliances and Gandhi Shipping, and Taj Sari Palace, India Bookhouse and Journals, and (the author's favorite name) Annapurna Fast Food. West of California Avenue the area turns Jewish, with stores like Tel-Aviv Kosher Pizza and the honorary street sign reading GOLDA MEIR BOULEVARD.

To get to Andersonville, take the #22 bus on Clark Street north to Foster Avenue, or the Red Line L train to the Berwyn Avenue stop. For Rogers Park/West Ridge, ride the Red Line L to the Loyola stop and walk south to Devon Avenue, or take the #22 or #36 bus to Devon, then transfer to the #155 Devon bus. It's quite a haul on public transportation, and, frankly, it's better if you have access to a car.

A logical place to start in Edgewater is the **Swedish American Museum Center** (5211 North Clark Street), a nonprofit educational activity center "for the celebration and interpretation of Swedish American history and culture." Established in 1976 by Kurt Mathiasson, one of the leaders of the Andersonville community and an immigrant himself, it was located in a small storefront log cabin and was officially opened by none other than Carl XVI Gustaf, the king of Sweden. In 1987 the museum moved to its present location, and the gracious king put in a return appearance. Permanent exhibits under the general heading of "The Dream of America—Swedish Immigration to Chicago" include explanations for the immigration (crop failures of the 1860s, religious intolerance, social and political discontent, and the desire to escape compulsory military service); displays of folk costumes and folk music; objects (circa 1928 to the 1950s), such as dishes and playing cards from the Swedish-American (steamship) Line; a reproduction of a Swedish American parlor in Chicago in the 1920s; local organizations, such as the Svithiod Singing Club; a room dedicated to Raoul Wallenberg, the courageous Swedish statesman who saved Jews from the Nazi death camps; and a children's museum that includes a log cabin suitable for crawling inside.

The museum store sells appropriate items such as books, glassware, mugs, dolls, and blankets, and there is a library on the third floor. In addition, the museum sponsors special art exhibits like "Swedish American Artists in Chicago" and "Scandinavian Masters (1853–2001)"; perfor-

I Say Anderson . . . You Say Andersen

*T*here appears to be little argument that Andersonville, the neighborhood in Edgewater with the Swedish heritage, takes its name from the Andersonville School, which existed from 1855 to 1925 at Foster Avenue and Clark Street. What is in dispute is after whom the school was named. Some say it was John Anderson, a Swedish farmer and highway commissioner, while others believe it was the Reverend Paul Andersen, a minister, who, as one can tell from the spelling of his name, was—horrors—Norwegian.

mances such as "Swedish Folk Tales," featuring music, movement, and puppetry; family programs with titles like "Pancakes with Pippi Longstocking" and "Vikings 'r' Us"; a mother-daughter fashion show; classes from the Swedish language to candlemaking and folk dancing; screenings of Swedish films; concerts, lectures, and workshops; and traditional Swedish herring breakfasts. Open Tuesday through Friday from 10:00 A.M. to 4:00 P.M., Saturday and Sunday from 10:00 A.M. to 3:00 P.M. Phone (773) 728–8111, or check out www.samac.org.

Much smaller and much less well known than Ann Sather's across the street, *Svea* (5236 North Clark Street) features charming Swedish decor, including colorful artwork, ten or so tables, and a short counter. It's the kind of place that closes at four in the afternoon, yet offers dinner selections. That's all right. Svea's is most popular for its breakfasts, especially on weekends. Try the "Gothenburg Special" (two eggs with Swedish Falukorv sausage or salt pork and limpa [Swedish] bread), or the "Swedish Tease" (one Swedish pancake with two eggs and bacon or link sausages). There's also the "Stockholm Special" (ham, onion, tomato, and cheese omelet). For lunch, the menu includes Swedish meatballs and open-faced sandwiches, and for that early-bird dinner there are liver and onions, pork chops, and the inevitable meatballs. The staff is extremely friendly, although the credit card policy (cash only) isn't. Open every day from 7:00 A.M. to 4:00 P.M. Phone (773) 275–7738. Inexpensive.

The mission of **Women & Children First** (5233 North Clark Street) is evident from its title. The independent bookstore, which has been around for over twenty years in three different locations, sells works of interest to those two groups. Founders/owners Ann Christophersen and Linda Bubon envisioned a store "that would define 'feminist' inclusively, as encompassing the interests and lifestyles of women whether they were heterosexual or lesbian; partnered or single; family-centered, career-centered, or both; and no matter what ethnic, racial, or spiritual background they came from." Titles run from Sara Paretsky mysteries, Alice Hoffman novels, and Molly Ivins's political observations to the collected stories of Colette and Jane Addams's autobiography, and there are categories like "Women's Music," "Violence Against Women," "Pregnancy," "Lesbian Mysteries," and, simply, "Work." Unlike a lot of stores, the kids' books are helpfully divided by ages. Women & Children First also sponsors Wednesday morning story hours for toddlers, speakers on women's issues ranging from local poets to nationally prominent

Sandburg on the Swedish

authors, and in-house appearances by such writers as Sandra Cisneros, Margaret Atwood, Gloria Steinem, Alice Walker, the late Gwendolyn Brooks, and Barbara Kingsolver. All this, and a cheerful, sunny ambience, too. Open Monday and Tuesday from 11:00 A.M. to 7:00 P.M., Wednesday through Friday from 11:00 A.M. to 9:00 P.M., Saturday 10:00 A.M. to 7:00 P.M., Sunday from 11:00 A.M. to 6:00 P.M. Phone (773) 769–9299, or log onto www.womenandchildrenfirst.com.

Historically, there has been a lot of back-and-forth bantering between Swedes and Norwegians—some of it good-natured, some not. "We sell Norwegian things because we have to," one staff member pleasantly jokes at **Wikstrom's Gourmet Food & Catering** (5247 North Clark Street), which has been in business over forty years, more than twenty-five at its present location. The colorful store sells such Scandinavian items as Swedish coffee roll mix and, yes, Norwegian salmon, along with delicatessen salads, herrings, cheeses, pumpernickel breads, jams, syrups, and appropriate children's books like the Pippi Longstocking series and others with such titles as *Flicka, Ricka, Dicka, and the Big Red Hen*. In the one-world spirit, there's even a sign that reads PARKING FOR DANES ONLY. Open Monday through Saturday from 9:00 A.M. to 6:00 P.M., Sunday from 11:00 A.M. to 4:00 P.M. Phone (773) 275–6100.

Surviving in business for over seventy-five years, the Swedish-owned **Erickson's Delicatessen** (5250 North Clark Street) offers all kinds of Scandinavian items, from bottles of glögg (a port wine-based holiday beverage) to crispbreads and flatbreads, Swedish Wild Delights cookies, hot mustards, lingonberry preserves, Swedish pancake mix, Norwegian cheese and sardines and fish cakes and chocolates, all kinds of pickled herring, and potato sausage (thousands of pounds are sold each year). The store also ships all over the United States (including Alaska and Hawaii) to those, apparently, living in the Scandinavian diaspora. Many have moved away from Andersonville, the staffer adds, but return to shop during the holidays: "At Christmas, we take back the neighborhood." Open Monday from 9:00 A.M. to 5:00 P.M., Tuesday through Friday from 9:00 A.M. to 6:00 P.M., Saturday from 9:00 A.M. to 5:00 P.M., Sunday from 11:00 A.M. to 4:00 P.M. Phone (773) 561–5634.

Incongruously, in an area settled by the Swedish, there are more Middle Eastern restaurants these days than Scandinavian. The granddaddy of them all is **Reza's** (5255 North Clark Street), presenting Persian food in a rather vast but still warm setting, aided by an attractive blend of light wood and exposed brick. There are more kebabs than you can shake a skewer at—shrimp, lamb, chicken, scallop, turkey breast, steak, fish—along with such other offerings as duck breast in pomegranate and walnut sauce and more than twenty-five vegetarian dishes. For parties of four or more, there are family-style dinners. Dill rice is a house specialty, and meals come with feta cheese and radishes. Open every day (including New Year's, Thanksgiving, and Christmas) from 11:00 A.M. to midnight. Touching all bases, the restaurant also offers delivery and carry-out. Phone (773) 561–1898. Moderate.

Kopi, A Traveler's Cafe (5317 North Clark Street) located in an intimate space overseen by a cordial staff, blends coffeehouse and boutique offerings. On the food side, there are fifteen or so tables, all kinds of coffee (or, as they say in Indonesia, *kopi*), along with soups and salads, burgers and burritos, and smoothies, frappes, and even New York egg creams. Along one wall, Indonesian masks are on sale, and along another there are travel books and clocks showing the times in places like Kyoto, Denpasar, and Rotorua. In the back there are sarongs and shawls, wall hangings, jewelry, pottery, batik scarves, vases, kiddie mittens, dresses, and blouses. Open Monday through Thursday from 8:00 A.M. to 11:00 P.M., Friday from 8:00 A.M. to midnight, Saturday from 9:00 A.M. to midnight, Sunday from 10:00 A.M. to 11:00 P.M. Phone (773) 989–5674.

"This is *not* a gallery," insists Stan Jones, co-owner of *American Hands* (5311 North Clark Street). "Galleries belong down on Michigan Avenue. We are a store, a shop." In fact, it's a very impressive shop that sells handcrafted items by American artists. Among the offerings—from classic designs to pop art—are funky clocks, beautiful wood clipboards, carvings based on ancient-culture images, leather animal figures, vases recycled from an old American chestnut split-rail fence, jewelry boxes, incense holders, backgammon boards, paperweights, wonderful wooden puzzles, art glass, baby rattles, and fun things like containers to hold "ashes of problem clients." Open Tuesday through Friday from 10:00 A.M. to 6:30 P.M., Saturday from 10:00 A.M. to 6:00 P.M., Sunday from 11:00 A.M. to 4:00 P.M. Phone (773) 728–4227.

The Swedish Bakery (5348 North Clark Street) is currently not owned by someone of Swedish descent, but not to worry. The always-busy store is full of tantalizing smells and sights, as it fills its cases with the likes of coffeecake made with cardamom dough with a light almond/cinnamon filling, marzipan cake, morskaka (sweet white dough blended with raisins), fruitcakes, tarts, Swedish semlor (traditional Lenten goodies), and sweets with intriguing names like rum rolls, coconut logs, and nut horns. And there's a dessert that transcends all nationalities: Chocolate Suicide Cake. Open Monday through Thursday from 6:30 A.M. to 6:30 P.M., Friday from 6:30 A.M. to 8:00 P.M., Saturday from 6:30 A.M. to 5:00 P.M. Phone (773) 561–8919.

The Griffin Theatre (5404 North Clark Street) puts on its share of plays for adults, but has become best known for its children's shows, which come with whimsical titles like *The Stinky Cheese Man & Other Fairly Stupid Tales* and *Sleeping Ugly*. These original presentations have been among its most critically and commercially successful productions. One of their unusual features is that they run two hours plus rather than the usual one hour. Griffin has also undertaken national tours with hits like *There's a Boy in the Girls' Bathroom*.

"There are other theaters in Chicago that do children's programming, but we're careful to stay away from issue-based themes—AIDS, prenatal concerns—that some of them do," says managing director Bill Massolia. "Our shows are geared toward kids in grades three through six, and all of our stuff is based upon really popular children's contemporary literature, like the Newberry Award winners. We don't do fairy tales. I mean, we're not going to do any 'fuzzy bunny' stuff! We go for the more thought-provoking works where kids actually see themselves as the characters and can relate to what happens to them." Adds Rick Barletta, Griffin's artistic director: "One of the things I really like about doing the children's shows is that a lot of kids just never see any theater. I also like working with kids in shows, getting them to interact with one another instead of interacting with a computer keyboard. It's a completely different world for them. And they find out something about themselves. Incidentally, we also have this whole weird adult following. They come to the shows *without* children." For schedules and prices, phone (773) 769–2228.

A few blocks north and east of Andersonville but still accessible to intrepid walkers, *Broadway Antique Market* (6130 North Broadway) is a nostalgia nut's "retro" wonderland. Located, appropriately, in an art deco building, it's Pop Culture Central—lots of chrome and plastic and colored glass. Selling merchandise from over eighty-five dealers in a sprawling space that goes on and on, the market offers up everything from Dad's (root beer) clocks to Elvis magazines to Aunt Jemima artifacts. There are flamingo figurines, Bakelite flatware, spoons from Chicago's 1933–1934 World's Fair, *Life* magazines from the '40s, vintage pink and orange radios, and venerable tennis racquets and birdcages. Besides the general public, the place is frequented by representatives from movie companies that are on location in Chicago and looking for just the right prop. Open Monday through Saturday from 11:00 A.M. to 7:00 P.M., Sunday from noon to 6:00 P.M. Phone (773) 743–5475, or spin up www.BAMchicago.com.

Moving along to Rogers Park/West Ridge, either drive or take the #155 bus down Devon Avenue to Ridge Avenue. Eating lunch at *The Greenhouse Inn* (6300 Ridge Avenue) is a wonderfully uplifting experience. A very special place—open and bright, with lots of plants and flowers—it is operated by Misericordia, Heart of Mercy, a residential facility for over 500 children and adults with varying degrees of mental and physical disabilities. Some of them wait on tables at the Greenhouse, such as the cheery, efficient woman of indeterminate age with Down's syndrome who took menu orders and wished diners "a pleasant lunch," adding, "Bon appétit." The food is delicious and may be more reasonably priced than it should be. Customers mark their orders on cards that are color-coordinated with the main menu ("That's for our residents who aren't able to read," explained the supervisory hostess). There are salads and homemade soups, sandwiches, and other items such as open-faced sliced beef or pork, spinach and goat cheese omelet,

The Greenhouse Inn

and pasta shells with sliced grilled chicken breast and spinach. For dessert, try the apple crisp or the pumpkin slice with whipped cream, old-fashioned chocolate cake, or fruit medley. The restaurant attracts diners of all ages, from young children to seniors celebrating birthdays with their friends, and there's a pervasive feel-good atmosphere.

With the bill comes a note: "Your support of our restaurant gives our Misericordia workers an opportunity to experience the sense of self-worth that comes with doing a job well and serving the larger community. Your continued support helps us to provide a caring, challenging environment for all our residents." Tip money is placed in a common jar and used for a special fund to provide recreational opportunities at Misericordia, which opened in 1983 on pleasant, sprawling grounds of the former Angel Guardian Orphanage and resembles a small college campus. In addition to the restaurant, there's the in-house retail Hearts and Flour Bakery (also providing employment for the residents) and the Heartworks Gift Shop, selling "jewelry, bridal accessories, fine crystal, baby gifts, and many Irish items," along with artwork, crafts, and pottery created by those living in the facility. The Greenhouse Inn is open for lunch Monday through Friday from 11:00 A.M. to 2:30 P.M. and for brunch most Sundays from 10:00 A.M. to 2:00 P.M. The bakery and gift shop are open Monday through Friday from 10:00 A.M. to 3:00 P.M. Phone (773) 973–6300.

After lunch, walk over half a block north and take a look at the impressive *Angel Guardian Croatian Catholic Church* (6346 North Ridge Avenue), the third and last church built by the German-speaking parishioners of St. Henry's parish, founded in the 1850s. Later used by Angel Guardian Orphange from the 1930s to the early 1970s, it is now operated by the Croatian Catholic Church. If all this seems confusing, it is. A staff member says that it is currently the Angel Guardian Mission, and the church itself is St. Henry's (although a sign on the building reads ANGEL GUARDIAN). Whatever, the brick and limestone Gothic structure was consecrated in 1906 and designed by Henry J. Schlacks. Most distinctive are the clocks that fill the tops of the tower's arches. Tours are available with advance notice. Phone (773) 262–0535.

Head farther west on Devon to another main street, Western Avenue, and stop in at the *Rogers Park/West Ridge Historical Society* (6424 North Western Avenue), founded in 1975. The society houses an impressive collection of vintage advertisements, matchbook covers, and more than 4,000 historical photos, such as the construction of Mundelein College (1930); a scene at a poultry farm (1939), then thriving at Pratt and California Avenues; the now-departed, opulent Granada

Theater on Sheridan Road; and the also-departed streetcars on Western Avenue. Open Wednesday from 10:00 A.M. to 5:00 P.M., Thursday from 7:00 to 9:00 P.M., and Friday from 10:00 A.M. to 5:00 P.M. Phone (773) 764–4078, or log onto www.rpwrhs.org.

Now move on to **Regal Sarees** (2616 West Devon Avenue), and absorb some of the area's Indian atmosphere in this store that sells silk sarees (which the establishment also spells saris), suits, and colorful fabrics. Regal also sells, incongruously, such items as English sweaters and French perfumes. Open every day from 11:00 A.M. to 8:00 P.M. Phone (773) 973–1368.

Three Sisters Delicatessen (2854 West Devon Avenue) is an unpretentious Russian establishment filled with wonderful smells and products such as smoked sturgeon and herring, caviar, chocolate and tortes, homemade pirogi, cheese blintzes, Lithuanian rye bread and Ukrainian salami, candy and jams, and pickled mushrooms. In the front windows

---

Hot Dogs, Chicago Style

*C*hicagoans never think about what goes into *a hot dog (it's just as well), but what goes on one. The so-called Chicago-style hot dog (a.k.a. "red hot," "frank," "wiener") calls for definite ingredients: a Vienna beef dog served on a poppyseed bun (probably Rosen's) and topped with mustard, relish, tomatoes, onions, pickle slice, peppers, maybe celery salt—and, pul-leeze, hold the ketchup. Local newspapers and magazines are always running "best hot dog" contests, which will never settle anything, but as long as you're up around 6821 North Western Avenue, check out the red hots at the* **Original Fluky's** *(established at a prior location in 1929).*

If you're lucky enough to grab a booth, you also get a jukebox that plays such oldies as "The Great Pretender" by the Platters, "Walk Like a Man" by the Four Seasons, and Dion's "The Wanderer."

The decor centerpiece is a gross plastic representation of a hot dog, wrapped in the American flag and squirting itself with (heresy!) ketchup. Over the counter there are packs of Fluky's own hot dog bubble gum. Nearby is a sign that asks, HAVE YOU HAD YOUR BREAKFAST BURRITO TODAY? *but, come on, no one goes to Fluky's for the burritos (or breakfast, for that matter). And why in heaven's name would someone go there for a turkey burger or—get this—sprout salad? That said, Fluky's wants you to know "We Ship Anywhere in the USA." Open for breakfast Monday through Saturday from 6:00 to 11:00 A.M., Sunday from 7:00 to 11:30 A.M. Regular hours Monday through Thursday are 9:00 A.M. to 10:30 P.M., Friday and Saturday from 9:00 A.M. to 11:00 P.M., Sunday from 10:00 A.M. to 10:00 P.M. Phone (773) 274–3652. Inexpensive, of course.*

are gift items, including nesting dolls and fancy plates, cups, and glasses. It's been around for over twenty years, and perhaps so have many of the customers, mostly older with that distinctive "Old World" look. Open Monday through Saturday from 9:00 A.M. to 9:00 P.M., Sunday from 9:00 A.M. to 7:00 P.M. Phone (773) 464–6695.

Billed as "The Oldest and Largest Full Service Jewish Book Store in the Midwest," **Rosenblum's World of Judaica** (2906 West Devon Avenue) has been in business since 1941. Its books are sold under such headings as "Talmud," "Art Scroll," "Rabbinic Literature," and "Jewish Thought," and individual titles range from Irving Howe's *World of Our Fathers* and *The Art of Hanukkah* to *More of the Best of Milton Berle's Private Joke File*. In the children's section there are such books as *Seder with the Animals* and *Sammy Spider's First Passover*. Other items for sale include menorahs, seder plates, wedding cards, yarmulkes, CDs, toys and games, and *The Jerusalem Post*. Open Monday through Wednesday from 9:00 A.M. to 6:00 P.M., Thursday from 9:00 A.M. to 7:00 P.M., Friday from 9:00 A.M. to 2:00 P.M., and Sunday from 10:00 A.M. to 4:00 P.M. Closed Saturday. Phone (773) 262–1700, or call up www.rosenblums.com.

Back east now on Devon to Western, then head north to **Warren Park** (6601 North Western Avenue), a heavily used, sprawling public facility with a field house (including a basketball court), ice rink, tennis courts, playing fields, and even several baseball/softball batting cages. The field house is open Monday through Friday from 9:00 A.M. to 9:00 P.M., Saturday and Sunday from 9:00 A.M. to 5:00 P.M. Phone (773) 742–7888.

Just to the east of the park is **Robert A. Black Golf Course** (2045 West Pratt Avenue), a nine-hole public golf course on land formerly occupied by the private Edgewater Country Club's eighteen-hole course. Dedicated in 1980 and designed by the architects who also laid out well-known Kemper Lakes in Long Grove, Illinois, Robert A. Black was named after the late chief engineer for the Chicago Park District. The course is open all year (weather permitting) from dawn to dusk, and tee times may be made in person or by calling (312) 245–0909.

B.J. Furniture and Antiques (6901 North Western Avenue)—"Top Dollar Paid for Antiques 50 Years and Older"—is your mother's kind of place. Established more than twenty years ago, its rooms are filled with traditional, classic items such as figurines, curio cabinets, mahogany end tables and china cabinets, candelabras, mirrors, oil paintings of pastoral scenes, secretary desks, Victorian tables, crystal lamps, inlaid tea tables, and venerable music boxes. A sign in one of the rooms reads: THE TIME TO BUY AN ANTIQUE IS WHEN YOU SEE IT. YOU RARELY GET A SECOND CHANCE. True enough. Open Monday through Saturday from 10:00 A.M. to 6:00 P.M. Phone (773) 262–1000.

Walk north a couple blocks to Lunt Avenue and take the #96 bus east, get off at the Morse Avenue L station, and walk a block north to the *Heartland Cafe* (7000 North Glenwood Avenue), the kind of down-home place where the waitress calls you, alternately, "honey," "hon," and "babe." What's not to like? With a tie-dyed-type '60s feeling and decor and super-friendly attitude, the plain-and-simple restaurant (which has been around for over a quarter of a century) serves up good food in more than ample portions. The menu is all over the board. For breakfast, there are eggs New Orleans (same as Benedict but with spicy shrimp instead of ham), scrambled tofu, huevos rancheros, and peach pancakes. Later on, the appetizers include whole wheat blinis and mushroom caviar, and the main dishes run from pasta of the day to burritos and quesadillas, buffalo cheeseburger, chicken chardonnay, red and black bean buffalo corn chili, and the Heartland macro plate (brown rice, beans of the day, steamed greens, mushroom gravy, and gamashio—a crushed sesame seed and salt mix). The cafe, nestled alongside the L tracks, also harbors the Buffalo Bar, specializing in international draft and bottled beer, and the General Store, which sells everything from work gloves to drawing pencil kits and Audubon bird calls. What's more, there's entertainment several nights a week: jazz, bluegrass, folk-pop, "funky rock," and even "rockin' harmonica." The kitchen is open Monday through Thursday from 7:00 A.M. to 10:00 P.M., Friday from 7:00 A.M. to 11:00 P.M., Saturday from 8:00 A.M. to 11:00 P.M. The bar is open Monday through Thursday from 7:00 A.M. to 1:00 A.M., Friday from 7:00 A.M. to 2:00 A.M., Saturday from 8:00 A.M. to 3:00 A.M. The store is open Monday through Saturday from 11:00 A.M. to 11:00 P.M. Phone (773) 465–8005. Inexpensive.

Another option is to head east a short way to Sheridan Road and walk slowly into the *Ennui Cafe* (6981 North Sheridan Road), a friendly and funky, throwback kind of coffeehouse with loads of plants, beat-up tables and chairs, a bookcase full of battered paperbacks, well-thumbed copies of the morning's newspapers, and a popular smoking section. Ennui offers things like soups, sandwiches, and bagels, but most customers—many of whom seem to be perpetual students—seem to settle for the assortment of coffee. Outside, the cafe displays two, well, far-out pieces of sculpture, "Chicago Good Year Construction" and "Empress Fan," made of an old tire and rusty metal pieces and created by Rogers Park resident Bill Boyce, who uses "industrial and urban jet-sam" and believes, "These junk trucks full of scrap . . . these guys have gold mines and don't know it!" Ennui is open Sunday through Thursday from 7:30 A.M. to 11:00 P.M., Friday and Saturday from 7:30 A.M. to 1:00 A.M. Phone (773) 973–2233.

Helping folks make a more melodic world since 1976, *Flatts & Sharpe Music Company* (6749 North Sheridan Road) specializes in selling acoustic and electric guitars, and has a small collection of wonderful old Hawaiian guitars from the '20s and '30s. Other items include a wide assortment of harmonicas, pennywhistles, and bamboo flutes; keyboards and amps; instruments for kids such as triangles, sweet potatoes (ocarinas), and glockenspiels; and an assortment of instrumental and vocal books featuring the sheet music of such performers as John Prine, Carly Simon, Van Halen, and Patsy Cline. Open Monday and Friday from 11:00 A.M. to 6:00 P.M., Tuesday, Wednesday, and Thursday from 11:00 A.M. to 8:00 P.M., and Saturday from 11:00 A.M. to 5:00 P.M. Phone (773) 465–5233.

One of the best kept secrets in the city is *The Martin D'Arcy Museum of Art* (6525 North Sheridan Road) in the lakefront Cudahy Library on the campus of Loyola University. Founded by Donald Rowe, S.J., who served as its director from 1969 to 1991 and is the former president of the highly regarded St. Ignatius College Prep, the museum was named for an

Pottawatomie Heritage

*F*or a look at a quintessential Chicago neighborhood park, check out **Indian Boundary,** headquartered at 2500 West Lunt Avenue. Established in 1916, the park commemorates the Treaty of 1816, which established the land boundaries of the Pottawatomie Indians. The park's thirteen acres pack in a lot, including a handsome, vintage field house; a small, duck-filled lagoon and geyser; tennis courts; a children's wading pool with a summertime spraying apparatus; an imaginative, wooden-structure play-ground; and even a small, rather pathetic, but somehow appealing zoo that has been there for years and now features mute swans, white-tailed deer, alpaca, and, mostly, goats. A plaque near the playground notes that various tribes of Native Americans lived in villages on the Indian Boundary line, which runs through the park. First there was the Illinois tribe, followed by the Ottawa, Chippewa, and, especially, the Pottawatomie (which means "People of the Place of the Fire"). The park may be reached by boarding the #96 Lunt bus at the Morse Avenue L station, but it's much easier to get there by car. Open daily from 6:00 A.M. to 11:00 P.M. Phone (312) 742–7887.

Oxford University priest, author, and philosopher who was involved with the arts. Situated in a lovely, classical setting that serves as a welcome refuge from nearby bustling Sheridan Road, the museum has beautiful European paintings and other works, mostly religious, made of various materials: tempera, copper repoussé (beaten copper), oak, cast and engraved silver, lead-glazed earthenware, and carved ivory. The distinc-, tive items include a late-sixteenth-century Italian prie-dieu (kneeler); a seventeenth-century German elephant automaton clock; a cast bronze seventeenth-century German or Flemish figure of a "birdcatcher"; an eighteenth-century Spanish Christ on the cross figure made of ivory, silver, glass, and ebony; a carved lindenwood St. Christopher and the Christ child from Germany, circa 1500; a 1487 Latin vulgate Bible translated by St. Jerome; a fifteenth-century Italian processional cross; and a Spanish silver gilt and base metal altar card (circa 1650), which served as a memory aid for the priest celebrating Mass. The museum also presents various lectures on subjects from "The Buddhist Guardians: Icons of Protection" to "Artemisia Gentileschi: Trials and Triumphs of a Woman Painter in Baroque Italy." Open Tuesday through Saturday from noon to 4:00 P.M. Phone (773) 508–2679, or log onto darcy.luc.edu. Free.

PLACES TO EAT IN
EDGEWATER AND ROGERS
PARK/WEST RIDGE

Ann Sather,
5207 North Clark Street;
(773) 271–6677.
Undoubtedly Chicago's best known Swedish restaurant, Ann Sather was founded in 1945 by Ms. Sather—of all things, a *Norwegian*. And the current owner, it has been publicly admitted, is *Irish*. No matter. The food is plentiful and delicious. Not as high profile as the Sather flagship on Belmont Avenue in Lakeview, the two-story Clark Street version is nevertheless lighter and cheerier, with colorful

Scandinavian art brightening the scene and creating a sort of country kitchen effect. Although lunch is served (Swedish meatballs, sandwiches, salads), Sather's is best known for its breakfasts. Selections include the ever-popular Swedish pancakes with lingonberries, the rather peculiar combination of two pancakes and four meatballs, and anything that includes Sather's famous cinnamon rolls, better known as "sticky buns." Also on hand are various omelets—including spinach, broccoli, and peach—along with "selections of [eggs] Benedict" (from traditional to smoked salmon and crab cake), homemade hash

(corned beef, turkey, vegetarian), apple-cranberry pancakes, whole wheat pecan waffles, and fresh orange and grapefruit juice. Open Monday through Friday from 7:00 A.M. to 3:30 P.M., Saturday and Sunday from 7:00 A.M. to 5:00 P.M. Inexpensive.

Atlantique,
5101 North Clark Street;
(773) 275–9191.
Chef-owner Jack Jones's upscale seafood spot combines a friendly atmosphere, superb service, and exquisite food that creates an enthusiastic repeat clientele. Appetizers run from Louisiana crab cake Napoleon to sautéed Hudson Valley foie gras on brioche, and the inventive

salads have to rank among the best in the city. For the main course, try the grilled wild striped bass over herbed risotto with mussels and clams, the seared dry pack scallops with lobster and mushroom polenta, or the grilled Atlantic salmon with pureed potatoes, creamed leeks with rock shrimp, and a fava bean coulis. And there's an ambitious wine list. One small drawback is the surprisingly trite decor, from the marlin over the bar to the mermaid and Neptune on the rest room doors. Open Monday through Thursday from 5:30 to 10:00 P.M., Friday and Saturday from 5:30 to 11:00 P.M., Sunday from 5:00 to 9:00 P.M. Expensive.

The Greenhouse Inn,
6300 Ridge Avenue;
(773) 973–6300.
See page 113 for full description.

Heartland Cafe,
7000 North Glenwood Avenue;
(773) 465–8005.
See page 117 for full description.

La Donna,
5146 North Clark Street;
(773) 561–9400.
A family restaurant specializing in Italian cuisine, La Donna operates out of a low-ceiling, intimate space with decor centering on framed, art decoish Italian posters. For lunch, you might pick the delicious linguine with fresh salmon and mussels, the bow tie pasta tossed in a creamy saffron and vodka sauce, or the risotto with Parma ham, leaks, and spinach. Dinner appetizers include an antipasto plate of prosciutto di Parma and tuna carpaccio with ginger and citrus dressing. Besides exotic kinds of pizza (radicchio, salmon, and onion) and homemade pasta, entrees range from risotto with jumbo shrimp to veal and prosciutto rolls, tiny veal meatballs braised with savoy cabbage and white wine, grilled Chilean sea bass, and chicken breast sautéed with shiitake mushrooms, spinach, and sundried tomatoes. There's an extensive wine list and martinis with contrived names like "French Kiss." The service can be rather relaxed. Open Monday through Saturday from 11:00 A.M. to 11:00 P.M., Sunday brunch from 10:00 A.M. to 3:30 P.M., dinner to 11:00 P.M. Moderate.

Leona's,
6935 North Sheridan Road;
(773) 764–5757.
One of nine or ten entries in a popular family-run chain born in 1950, this one is roomy and pleasant and is a survivor in a Rogers Park location near the lakefront that, for some reason, has had a fair amount of restaurant turnover. The food is solid and the portions more than ample, although those who can't abide cutesy menus and "Divine Delivered Dining" are advised to stay away. Others might try the Bodacious Burgers, Carnivorous Combo (Italian sausage and beef with tricolored peppers), Garbage Pasta Salad, Kickass Garlic Bread, Saucy Salmon Grill, Killer Shrimp, Psychedelic Salad, and Vegetarian Thang! which means thangs like marinated Italian tofu and vegetable skewers. Open Monday through Thursday from 11:30 A.M. to 11:00 P.M., Friday from 11:30 to 12:30 A.M., Saturday from noon to 12:30 A.M., Sunday from 10:30 A.M. (brunch) to 10:30 P.M. Inexpensive.

Pasteur,
5525 North Broadway;
(773) 878–1061.
Formerly located in a plain space with basic furnishings, Pasteur in recent years transformed itself into a stylish place with elegant decor (and higher prices). Serving fine, inventive Vietnamese fare, the restaurant offers such appetizers as a Saigon-style crepe filled with chicken, shrimp, and mushrooms and shrimp paste wrapped around fresh sugarcane. Among the unusual salad choices are shredded lotus stem mixed with shrimp, chicken, sliced apple, herbs,

and a fish sauce dressing and shredded green papaya tossed with shrimp and mint leaves and topped with peanuts and a fish sauce. Entrees include sautéed shrimp and chicken with rice noodles, steamed bass with ginger, grilled rainbow trout marinated in lemongrass and wrapped in banana leaves, and Asian vegetables with tofu and coconut milk. Moderate.

Reza's,
5255 North Clark Street; (773) 561–1898.
See page 110 for full description.

Svea,
5236 North Clark Street; (773) 275–7738.
See page 109 for full description.

Viceroy of India,
2516 West Devon Avenue; (773) 743–4100.
There is a plethora of establishments serving Indian food along West Devon, and one of the best is Viceroy (which also offers catering and carry-out). Besides its bargain-price, sinus-clearing lunch buffet, the restaurant with the plain, formal dining room offers three dinner chef's specials: the Tandoori Mix Grill, Vegetarian Bhojan, and Special Dinner (featuring tandoori chicken). Entrees include fish tikka (fish pieces marinated and roasted in a charcoal clay oven), reshmi kabab (barbecued ground boneless pieces of chicken, served with onions and lemon), and various lamb, seafood, chicken, rice, and vegetarian specials. For dessert, there is a wide selection, including mango ice cream. Open for buffet every day from noon to 3:30 P.M., for dinner Sunday through Thursday from 5:00 to 10:00 P.M., Friday and Saturday from 5:00 to 10:30 P.M. Inexpensive.

SOUTH LOOP AND NEAR SOUTH SIDE

For years the South Loop was overwhelmed by railroad tracks, particularly those of the Illinois Central Gulf Railroad, as well as several freight lines. By 1903 there were four major train terminals: the Illinois Central's Central Station, the Dearborn Street Station, the Chicago Grand Central Depot, and the LaSalle Street Station. It was at the Central Station (12th Street and Michigan Avenue) that a young jazz trumpet player named Louis Armstrong arrived from New Orleans to join mentor King Oliver at a South Side club and was promptly intimidated by the city's tall buildings, thinking they might all be part of universities. Three of the stations have been long demolished, and only the Dearborn (1885) remains. It was near this station that the city's printing industry started up, in an area just south of Congress that is now known as Printer's Row. After World War II, the industry moved out, and many of the buildings were abandoned, only to be restored in the late 1970s. Overall, the area experienced considerable decline, and as rail traffic decreased sharply after World War II, the railyards gradually were abandoned. The blocks—just a short walk west of Michigan Avenue—were full of disreputable bars and porno palaces. Then, in the '70s a group of business leaders formed a committee proposing that the railyard space be used for middle-class housing. The result was the successful development known as Dearborn Park, south of the Dearborn Station, which, joined by trendy Printer's Row in the early '80s, brought the area back to life.

In the late 1800s and early 1900s, big hotels went up along Michigan Avenue between Congress and Roosevelt, capped in 1927 by the ultra-swank Stevens Hotel, now the Chicago Hilton and Towers. (See "Places to Stay" at the end of this chapter.) The Michigan Avenue hotels today are within walking distance of the Museum Campus, housing three of the city's biggest institutions—the Field Museum of Natural History, John G. Shedd Aquarium, and Adler Planetarium—as well as Soldier Field, which became the site of famous sporting events, including the second fight between Jack Dempsey and Gene Tunney in 1927, and is now the home of the Chicago Bears and Chicago Fire (soccer).

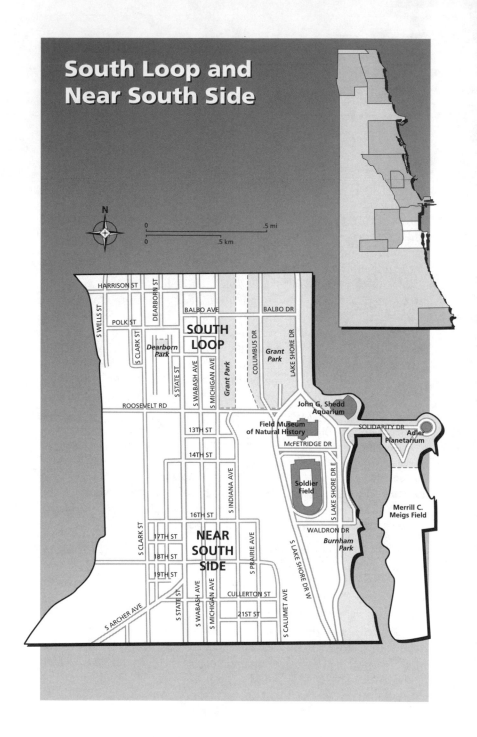

South Loop and Near South Side

SOUTH LOOP AND NEAR SOUTH SIDE

Top Attractions in the South Loop and on the Near South Side

The Columbia College Chicago Center for Book & Paper Arts

Glessner House Museum

Henry B. Clarke House

Willie Dixon's Blues Heaven Foundation

Quinn Chapel African Methodist Episcopal Church

Before Chicago was incorporated as a city in 1837, the area south of 12th Street (now Roosevelt Road) was a sandy stretch crossed by wagon trails. Its first residents were poor Germans and Irish who came to work on the Illinois and Michigan Canal between 1836 and 1848. The first large development occurred in the 1850s, with the arrival of the railroads, and the Near South Side was spared by the 1871 fire. During the 1880s and 1890s, the Prairie Avenue section between 16th and 22nd Streets became Chicago's original "Gold Coast," with more than fifty mansions belonging to such tycoons as Marshall Field, George Pullman, Philip Armour, and William Kimball (the piano and organ manufacturer). But the Near South Side was also home to many poor people. Prairie Avenue began declining rapidly around the turn of the twentieth century, due to several factors, including the noise and dirt created by the nearby railyards, and the spread of commerce and industry. The first automobile showrooms opened on Michigan Avenue in 1908, and by 1911 there were more than twenty-five auto businesses along Michigan. By the 1920s many of the old mansions were converted into rooming houses or torn down to make way for factories and warehouses.

During and after World War I, there was a great influx of blacks, many from the South, who took up housing in the low-rent areas, which led to the former residents, mostly Irish and German, moving elsewhere. The Prohibition years of the 1920s gave Chicago an unwanted reputation it is still trying to live down. Al Capone's headquarters was at the Lexington Hotel, Michigan Avenue and Cermak Road. Following the decline that accelerated after World War II, much of the Near South remained for years a deteriorating, impoverished, unsafe area. But in recent times it has experienced somewhat of a renaissance, with the construction of many new town houses, condominiums, and lofts and the influx of new businesses (including restaurants). Tourism continues to thrive in the Prairie Avenue Historic District, designated in 1973. And every year McCormick Place on the lakefront—opened in 1960 and rebuilt after a fire in 1967—attracts dozens of trade shows.

Attractions in the South Loop area may be reached by walking or taking the #22 or #36 bus (board both downtown). As for the Near South Side, many of the places covered in this chapter are open only in the daytime. Either take a taxi or the #3 or #4 bus, which run south on Michigan Avenue to 22nd Street. (Board on Michigan Avenue south of Randolph

Street.) Visitors are definitely advised not to walk around the Near South at night. The area is slowly becoming upgraded, but there are still rough spots. Take a cab to a definite destination, for sure.

A good place to start walking around the South Loop might be south on Michigan from Congress. Or take the Red Line subway to the Harrison stop, and walk east to Michigan. Over the years, Columbia College Chicago, a four-year private institution, has become widely known throughout the area as a leader in training students in the performing and visual arts, as well as communications (which the college, for some reason, also insists on calling an "art"). Columbia's *Museum of Contemporary Photography* (600 South Michigan) lists itself as "the only museum in the Midwest with an exclusive commitment to the medium of photography." The museum features exhibits by photographers employing such techniques as enlarging Polaroid images and incorporating them into elements of collage, using enamel paint to both obscure and frame details, and staging apparently intimate "candid" snapshots of family and friends. Those who have exhibited include Wojciech Prazmoski, who works with photomontages; Clement Cooper, who has produced a series of portraits of inner-city schoolchildren of diverse races in Birmingham, Preston, and Manchester, England; Antonia Contro, who creates images of objects and landscapes, combining them with objects such as antique maps and written notes; and Maurizio Pellegrin, whose wall collage, *Cameras,* incorporates old cameras and photo-related equipment. The museum, which also sponsors periodic "Gallery Talks" with the exhibiting photographers, is open Monday through Friday from 10:00 A.M. to 5:00 P.M., Thursday from 10:00 A.M. to 8:00 P.M., Saturday from noon to 5:00 P.M. For more information, phone (312) 663–5554, or check onto www.mocp.org. Free.

Perhaps the least known space in the *Spertus Museum* (618 South Michigan) is its downstairs *Rosenbaum ARTiFACT Center,* a wonderfully creative, interactive place for youngsters. The centerpiece is the model tel, which is a mound built up over the years by layers of successive ancient civilizations. On the tel, children (and, presumably, adults with well-honed imaginations) can pretend they're archaeologists by digging in the sand and coming up with shards of pottery and other artifacts. Friendly staff members are on hand to explain how to use the tools. Nearby, preschoolers and kindergarten students play in the Israelite House, filled with props, including puppets and a baking oven. Spots in the ARTiFACT Center for older children include "The Marketplace," a group of market stalls where one can examine objects from ancient Israel and participate in various hand-on activities such as clay sculpture and water conservation; "Music in the Marketplace," focusing on ancient instruments such as lyres, lutes, harps, and shofars ("Push to hear King Tut's trumpets"); and "The Trade and Travel Game," which explains barter and trade. The Rosenbaum ARTiFACT Center is open Sunday through Thursday (except holidays) from 1:00 to 4:30 P.M., with mornings reserved for group tours. For tour reservations and fee and program information, phone (312) 322–1747.

Upstairs, in the Spertus Museum itself—the largest Jewish museum between the East and West coasts—there are exhibitions about Jewish practices and traditions; the Zell Holocaust Memorial, North America's first permanent museum exhibition about the terrible events between 1933 and 1945; the Asher Library, the largest Jewish public library in the Midwest; and a gift shop offering everything from books and calendars to porcelain dolls, puppets, seder plate sets, prayer shawls, and CDs (Barbra Streisand to Jan Peerce). The museum is open Sunday through Wednesday from 10:00 A.M. to 5:00 P.M., Thursday from 10:00 A.M. to 8:00 P.M., Friday from 10:00 A.M. to 3:00 P.M. Suggested nominal admission, free on Friday. Phone (312) 322–1747.

Farther south, and a block west over on Wabash, *The Columbia College Chicago Center for Book & Paper Arts* (1104 South Wabash) started in 1992 when a group of book artists, papermakers, printers, designers, and calligraphers decided to form a center that would train people to become book and paper artists, and did just that. Facilities in the

Fishy Fare

The proclaimed lofty mission of the John G. Shedd Aquarium (1200 South Lake Shore Drive) is to "promote the enjoyment, appreciation, and conservation of aquatic life and environments through education, exhibits, and research." An admirable goal, indeed. Which is why it's such a surprise to enter the Shedd's Soundings restaurant (great lake views, by the way) and look at the menu, which lists such items as hamburgers, grilled chicken sandwiches, and . . . baked halibut filet and sautéed tilapia almondine. That's right. Those very finny creatures it is enjoying, appreciating, and conserving are also being served up for your dining pleasure. Oh, well. If you or your children feel squeamish about ordering such fare, you can always opt for the vegetarian wrap.

sprawling 20,000-square-foot space include two galleries, a papermaking studio, a bindery, a letterpress studio, and a computer lab, along with 500 drawers of type, hundreds of brass tools for decorating books, and such arcane equipment as board shears, job backers, hot stampers, a guillotine, and Vandercook presses.

For those not into stampers or Vandercooks, or not looking to get a master's of fine arts in interdisciplinary book and paper arts, the Center presents all kinds of exhibitions and events, such as "The Manuscript Illuminated," which explores unusual perspectives on typography; a display of pop-up children's books; a droll collage of homework excuses ("I Don't Understand the Concepts"); and, if you really want to know, "The Edible Book Show and Tea," in which participants concoct book-like sculptures made out of food like peanut butter and salami. The center also offers classes and workshops for the community in bookbinding, linoleum block printing, papermaking ("wear galoshes or boots and expect to get wet"), and letterpress ("bring rubber gloves and an apron and prepare to get inky"). If you're lucky, one of the students working in the bookbinding studio or energetically making paper may volunteer to show you around. Open Monday through Friday from 9:30 A.M. to 5:00 P.M. Phone (312) 344–6630, or look up the Web site at www.colum.edu/centers/bpa.

If you're in the South Loop at night, all kinds of music rings out loud at **HotHouse,** a lively, sprawling club at 31 East Balbo Avenue, a block west

Of Pigs and Men

*H*og Butcher for the World,

Tool Maker, Stacker of Wheat,

Player with Railroads and the Nation's Freight Handler;

Stormy, husky, brawling,

City of the Big Shoulders . . .

—Carl Sandburg, "Chicago" (1914)

"Hog Butcher for the World. Not any more, Carl. Not for some time. The song is ended, though for a visitor from far off the melody lingers on. Vere are the shtockyards? may be his first question. I'll tell you, Günter or Jean-Louis or Marcello or Niels. Cattle and swine are no longer shipped on the hoof. They are done in close to the feedlots in such places as Greeley, Colorado; Logansport, Indiana; Guyman, Texas; and Clovis, New Mexico. Sic transit gloria porko."

—Studs Terkel, "Chicago" (1985)

of the Chicago Hilton and Towers. Performers in one schedule span included the likes of the J. Davis Trio, which belts out what it calls "martini-styled hip hop"; the Odd Assortment, traditional Irish folk music; Deanna Witkowski, a pianist, vocalist, and composer whose music is a fusion of jazz, Afro-Latin, and classical; jazz vocalist Dee Alexander, who has been compared to Sarah Vaughan; Mambo Express, an Afro-Cuban ensemble; and Bucky Halker and the Complete Unknowns, which recorded a collection of labor protest songs from 1886 to 1950. For something completely different, every month there's the Backyard Variety Show, a showcase of vaudeville-style performers who include acrobats, torch singers, magicians, and (how retro can you get?) fire-eaters. Open Sunday through Friday from 5:00 P.M. to 2:00 A.M., Saturday from 6:00 P.M. to 3:00 A.M. For performance times and (varying) admission prices, phone (312) 362–9707, or check out www.hothouse.net.

Another way to investigate the South Loop is to head over to the area south of Congress down to Polk Street, and approximately between Clark and State Streets, known as Printer's Row. *Sandmeyer's Bookstore* (714 South Dearborn) is a twenty-year-old Printer's Row fixture located in the Rowe Building, a former printing arts factory built in 1892. A good example of the late-nineteenth-century Romanesque Revival, it was designed by influential architect William Le Baron Jenney and renovated in 1980. The attractive store specializes particularly in fiction, travel, and children's books, with other sections devoted to, among other things, cooking, music, drama, and biography. Open Monday through Wednesday and Friday from 11:00 A.M. to 6:30 P.M., Thursday from 11:00 A.M. to 8:00 P.M., Saturday from 11:00 A.M. to 5:00 P.M., Sunday from 11:00 A.M. to 4:00 P.M. Phone (312) 922–2104.

Wrapped in attractive Victorian furnishings, *Printers Row Fine & Rare Books* (715 South Dearborn) was started in 2001 by Doug Phillips, whose previous occupation was in something not so rare: his family's insurance business. Phillips, a longtime collector of rare and first-edition books, says his most popular volumes are works by what he calls "The Big Four": Hemingway, Fitzgerald, Steinbeck, and Faulkner. Located in an old printing building, where the first edition of L. Frank Baum's *The Wonderful Wizard of Oz* was printed in 1900, the store offers anywhere from 8,000 to 10,000 rare volumes, either on display in bookcases or on Phillips's computer database. The specialties are nineteenth- and twentieth-century American, British, and continental fiction. Most of the titles are first editions and are signed. The proprietor also sells autographed framed letters and manuscripts from the likes of Aldous Huxley, Theodore Dreiser, and James Joyce. A note of caution: Rare book stores in Chicago tend to have a short shelf life, so be sure to call first (312–583–1800). Open Monday through Saturday from noon to 5:00 P.M., mornings and Sundays by appointment.

Chicago's train stations were once the O'Hares of transportation. The former Dearborn Station, which hasn't seen a train arrive or depart in over twenty-five years, sits at 47 West Polk at Dearborn. Designed by Cyrus L. W. Eidlitz and built in 1885, it was reconstructed in 1922 after a fire and converted into a cornucopia of eating spots, shops, and offices in the mid-1980s. Even in its present incarnation, the *Dearborn Station Galleria,* the Romanesque Revival structure stands tall and handsome, with its red-brick facade and charming Italian brick clock tower. Inside the pleasant, airy interior, which includes a mezzanine walkway, is a food court (good place to take a tour break), as well as a hair salon, dry cleaner's, bank, real estate firm, law offices, and a music school. The galleria is open Monday through Friday from 7:00 A.M. to 9:00 P.M., Saturday from 8:00 A.M. to 5:00 P.M. Phone (312) 554–8100.

Lunch time? BETTER FOOD THAN MOST HOSPITALS, proudly declares the sign over the front door of *Blackie's* (755 South Clark Street), a cheery, woody, friendly place, where, if everybody doesn't know your name, they certainly aren't letting on. Established in 1939, the family-owned restaurant, in which four generations have been involved, attracted a clientele in the '40s and '50s that included Glenn Miller and Tommy Dorsey, the Harlem Globetrotters, Rocky Marciano, the Three Stooges, and the Marx Brothers. You won't see them around these days, of course, unless you believe in reincarnation and Groucho comes back as a liver sausage on rye. The wide-ranging menu lists items from lemon broiled chicken breast and pasta shells marinara to steak sandwiches and cheeseburgers, and, yes, it *is* better than most hospitals. Open for breakfast Friday from 7:30 to 10:30 A.M., Saturday and Sunday from 7:30 A.M. to 1:30 P.M.; for lunch every day from 11:00 A.M. to 3:30 P.M.; and for dinner Tuesday through Friday only, from 5:00 to 11:00 P.M. Phone (312) 786–1161. Inexpensive.

Two nighttime attractions farther south on the Near South Side are situated on Michigan Avenue. (Again, take a taxi.) Located for years in a funky space in Uptown on the North Side, the *Dance Center of Columbia College Chicago* moved south a while back to a new three-story, 33,000-square-foot home at 1306 South Michigan. The center, more than thirty years old, presents contemporary dance in a 272-seat space performed by groups with contemporary names like Mad Shak Dance Company, Jump Rhythm Jazz Project, Luna Negra Dance Theater, and 33 Fainting Spells. But lots of things go on here. Studying in the building's

Dearborn Station

several studios, students take classes in ballet, jazz dance, ethnic traditions, and modern movement. The Dance Center offers a FamilyDance Matinee Series, with each one-hour show including a hands-on movement workshop for children and adults taught by members of the performing companies, and the Community Outreach and Education division runs DanceMasters, a series of workshops and technique classes (open to the public) with featured choreographers and dancers. Phone (312) 344–8300, or check out www.dancecenter.org.

Live jazz and blues are served up at the *Cotton Club,* a friendly, cavernous place at 1710 South Michigan that features performers in the Cab Calloway Room and bands for dancing in the Gray Room. It doesn't have the big-name owners like two other clubs in the area—Buddy Guy's

Legends and Koko Taylor's Celebrity—but that's all right. Chances are you won't see those folks at their own places anyway. The Cotton, though, does have folks like Killer Ray and the Killer Players, and, depending on the night, there's also comedy and open mike poetry readings and a complimentary buffet on Fridays and Saturdays. For show times and admission, phone (312) 341–9787.

Michigan Avenue is also the place for an excellent choice for lunch or dinner. Opened in the spring of 2000 and quickly becoming a success, the cheery *Chicago Firehouse Restaurant* (1401 South Michigan Avenue)—next door to the National Association of Letter Carriers—is, not surprisingly, located in a former Chicago firehouse. Originally constructed in 1905 to house Engine Company C F 104, the space has been marvelously converted, full of mahogany, while retaining everything from the tin ceiling to the brass fire pole. Along with private rooms, the two dining areas are the main dining room and the cozier, more casual quarters in the pub, which one noontime attracted extremely casually dressed workers from nearby businesses along with the dapper Illinois secretary of state. The restaurant serves deliciously prepared American cuisine rarely seen, one surmises, in a firehouse. Appetizers include roasted mushrooms and blue crab cakes, with entrees ranging from pan-fried rainbow trout and grilled coriander-crusted salmon to slow-cooked pot roast, barbecue ribs,

Of Moose and Teapots

*B*ecause of the convenience of rail transportation, for the first twenty years of the twentieth century, Chicago's Near South was a political mecca. The (since-demolished) Coliseum at Wabash Avenue and 15th Street was the site of six national conventions. In 1904 the Republicans nominated "the Cowboy President," Theodore Roosevelt, and his ample-girthed secretary of war, William Howard Taft, in 1908. Taft won the bid again in 1912, when one of his challengers was none other than his onetime mentor, Mr. Roosevelt, who switched over as the candidate of the third-party Progressive Republicans.

With T.R. proclaiming he felt "as strong as a bull moose," his followers naturally became known as the "Bull Moosers." (The winner nonetheless was the Democrat, Woodrow Wilson.) Again, in 1916, the Republicans congregated on the Near South Side, nominating a Supreme Court justice (and another ultimate loser), Charles Evans Hughes, and then in 1920 finally put up another winner, Warren G. Harding of Ohio, who quickly became a loser. Harding's abbreviated, corruption-plagued term (he died in 1923) was best known for the Teapot Dome naval oil reserves bribery caper and other scandals.

shrimp and pasta, and grilled pork loin. Among the desserts are flourless chocolate cake with raspberry coulis, carrot cake with cream cheese icing, and lemon tart with crème Anglaise. Open for lunch Tuesday through Saturday from 11:00 A.M. to 3:00 P.M. and Sunday from 11:00 A.M. to 4:00 P.M., and for dinner Tuesday through Thursday from 5:00 to 10:00 P.M., Friday and Saturday from 5:00 to 10:30 P.M., Sunday from 4:00 to 9:00 P.M. Phone (312) 786–1401. Moderate.

If it's the daytime, either walk south on Michigan or take Michigan's #3 or #4 bus. At 18th Street, take a left 1 block to Indiana Avenue, where you'll find the **National Vietnam Veterans Art Museum** (1801 South Indiana Avenue). Following a nearby temporary venue, it opened in its present location in 1996 in a previously abandoned warehouse donated by the city. It characterizes itself as "the only museum in the world with a permanent collection focusing on the subject of war from the personal point of view" and is "adamantly apolitical and without bias." It has its genesis in the Vietnam Veterans Art Group, formed in 1979–1980. Featured are over 700 works of art—paintings, watercolors, charcoals, sculptures, collages, and photographs—created by more than one hundred artists from the United States, Australia, Cambodia, Thailand, and North and South Vietnam who served in the military during the Vietnam War. One artist named Joseph Fornelli remembered he created drawings "done with C-ration coffee and river water," while Richard Yohnka wrote: "My art is not pretty to look at, but I have a statement to make about the negative side of man. War is my nightmare and that of thousands of other soldiers. . . . I want my paintings to be read as violent, emotional poems."

Some of the works are jarringly graphic, powerfully disturbing and intense—the viewing experience is deeply moving—with titles like *Battling Freaks, A Naked Woman Offers Death on a Sunday Afternoon, Napalm Sky Ride, Survivor Guilt,* and, simply, *Fear.* There's a good amount of bitter political commentary, like the painting of generals playing a Monopoly-like *War Games,* and there are a lot of images of skulls and the specter of Death. There's a series of three sculptures centered around a prisoner of war and entitled *Pride, Broken, Death.* A sculpture, *Dressed to Kill,* uses teakwood and .50 caliber brass shell casings. A painting showing the legs and feet of three army corpses is entitled *Class of '67.* Along with the artworks, the museum displays a collection of North Vietnamese and Viet Cong weapons, uniforms, and medals, and presents a twenty-minute slide show of the artists when they were in the war. On the ceiling of the central atrium is a huge wind chime–like memorial made of thousands of dog tags (stamped out by an in-house machine) as a remembrance to those who never returned.

The museum, which has a coffee shop and gift shop, is open Tuesday through Friday from 11:00 A.M. to 6:00 P.M., Saturday from 10:00 A.M. to 5:00 P.M., Sunday from noon to 5:00 P.M. During Chicago Bears games at nearby Soldier Field, an answering-machine message dryly reveals, the museum is closed because of traffic problems. Phone (312) 326–0270, or look up www.nvvam.org.

Just east of the museum is the Prairie Avenue Historic District, where two buildings—the Kimball House (1801 South Prairie Avenue) and the Coleman-Ames House (1811 South Prairie Avenue)—are both owned by the United States Soccer Federation. You can read about their history on signs in front, but they are *not,* a receptionist promptly and rather haughtily informed me, open to the public. That's all right. Two others are. So there.

The coach house/gift shop of **Glessner House Museum** (1800 South Prairie Avenue), is the starting point of tours for both Glessner and the adjacent **Henry B. Clarke House** (1855 South Indiana Avenue). The latter is also known as the Widow Clarke House, although it might more appropriately be called the Wandering Clarke House. Reportedly Chicago's oldest surviving building, it was built in 1836 on twenty acres of land on what is now the 1700 block of South Michigan—an area so remote that Clarke would put out a lantern at night to help guide his guests. Built in a Greek Revival style, supplemented by an Italianate cupola, it was meant to resemble top-drawer houses in the Clarkes' native upstate New York.

The house, which, unlike the privately run Glessner House, is owned and maintained by the city, is also distinctive for having been moved two times. The first time, after the death of both Clarkes, was in 1872, when the new owner took it to a spot farther south in the "country" (45th and Wabash Avenue). The second was in 1977, when the city bought the place. Through an unusual plan, the house was lifted hydraulically over the CTA elevated tracks at 44th Street between Calumet and Prairie Avenues. Problem was, the excellent docent guide said, things froze, and the house was left suspended in the air for ten days. She also noted that most of the furnishings are not the originals, that the Clarkes only addressed each other by their first names in the privacy of their bedroom, and that Henry eventually went bankrupt in the hardware and banking businesses and subsequently turned half the house into a cold storage area for the game he killed and sold to restaurants to make ends meet. Among the items on display are a unique combination cradle/rocking chair and a wonderful doll house.

You may very well find it a more interesting experience wandering through the John J. Glessner House, built from 1885 to 1887 and designed by Boston architect Henry Hobson Richardson, a heavy-set, flamboyant man who liked to dress up in a monk's habit. Best known for Trinity Church in Boston, he had no reservations about creating a private residence, stating that he took on "everything from cathedrals to chicken coops—that's how I make my living." Richardson died before the house was completed, sparing him the anger of the Prairie Avenue neighbors, who thought it resembled a fortress. (Actually, it does.) Huffed railroad car magnate George Pullman (whose own residence no long exists): "I do not know what I have ever done to have that thing staring me in the face every time I go out of my door." If the Romanesque granite exterior is forbidding, the handsome oak-paneled English Arts and Crafts interior is considerably more inviting. The tour guide pointed out that the owners—John Glessner was in the farm machinery business—made sure their living quarters faced the sunny south, while the servants had to deal with the northern light, made even darker by narrow slit windows.

Among the highlights (almost all of the furnishings, unlike those in the Clarke house, are original) are the exquisite carved picture frames and cabinetry of Isaac Scott, the ceramic tiles of William Morris, a small gallery where members of the Chicago Symphony would play at parties (both patrons of the arts, the Glessners helped found the orchestra), a partners' desk in the library (Frances Glessner was one of the few wives in those days actually allowed in a home library), and, in the "Upstairs/Downstairs" mode, an ingenious kitchen "annunciator" designed to summon the servants, who, not so incidentally, worked fourteen-hour days and were paid on the average $500 a year.

For a nominal fee (free on Wednesday), both the Glessner and Clarke houses may be visited through tours only (one hour each) Wednesday through Sunday departing at noon, 1:00 and 2:00 P.M. (Clarke) and 1:00, 2:00, and 3:00 P.M. (Glessner). There are also guided walking tours of the historic district on Saturdays May through September. Throughout the year the Glessner House Museum sponsors public programs such as a series in art history and architecture; lectures on such diverse topics as "The Style, Decorating, and Taste of Three Nineteenth-Century Families," "The Costumes of Oscar Wilde," and "The Chicago Fire: The Fireman's Perspective"; and special seasonal events such as the annual readings of the work of Edgar Allan Poe. Phone (312) 326–1480, or call up www.glessnerhouse.org.

Right down the street at 1900 South Prairie Avenue is the ***Woman Made Gallery,*** formed in 1992 and "dedicated to cultivating women's visions and experiences through monthly thematic exhibitions, readings, lectures, and performances." Certainly, the offerings—all original, most by local women—are eclectic; one exhibition included works from patch-work pillows to *Nancy Drew* screen prints. The gallery also maintains a gift shop, as well as holding for-a-fee workshops on such topics as "Exhibiting Professionalism," offering free Women's Art Critique work-shops on the fourth Sunday of each month for both advanced and begin-ning artists, and conducting guided tours for groups. In the spring, there's a soirée/art auction benefit and in November/December a holi-day bazaar. Open Wednesday, Thursday, and Friday from noon to 7:00 P.M., Saturday and Sunday from noon to 4:00 P.M. Phone (312) 328–0038, or check out the Web site at www. womanmade.org.

Next, walk back to Michigan for a remarkable aesthetic experience. When it was located at the corner of Washington Street and Wabash Avenue, **Second Presbyterian Church,** now at 1936 South Michigan (corner of Cullerton Street), was known as the "Spotted Church" because of the mottling in its gray-white limestone blocks. But the Great Fire of 1871 destroyed all that, and the present church—designed by East Coast architect James Renwick, who also did the original and whose other credits included St. Patrick's Cathedral in New York and the Smithsonian

. . . In My Merry Locomobile

*T*hese days, looking up at 2000 South Michigan Avenue, you'd never know there was a Locomobile show-room (what, you never even heard of a car called the Locomobile?), except that the company's terra-cotta logo distinctly remains. By 1910, the then-fashionable stretch on Michigan—mostly between 14th and 24th Streets—was known as "Motor Row," an area that at the time Architectural Record called "the longest and best automobile course in any city of this country." Cars were either sold or ser-viced in more than fifty establish-ments, situated in buildings designed by such prominent architectural firms as Holabird & Roche and Jenney, Mundie & Jensen—which is why in 2001 the Chicago Commission on Landmarks obtained landmark status from the City Council. (Not surpris-ingly, developers were salivating over the prospects of tearing down these structures and adding still more con-dos to the increasingly upscale Near South stretch.) A careful look at the top of some of the extant structures reveals traces of those glory days. Besides "Locomobile," there are medal-lions with the letter H (for the Hudson Motor Company of Illinois) that sit atop 2222–2228 Michigan above the Palladian window, and high up at 1454, there's "Buick." But there isn't much else. The area still has some car dealerships, both new and used, but a good many of the buildings have been boarded up, while South Michigan accommodates other businesses from sports novelties to hair-care products to a Burger King.

Institution in Washington—was dedicated in 1874 in the city's then-most-exclusive residential neighborhood. The still-imposing limestone structure, with square, turreted belfry and exterior gargoyles and sculptures, is reminiscent of fifteenth-century English Gothic churches.

In 1900 fire raged again, destroying the roof and causing extensive smoke and water damage in the sanctuary. The interior was rebuilt in the English Arts and Crafts style by socially prominent architect Howard Van Doren Shaw (known as "the most rebellious of the conservatives and the most conservative of the rebels") and muralist Frederic Clay Bartlett, both members of the wealthy congregation, which also included the "Prairie Avenue Set" (the George Pullmans, George Armours, John Glessners, etc.).

The twenty-two magnificent stained-glass windows in the sanctuary, fourteen from the studios of Louis Tiffany and one from chief competitor John La Farge, are some of the finest in the country. Three decades of Tiffany's work are represented, including, on the north wall, the striking *Pastoral Window,* for some reason the only signed Tiffany in the church (all the others have been documented), and, on the east wall, *The Ascension,* weighing 4 tons and consisting of some glass pieces 6 inches thick. The two windows at the entrance, *St. Margaret* and *St. Cecilia,* were designed by Pre-Raphaelite painter Sir Edward Burne-Jones and executed by the famous William Morris studio in England. Extremely rare in this country, they're replicas of windows in Christ Church Cathedral, Oxford. Bartlett's murals include scenes from Genesis and Revelations, and Shaw's candelabra represent the Four Gospels, Jesus' parable of the Five Wise and Five Foolish Virgins, and the Seven Churches of Asia Minor. An ecclesiastical trivia note: Throughout the sanctuary, more than 175 different angels are depicted in sculpture, frescoes, carvings, and the windows. Church tours are available from 8:00 A.M. to 5:00 P.M. Monday through Friday, but call first (312–225–4951) to make sure a staff member is available.

Dedicated to preserving the heritage of the blues and the legal rights of those who perform them, **Willie Dixon's Blues Heaven Foundation** (2120 South Michigan Avenue) is located in the former headquarters of Chess Records, at one time the only building in Chicago earmarked solely for recording blues music. Under the ownership of the brothers Chess, Leonard and Phil, the company from 1957 to 1967 recorded blues numbers by such musicians as Muddy Waters, Howlin' Wolf, and Sonny Boy Williamson, along with the early rock 'n' roll of Chuck Berry and Bo Diddley and even the Rolling Stones, who recorded "2120" in 1964 as a tribute to Chess. The building, originally built in 1911, was accorded landmark status by the city of Chicago in 1989, and the foundation opened its blues archives there in 1997 following an extensive restoration. It was here, said the guide conducting a tour, that Berry went through 102 takes recording his hit "Maybellene," and it was here that the musicians were made to use the back door. ("It was a racial thing.")

The late, legendary Dixon, who died in 1992, has been cited as "the most important behind-the-scenes figure in blues history" by *Rolling Stone* magazine. He was Chess's house songwriter ("Hoochie Coochie Man," "I Can't Quit You Baby," etc.) and producer, as well as a singer and bassist, and produced the first Chicago Blues Festival in 1969. Dixon created the Blues Heaven Foundation in 1981 and later bought the historic building, which subsequently was turned into a blues memorial, filled now with such mementos as John Lee Hooker's guitar, Koko Taylor's dress, Diddley's outfit, an old 78 record by Howlin' Wolf, and a harmonica belonging to Willie Mae Thornton, better known as "Big Mama." There's also a photo gallery including shots of Buddy Guy, Memphis Slim, James Brown, Junior Wells, Albert King, and Sunnyland Slim, along with a gift shop offering harmonicas, CDs, T-shirts, posters, and blues "license plates" with lettering boasting HOOCHIE COOCHIE MAN. In the summer there are blues performances in the adjacent garden.

The Blues Heaven Foundation not only preserves the blues tradition but also sponsors "American Blues Children," hands-on instruction with established artists and programs in which participants receive a donated instrument; "Blues in the Schools," a nationwide program designed to present the blues as an art form and possible career; "What It Takes" workshops, geared toward career development, including music publishing, publicity, "How to Negotiate in the Music Business," and "Women in Music." The foundation also sponsors scholarships in the name of Waters, Hooker, Taylor, and Albert King,

Dubious Distinction Award

*C*hicago, apparently, is no longer just Second City. It's also, according to one source, Rather Fat City. A while back, a national survey ranked Chicago as the tenth-fattest town in the country, citing the locals' love for belt-busters like sausage (especially on pizza) and fondness for beer with that pizza. Even more pudgy places included Houston, Philadelphia, and New Orleans. Chicago also was cited for its "Least Fitness-Friendly Climate," lagging behind (editorial judgment coming up here) lean-and-mean wimp centers San Diego, San Francisco, and Honolulu.

and conducts programs to educate musicians about legal issues such as royalties and contracts.

To support its efforts, the foundation conducts tours of its archives. As of this writing, the cost was $10 and the times were Monday, Wednesday, Friday, and Saturday from noon to 2:00 P.M. for drop-in individuals, and the same hours Tuesday and Thursday for groups reserving in advance. But, hey, anyone who knows anything about the blues knows how things change, so you better call (312) 808–1286, or strum onto the Web site at www.bluesheaven.com.

For those willing to go even farther off the beaten track, either take the #1 bus south on Michigan to 24th Street or walk about ten minutes to 24th and Michigan—offices of the *Chicago Daily Defender,* one of the country's leading African-American newspapers since the 1920s. The Spanish mission–style building, opened in 1936, was built on the site of the Standard Club (1887) and originally housed the Illinois Automobile Club.

Then walk a block west to Wabash Avenue, and the *Quinn Chapel African Methodist Episcopal Church* (AME) at 2401 South Wabash. Built in 1892 and declared a Chicago landmark in 1977, the church is the home of the oldest black congregation in Chicago, tracing its origins to 1844. It was named after the AME bishop William Paul Quinn, one of the most prolific circuit-riding preachers of the 1800s, and its first project focused on the abolition of slavery. At one point, in fact, members provided a stop on the Underground Railroad. After worshipping in ten different locations, the congregation—some former slaves themselves—helped erect the present Victorian Gothic building from 1891 to 1894. At one point, the church raised funds by scheduling appearances by, among others, President William McKinley, Dr. Booker T. Washington, and social worker Jane Addams. Subsequent guest visitors, speakers, and artists have included Dr. Martin Luther King, Jr., Branch Rickey (who desegrated major league baseball), Lionel Hampton, actors Ossie Davis and Ruby Dee, Duke Ellington, and Wynton Marsalis.

The church proper, with well-worn pews forming a curved pattern, contains exquisite stained-glass windows along the sides and on the second floor in back. The ceiling has an almost Moorish look. Above the altar and pipe organ (purchased from the 1893 World Exposition) is a mural of a black Christ, Mary, and angelic cherubs. At the front of the church, one might be surprised to find a set of drums—definitely, a church staff member confirms, used in Sunday morning services. Quinn Chapel is open during the week at various hours. Phone (312) 791–1846 beforehand to make sure someone is there to let you in. (To get back downtown—it's quite a ways at this point—walk back to Michigan and 22nd and take the #3 or #4.)

PLACES TO STAY IN THE SOUTH LOOP AND ON THE NEAR SOUTH SIDE

Best Western Grant Park Hotel,
1100 South Michigan Avenue;
(800) 528–1234 or (312) 922–2900.
Even closer to the museums and football/soccer stadium than the Essex Inn, the Best Western has 172 small but pleasant rooms, some with great views; an outdoor pool and exercise room; and a full-service restaurant. Moderate.

Chicago Hilton and Towers,
720 South Michigan Avenue;
(800) HILTONS or (312) 922–4400.
In its various incarnations, this establishment has had a decidedly colorful history. Originally the Stevens Hotel (opened in 1927), it boasted 3,000 rooms, an eighteen-hole rooftop grass miniature golf course, and a 1,200-seat theater with "talking motion picture" equipment. During World War II the hotel became an Army barracks, with the immense, luxurious Grand Ballroom housing the mess hall. Years later, as the Conrad Hilton, its ground-floor lounge became the center of international attention during the notorious 1968 Democratic Convention, when protesters, according to the combative Chicago police, "jumped" through its glass windows. (Sure.) The hotel, which in recent years underwent a $185 million renovation (marble and all), is huge. Crowds milling around the sprawling lobby could easily outnumber the population of a small town. There are a whopping 1,543 rooms (not so whopping by 1927 standards), all with cherry furnishings, many with two bathrooms, and some with lake/park views; an indoor pool and athletic club; and five restaurants and/or bars. Moderate.

The Essex Inn on Grant Park,
800 South Michigan Avenue;
(800) 621–6909 or (312) 939–2800.
A good choice for budget-conscious travelers, the Essex's slogan is "You pay less on the room, so you can do more on the town." The hotel is, in fact, within walking distance of the Museum Campus, home of three of the city's major institutions: the Field Museum of Natural History, the Shedd Aquarium, and the Adler Planetarium. It's also near Soldier Field. But be aware: This and the other South Michigan Avenue hotels are not close to much else at night. The Essex has 254 renovated rooms, some with fine views of Grant Park and the lake; in-room data ports; a fitness center and indoor pool; and a modestly priced restaurant. Guest parking is available at the attached garage. Inexpensive.

Hyatt on Printer's Row,
500 South Dearborn Street;
(312) 986–1234.
In creating its attractive setting, the Hyatt combined new construction with two venerable historic buildings—the Duplicator (1886) and the Morton (1896). Within walking distance to many Loop attractions, the hotel, with its Frank Lloyd Wright–inspired decor, has 161 European-style "boutique" rooms, meeting rooms, and a fine restaurant, Prairie (see "Places to Eat"). Moderate.

PLACES TO EAT IN
THE SOUTH LOOP AND
ON THE NEAR SOUTH SIDE

Blackie's,
755 South Clark Street;
(312) 786-1161.
See page 130 for full
description.

**Chicago Firehouse
Restaurant,**
1461 South Michigan
Avenue;
(312) 786-1401.
See page 132 for full
description.

Gourmand Coffeehouse,
728 South Dearborn Street;
(312) 427-2610.
Here's a popular neighborhood spot with lengthy
hours that serves not only
an assortment of brews but
also an eclectic array of
dishes, from "eggs
espresso" to quiche, veggie
burritos, spinach lasagna,
and vegetarian chili. Open
Monday through Thursday
from 7:00 A.M. to 11:00 P.M.,
Friday from 7:00 A.M. to
midnight, Saturday from
8:00 A.M. to midnight, Sunday from 8:00 A. M. to 11:00
P.M. Inexpensive.

Prairie,
Hyatt on Printer's Row,
500 South Dearborn Street;
(312) 663-1143.
This exquisite, intimate
restaurant is blessed with a
Frank Lloyd Wright–like
Prairie School low-ceiling,
earth-tones setting—hence
its title. In the '20s and
'30s, it would have been
characterized as "smart."
It's the kind of place where
the prices on the menu are
spelled out rather than
stated in crass dollar-sign
terms. Chef Kevin Cooper's
Midwestern fare is elegant,
too, as is the crisp but
warm service. Starters
include roasted butternut
squash soup, pheasant and
rabbit turnover, and
ostrich-filled herb pasta,
and among the salads are
the smoked goose and
lamb loin. For a main
course, try the oven-
roasted Minnesota stur-
geon (when's the last time
you saw sturgeon on a
menu?) with shredded
potato, horseradish, and
red wine butter sauce, or
the roasted Wisconsin
pheasant with stuffed,
poached pear, dried fruits,
and lentils. Open every day
(it *is* in a hotel), with breakfast from 6:30 to 10:00 A.M.,
lunch from 11:30 A.M. to
2:00 P.M., and dinner from 5
to 10:00 P.M. Expensive.

Printer's Row,
550 South Dearborn Street;
(312) 461-0780.
Restaurants come and go,
but this one has been a
longtime (twenty years
plus) anchor in the historic
South Loop district. Billing
itself as "an original American bistro," it presents a
simple, woody decor that
has a masculine feel,
although one noontime the
diners included not only
lawyer types discussing
their latest cases but also a
party of snazzily dressed
"ladies who lunch." Lunch
menu offerings from chef-
restaurateur Michael Foley
can be quite unusual, such
as venison meatloaf and a
smoked salmon club sand-
wich, while dinner items
include mushroom ragout
and clam bisque for appe-
tizers and roasted radicchio
risotto with rosemary,
roasted anise-scented loin
of veal, and portabella, pur-
ple, and white sticky rice
with Japanese eggplant
"steak." The service is
sharp and attentive. Open
for lunch Monday through
Friday from 11:30 A.M.
to 2:15 P.M., and dinner
Monday through Thursday
from 5:00 to 9:00 P.M., Friday and Saturday from 5:00
to 10:00 P.M. Expensive.

Hyde Park

For years Hyde Park—composed of everything from modest frame cottages to lakefront high-rises to lavish residences built for faculty members at the University of Chicago (popularly known as "the U of C")—was known for its number of Nobel Prize winners (at the U of C, of course), and crummy restaurants. Twenty years ago, when the *Chicago Tribune*'s Sunday Magazine assigned two writers—one who lived in Hyde Park, the other in Lincoln Park—to take playful swipes at each other's neighborhood, the Lincoln Parker stated that the two main problems with Hyde Park were dullness and haughtiness associated with its university/centerpiece. He proceeded to quote a U of C employee who said, "It's like living in a middle-size university town, but along with that sense of community comes the inflated egos of these faculty types—the arrogance of these prima donnas."

However, these days there are actually a handful of good eating establishments with varied, ambitious cuisine, and the longtime-insular neighborhood seems more accessible to outsiders. In 1853 a young lawyer named Paul Cornell, who had moved to Chicago from New York, bought 300 acres of uninhabited lakefront land, planning to build a suburb. He named this place Hyde Park after swank areas in London and upstate New York, and in 1856, he persuaded the Illinois Central Railroad to build a station at what is now 53rd Street. In 1861 the town of Hyde Park was incorporated, eleven years later it was incorporated as a village, and in 1889 Hyde Park Township was annexed to the city of Chicago. Earlier, in 1869, the South Park Board was formed to create plans for what are now Washington and Jackson parks and the Midway Plaisance, designed by Frederick Law Olmsted and Calvert Vaux. Two major developments in the 1890s added to the thriving expansion: construction of the World's Columbian Exposition in Jackson Park, which opened in 1893 (as the four hundredth anniversary of Columbus's arrival in the New World) and caused a burst of hotel and apartment building, and the founding of the university in 1890. By the 1920s, the ethnic groups included Irish, German and Russian Jews, and blacks.

Hyde Park

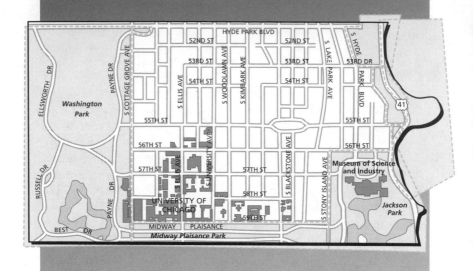

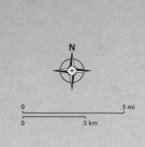

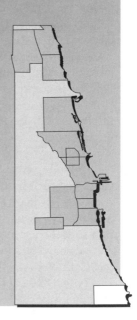

HYDE PARK

TOP ATTRACTIONS IN HYDE PARK

Powell's/O'Gara and Wilson's bookstores

David and Alfred Smart Museum of Art

Promontory Point

After World War II, many of the structures built for the 1893 exposition had fallen into disrepair, and residents formed the Hyde Park–Kenwood Community Conference to stop urban blight and encourage racial integration. Also in the 1950s, the U of C sponsored the South East Chicago Commission to fight crime and encourage commercial development. The retail complex known as Harper Court opened in 1965. These days, the only survivor from the Columbian Exposition is the pride of Hyde Park, the world-class Museum of Science and Industry at South Lake Shore Drive and 57th Street. Designed by Charles B. Atwood and originally built as the Palace of Fine Arts, the building housed the Field Museum of Natural History (now farther north on the Museum Campus) until 1920. A portion of the present museum opened in 1933 to coincide with the Century of Progress International Exposition, and full renovation was completed in 1940, as the museum subsequently became known particularly for its operating coal mine and captured World War II German submarine.

The Metra runs trains to Hyde Park from its downtown station at Randolph and Michigan, but for most of the day the departures are an hour apart. For a more timely, comfortable, and painless trip, board the #6 Jeffery Express along State Street at either Washington (across from Marshall Field's), Monroe, or Jackson, or at Wabash/Congress or Michigan/Congress. A speedy, nonstop ride once it leaves Michigan and Balbo, it goes along the lakefront, and takes about fifteen or twenty minutes. In Hyde Park, a good place to get off initially is 57th Street and Stony Island Avenue near the Museum of Science and Industry.

If the weather is nice, you might want to walk over to an area of Jackson Park just south of the Museum of Science and Industry (Lake Shore Drive and 57th Street) known as the **Wooded Island.** It's a favorite spot for birdwatchers, although one knowledgeable Hyde Park birder recommends using caution—always good advice in city parks—if you're in the area before dawn. Besides its lovely natural elements, including lagoons connected by bridges, Wooded Island is home to the Japanese-style **Osaka Garden** (so named in 1993), which features a pavilion and arched moon bridge that were built in 1981. The original Japanese Garden, created for the 1893 World's Columbian Exposition, was destroyed by fire at the outset of World War II. North of Wooded Island is the Columbian Basin, a reflective pool, at the south end of which is the **Clarence S. Darrow Bridge,** named for the renowned lawyer most famous for defending the teaching of evolution in the 1925 Scopes "Monkey Trial."

Now go back for a pleasant stroll down 57th Street—where many of Hyde Park's attractions are located—and head west. Almost directly across the street from one another are Hyde Park's two most noted used book stores. Crammed with all kinds of volumes, **Powell's Bookstore** (1501 East 57th Street) specializes in scholarly books, particularly philosophy and ancient and medieval history. If those don't attract you, there are great bargains in dozens of other categories, including "American History—Civil War," "Literary Criticism," "Music" (works such as *Red River Blues*), and even "Sports" and "General Pets" (*All About Breeding Canaries*). Down in the basement, there's a large paperback mystery section that's to die for. Open every day from 9:00 A.M. to 11:00 P.M. Phone (773) 955–7780, or browse through www.powellschicago.com.

Founded in 1936, *O'Gara and Wilson Booksellers, Ltd.* (1448 East 57th Street) is a much smaller, tidier, and seemingly more manageable shop which, unlike Powell's, disdains "remainders" and instead buys books only from private individuals and estates. The focus, according to proprietor Doug Wilson, is on "good books in the humanities, with no textbooks and very little popular fiction." (There is also, which he didn't note, a shelf devoted to comic books.) Among the works offered one late-winter afternoon were the five-volume memoirs of Maximilian de Bethune, prime minister to King Henry IV ($150), and *Travels in Mesopotamia* (1827), two volumes ($1,250), along with a selection of pencil sketches and hand-colored engravings. Open Monday through Thursday from 10:00 A.M. to 9:00 P.M., Friday and Saturday from 10:00 A.M. to 10:00 P.M., Sunday from noon to 8:00 P.M. Phone (773) 363–0993.

A longtime Hyde Park favorite, especially with students and other University of Chicago types (Nobel Prize winners?), *Medici on 57th* (1327 East 57th Street) is housed in well-worn quarters with funky art and battered wooden booths, carved up with years of graffiti, most of it pedestrian stuff revealing who loves whom. (Occasionally, creativity comes to the fore with Charlie Chan-like aphorisms such as "A shut mouth gathers no foot.") The staff is laidback but attentive—almost motherly, in some cases: waitresses without attitude. The food is decent enough, and certainly reasonable. Medici specialty pizzas include spinach goat cheese, smoked German ham (listed as the owner's personal favorite), and the Medici Classic, proudly touted as the "Garbage" pizza (sausage, ground beef, pepperoni, Canadian bacon, peppers, onions, and mushrooms). There are the usual sandwiches with an occasional surprise (grilled portabella mushrooms, grilled tuna steak, Stroganoff burger), pastas, barbecued chicken, and, for something completely different, Moroccan ragout (a spicy lentil and vegetable stew). Desserts include fudge-banana-nut-blend shakes and malts, Gracie's apple pie and (remember, this is Hyde Park) the Vaguely Reminiscent (frozen mocha pie with rum-flavored whipped cream). Open Monday through Thursday from 7:00 A.M. to 11:30 P.M., Friday from 7:00 A.M. to 12:30 A.M., Saturday from 9:00 A.M. to 12:30 A.M., Sunday from 9:00 A.M. to 11:30 P.M. Phone (773) 667–7394. Inexpensive.

Then, more books. A branch of the Seminary Co-Op Bookstore, *57th Street Books* (1301 East 57th Street) is a sprawling yet cozy below-street-level place to find new hardcover and paperback books. Customers may wander through its five rooms, moving deeper and deeper into the seemingly endless, labyrinthine space. Extensive sections include mystery, science fiction, art, film, photography, African-American studies, cookbooks, and children's books. The store obviously welcomes browsers and even has its own information desk. It also sponsors poetry readings, author appearances, workshops, children's story hours, and a monthly adults' evening reading group. On the weekends, of course, there's always the Bible of Hyde Park—the Sunday *New York Times*—for sale. Open Monday through Saturday from 10:00 A.M. to 10:00 P.M., Sunday from 10:00 A.M. to 8:00 P.M. Phone (773) 684–1300.

You're now approaching the University of Chicago campus. Turn left (south) a block and zero in on the *Robie House* (5757 South Woodlawn Avenue). Undergoing a $7 million, ten-year renovation that began in the mid-1990s, it represents the marvelous culmination of Frank Lloyd Wright's Prairie style and is one of the cornerstones of modern architecture. Built in 1910 for Frederick C. Robie, who was involved in motorcycle and car design, the National Historic Landmark is noted for its sweeping horizontal planes, dramatic cantilevers, continuous limestone sills, and

Telling It Like It Was

"*Yes, Chicago. First in violence, deepest in dirt; loud, lawless, unlovely, ill-smelling, irreverent, new; an over-grown gawk of a village, the 'tough' among cities, a spectacle for the nation. . . . They can balance high buildings on rafts floating in mud, but they can't quench the stench of the stockyards.*"

—Lincoln Steffens, The Shame of the Cities *(1903)*

A Wright Pronouncement

"A house, we like to believe, can be a noble consort to man and the trees."

—Frank Lloyd Wright

long rows of art-glass windows. The house contains some of the original materials and furnishings, including almost all of the 174 windows (but only 3 of the 92 sconces) and the very expensive red oak woodwork.

Basically two rectangles, the low-lying house demonstrates the influence of both nature and Japanese architecture on Wright, who designed Robie at age 41. On the tour you'll be able to pick up such tidbits as the fact that the exterior originally included a tall wall and gate because of Robie's fear that his son would be kidnapped. For years, the structure—now owned by the University of Chicago and operated by the Frank Lloyd Wright Preservation Trust—fell into disrepair, and at one point it was used as a dormitory, of all things, for the Chicago Theology Seminary. Wright himself was twice instrumental in saving the building from being demolished—not surprising since, incredibly, 29 percent of his houses were torn down during his lifetime. At one point, when Robie was used for U of C offices, students served as guide leaders, and, according to our guide, would make up stories. ("People who were on those tours ask me things today like, 'Where's the room where they had the orgies?'") Two pieces of Robie House trivia: (1) The Robies actually lived in the house for only a year, after which it was sold to pay off family debts and (2) Lora Robie was the first woman in Illinois to obtain a driver's license. Tours are offered on weekdays at 11:00 A.M. and 1:00 and 3:00 P.M., weekends from 11:00 A.M. to 3:30 P.M. every half hour. The fee is $9.00 for adults, $7.00 for seniors and children ages 7 to 18; free for children under 7. Phone (773) 834–1847, or sign onto www.wrightplus.org or www.nationaltrust.org.

An added bonus is the **Robie House Bookstore,** which sells much more than architecture books and videos and is one of the best places to shop in the city. Opened in 1997, the store offers wonderful items adapted from Wright designs such as a Robie vase, a Taliesin table lamp, a Guggenheim teapot, and a Prairie House block set, along with serving bowls, sculptures, umbrellas, coasters, urns, candlesticks, notepaper, a wall sconce, a wall clock, a magazine rack, a watch, and even a mug sporting the architect's signature. The bookstore is open every day from 10:00 A.M. to 5:00 P.M.

With over 100,000 artifacts, most of which were excavated by its own scholars, the **Oriental Institute Museum,** 1 block west at 1155 East 58th Street, is part of the university's Oriental Institute, which has supported research and excavation in the Near East since 1919. The collection has been housed in its current quarters since 1931, with an expansion and

Robie House

renovation completed in 1998. Permanent collections focus on the cultures of ancient Iran, Iraq, Israel, Syria, and Turkey. But the most interesting portion is the Egyptian Room, which contains such items as miniature tools, a water clock, and model boats, some with a square sail (buried with the deceased to give them the mobility to travel up and down the Nile). There are mummies and coffins, a model of an excavated tomb (complete with bones and pottery), a display of animals (baboons, frogs, lions, and scarab beetles) associated with the gods, and various papyrus documents, including a fragment of a poem and even something as mundane as a receipt for the delivery of fish. As the room's centerpiece, there's a 17-foot-4-inch-tall, 4-ton statue of King Tutankhamun, the famous pharaoh—the tallest ancient Egyptian statue in the Western Hemisphere. The museum also sponsors adult education classes, family programs, workshops, lectures, and films, and runs the small Suq (Arabic for "market") gift shop, offering rugs, jewelry, pottery, and the inevitable T-shirts. Open Tuesday and Thursday through Saturday from 10:00 A.M. to 4:00 P.M., Wednesday from 10:00 A.M. to 8:30 P.M., Sunday from noon to 4:00 P.M. Phone (773) 702–9514, or dig up the Web site at www.oi.uchicago. edu. Donation of $5.00 suggested.

Walk north on South University Avenue to the **Seminary Co-Op Bookstores, Inc.** (5757 South University Avenue), founded in 1961 by a group of 10 book lovers who pitched in $10 apiece. It now has over 40,000 members and maintains what it says is the largest selection of scholarly titles in the country. The store is located inside the Chicago Theological Seminary, an affiliate of the United Church of Christ, but its inventory is by no means limited to religious and philosophical volumes. A staff member said that books on the social sciences were especially popular, and among the works displayed in the packed, warrenlike rooms one afternoon were a biography of Bing Crosby, mystery writer Carl Hiaasen's *Sick Puppy*, fiction by Jane Smiley, and several volumes devoted to Monty Python. Open Monday through Friday from 8:30 A.M. to 9:00 P.M., Saturday from 10:00 A.M. to 6:00 P.M., Sunday from noon to 6:00 P.M. Phone (773) 752–4381.

Deeper into the campus there's **Mandel Hall** (1131 East 57th Street), a bustling, woody and worn building, one of several anchoring the northeast corner of the main quadrangle that are known as Hutchinson Court and the Tower Group. Built in 1903 and renovated in 1981, it houses the student union, along with meeting places for various organizations, which unfurl their banners all over the place. The handsome concert hall is the scene of a wide assortment of performances during the year that are open to the public, from those by the university's own symphony orchestra and wind ensemble to the Gilbert & Sullivan Opera Company's rarely seen *Princess Ida*. The building is open Monday through Friday from 7:00 A.M. to 2:00 A.M., Saturday from 8:00 A.M. to 2:00 A.M., and Sunday from 9:00 A.M. to 2:00 A.M. For performance times and prices, phone the box office at (773) 702–7300, or the university's music department (773–702–8484) or music office (773–702–8068). (They're separate.)

Overshadowed by the university's nearby and much better known, massive Rockefeller Memorial Chapel, the small **Joseph Bond Chapel,** connected by a cloister to the Divinity School's Swift Hall (1025–1035 East 58th Street), has a beautifully carved altar; simple, wooden pews; and lovely stained-glass windows on all sides, including depictions of Adam and Eve and an inscription of the Beatitudes. It was opened in 1926 and was designed by the firm of Coolidge & Hodgdon, which also did other U of C buildings as well as nearby St. Stephen's Church of God in Christ (Tenth Church of Christ, Scientist) at 5640 South Blackstone Avenue, McKinlock Court at the Art Institute of Chicago, and Temple Sholom on the city's North Side. Open daily from 8:30 A.M. to 5:00 P.M. when the university is in session, there's an ecumenical service Wednesday at 11:30 A.M. Phone (773) 702–8200.

Established in 1915, the **Renaissance Society** sponsors a museum devoted exclusively to contemporary art, with constantly changing exhibits. Over the years the society has presented groundbreaking exhibitions of such artists as Alexander Calder, Paul Klee, Diego Rivera, and René Magritte. The museum is located in the fourth-floor Bergman Gallery in the Gothic-style Cobb Lecture Hall (5811 South Ellis Avenue), the university's first building (1892). Open Tuesday through Friday from 10:00 A.M. to 5:00 P.M., Saturday and Sunday from noon to 5:00 P.M. Phone (773) 702–8670, or explore www.renaissance society.org. Admission is free.

Located in a starkly modern, rectangular limestone building at 5730 South Ellis Avenue on the west side of the Science Quadrangle, the four-story **John Crerar Library** houses many of the university's more than one million volumes in such disciplines as biomedicine (including natural history, microbiology, botany, zoology, human anatomy, physiology, and medicine), general science, technology, agriculture, veterinary medicine, and the physical sciences such as astronomy, oceanography, and physics. The Crerar is open to the public—unlike the gigantic Joseph Regenstein Library, where, a visitor was promptly told, one has to come highly recommended from another institution to gain admittance. Suspended from Crerar's three-story atrium skylight is *Crystara* (1984), a complex sculpture of aluminum and Waterford crystal by Chicago artist John David Mooney. Aside from looking over *Crystara*, the Crerar obviously is not for everyone, but if, for some reason, you want to look something up, it's refreshing that you're quite welcome to do so (although, of course, you can't check out the books). Public hours

Rosalie Villas

*S*till lined up along the 5700 and 5800 blocks of South Harper Avenue (alongside the Metra tracks) are many of the Queen Anne–style houses that were built as part of **Rosalie Villas,** Hyde Park's first planned community that sprang up in the 1880s. Originally, there were forty-two houses, the construction and design of which were supervised by architect Solon S. Beman, who had also overseen the company town of Pullman farther south in the city. The structures today are in various states of repair, from standing tall to barely standing, and display various shades of exterior color (including bright orange). Check out particularly the M. Cochran Armour House (5736 South Harper Avenue), perhaps the most opulent of the bunch, and the double house at 5832–5834, designed by Beman himself.

are Monday through Saturday from 8:30 A.M. to 5:00 P.M. (Leave a piece of identification at the entrance.) Phone (773) 702– 7720, or research at www.lib.uchicago.edu/e/crerar/.

Now walk north to 56th Street, then west past Cottage Grove Avenue and Washington Park to *The DuSable Museum of African-American History,* which was founded in 1961 (as the Ebony Museum of Negro History) and has been at its present location (740 East 56th Place in the park) since 1973. One of the few of its kind in the world, the museum is named after Jean Baptiste Pointe DuSable, a black fur trader who, in 1779, established the trading post and permanent settlement that would become Chicago. Containing more than 12,000 pieces, it houses a permanent collection of paintings and sculptures, including the works of Archibald Motley, William Edouard Scott, and Charles Sebrell; and special exhibits such as the exquisite work of the museum's founder, the multitalented Dr. Margaret Taylor Goss Burroughs, printmaker, oil painter, sculptress, and pen-and-ink artist.

One of the most moving exhibits is devoted to slavery. Included are slave shackles, a graphic statue of a bloody and shackled slave cringing from more blows, photographs of lynchings, a 1926 headline from the Chicago *Defender* ("Klansmen Burn Girl"), an auction billing ("All of My Ox Team, Six Head of Fox Hounds," "6 Negro Slaves") and a $200 reward notice for a twenty-year-old runaway slave. In contrast is the exhibit "From Trial to Triumph," including photos of opera singer Marion Anderson and track stars Jesse Owens and Ralph Metcalf. Also noteworthy is "Distorted Images," a collection of shameful stereotype products such as Aunt Jemima pancake mix, a *Topsy Turvy's Pigtails* book, a *Little Black Sambo* drawing book, and an ad for *Picaninny Freeze* ice cream. Among the other exhibits are African masks, displays of black inventors and aviators in World War II, and a replica of the office (and videos of) Harold Washington, the city's first African-American mayor, who died at his desk in 1987 and was "a catalyst who awakened in all of Chicago the realization that hopes and dreams could, in fact, be turned into reality."

The DuSable Museum also sponsors annual special events, such as a year-round jazz and blues concert series, a children's summer film series (July/August), and an African arts festival (September). Open Monday through Saturday from 10:00 A.M. to 5:00 P.M., Sunday from noon to 5:00 P.M. Phone (773) 947–0600. Admission is $3.00 for adults, $2.00 for seniors and children 14 and older, and $1.00 for children 6 to 13. Free on Thursday.

Back east now. The mission of **Court Theatre** (5535 South Ellis Avenue), as stated on one of its lobby walls, is to "celebrate the immutable power and relevance of classic theater," and its vision is to share "a collective aspiration to create a National Center for Classic Theatre." Affiliated with the University of Chicago—its faculty and staff founded it back on campus in 1955—the theater operates out of an intimately designed 250-seat space. The highly respected Court is noted for its new translations and adaptations of classic texts, and its presentations are all over the place. In a recent season, works ranged from Shakespeare (*Twelfth Night*) to Noel Coward (*Hay Fever*) and Tom Stoppard (*The Invention of Love*) to a new chamber opera (*In the Penal Colony*) by Philip Glass based on a story by Franz Kafka. Phone (773) 753–4472, or log onto www.courttheatre.org.

Undoubtedly, there have been hoary, dumb jokes such as: Why is the Smart Museum so named? (Answer: Because it's at the University of Chicago.) Actually, the **David and Alfred Smart Museum of Art** (5550 South Greenwood Avenue), the university's fine arts museum, was named after the founders/publishers of *Esquire* magazine. The facility, built in 1974 with a large gift from the Smart Family Foundation, contains over 7,500 objects. The collection—presented in rotating, thematic displays—includes ancient Chinese bronzes, Korean and Japanese paintings, calligraphies, ceramics, and medieval sculpture. There also are Old Master prints, Frank Lloyd Wright furniture, Tiffany glass, twentieth-century paintings and modern sculpture, German Expressionist graphics, and work by postwar Chicago artists such as Roger Brown and Ed Paschke. A typical eclectic exhibit range in the museum's pleasant, airy space was "Theatrical Baroque" (seventeenth-century French paintings), "Landscapes of Retrospection" (British drawings and prints, 1739–1860), "The Arts of Asia," "The Gothic Past," and "The Modern City."

The museum also conducts numerous education programs for university students, Chicago public schools, and neighborhood groups, along with workshops for teachers, an "Art Sundays" family series, and summertime "Family Days." There's a small gift area and a coffee bar, and, outside, a sculpture garden—which, frankly, needs a lot of work. Open Tuesday, Wednesday, and Friday from 10:00 A.M. to 4:00 P.M., Thursday from 10:00 A.M. to 9:00 P.M., Saturday and Sunday from noon to 6:00 P.M. Public tours of special exhibitions are offered on selected Sundays at 1:30 P.M., and guided group tours for adults are available by appointment for a nominal fee. Phone (773) 702–0200, or check out http://smartmuseum.uchicago. edu. Admission is free, box donations are appreciated.

In case all of this has created a terrific thirst, it might be time for a strategic pause. It's formally known as the **Woodlawn Tap,** but frequenters of this neighborhood institution at 1172 East 55th Street (at Woodlawn) wouldn't dream of calling it anything else but "Jimmy's," named after the proprietor, who died in the late 1990s. Born in 1952, this well-worn, dark, frill-free bar (not a cute sign or knickknack in sight) attracts university students and professors and normal neighborhood folks, who seem to coexist in a reasonably benign fashion. "It's a neat mixture," confirmed one barmaid (wearing a T-shirt that read "The Floggings Will Continue Until the Morale Improves"). "It's very academic, but also laid back." (In fact, the bartenders reportedly keep the *Encyclopedia Britannica* handy to settle arcane disputes—which I was going to verify before getting caught up in the always-difficult choice of picking one of fifty or so different beers.) There's a long, always-occupied bar, home to transient drop-ins along with the "Cheers"-like regulars, and there are four resident TV sets (during the

Fight Fiercely, Chicago

S*tarting in the late 1800s and early 1900s, the University of Chicago—a charter member of the Big Ten— played big-time intercollegiate football, even whipping powerhouses like Notre Dame and Michigan. But in 1939 university president Robert Hutchins dropped the sport, declaring that "the game has been a major handicap to education in the United States." However, football was resumed in 1969, accompanied by characteristic wry, ironic spin. Instead of a precision marching band, there was a marching kazoo band playing tunes like "Joy to the World" upon the home team's successful completion of a pass. The student body, naturally, put its collective thinking hat on and came up with cheers like, "Refract them, Maroons!" and "Restrict their kinesthetic movement!" and "Themistocles, Thucydides / Peloponnesian War / X square, Y square / H$_2$ SO$_4$!" It all recalls*

a classic Second City sketch entitled "Football Comes to the University of Chicago," in which one player describes the ball as having the shape of a demipolytetrahedron, another confuses left guard with Kierkegaard, and the center is reluctant to hand the ball to the quarterback between his legs because he hardly knows him.

If you're around on a fall Saturday afternoon, the school these days plays opponents like Washington University, Carnegie-Mellon, and the University of Rochester at Stagg Field, 56th Street and Cottage Grove Avenue, which replaced the historic Stagg Field, ripped down in the 1960s to make room for the Regenstein Library. The "new" field is less than imposing. "One year the Sewanee team got off the bus and asked me where the stadium was," recalled one journalist. "I said, 'You're standing in it.' "

season, it's a good bet the South Side's White Sox will be on), and over the cash register sits the U of C crest. There's also a sign stating that food is offered—burgers, hot dogs, grilled American cheese, fries—but why bother? For you creative types, Jimmy's also hosts Monday night poetry slams ("Poetic Spirits to Quench Your Soul"). Open Sunday through Friday from 10:30 A.M. to 2:00 A.M., Saturday from 10:30 A.M. to 3:00 A.M. Phone (773) 643–5516.

Farther east and then north, you might want to stop at Harper Court, a small cluster of restaurants and shops near 52nd Street and Harper Avenue, and enjoy a meal at the ever-popular *Dixie Kitchen & Bait Shop* (5225 South Harper Avenue). This is the Cajun/Creole place where the Reverend Jesse Jackson took Al Gore during the 2000 political campaign. The restaurant is studiously cluttered with reproductions of old automobile and chewing tobacco ads; an old, battered gas pump; vintage Jays Potato Chip and Carnation Malted Milk cans hanging from the ceiling; and signs like the wonderful one that reads WANTED: GOOD WOMAN. MUST BE ABLE TO CLEAN, COOK, SEW, DIG WORMS, AND CLEAN FISH. MUST HAVE BOAT AND MOTOR. PLEASE SEND PICTURE OF BOAT AND MOTOR. Happily, all the decorative shtick is not a cover-up for the food, which is plenty good. For starters, there are fried green tomatoes ("movies are made of this"), crayfish and corn fritters, and, for something completely different, peach-glazed chicken wings. The gumbo (of sinus-clearing strength) is great, and other specialties include the Southern sampler (jambalaya, gumbo, and red beans and rice) and shrimp creole. Among the sandwiches are North Carolina pulled pork and three po'boys (oyster, catfish, and shrimp), while the desserts are bread pudding with whiskey sauce, peach cobbler, and pecan (that's "PE-kin") pie. Open Sunday through Thursday from 11:00 A.M. to 10:00 P.M., Friday and Saturday from 11:00 A.M. to 11:00 P.M. Phone (773) 363–4943. Inexpensive.

Even farther east, there's more on the other side of the railroad tracks. Admittedly, Hyde Park is not exactly a visiting child's paradise, but if you're touring with young children a perfect place for a kiddie detour is *Harold's Playlot* in Harold Washington's Park—formally part of Burnham Park—off Hyde Park Boulevard between 51st and 53rd Streets. The colorful, creative area is named for the late Mr. Washington, a neighborhood resident and the city's first African-American mayor, who said things such as "I see a Chicago of educational excellence and equality of treatment in which all children can learn to function in this ever-more-complex society." One afternoon a little boy may not have known about functioning, but when he saw the play lot, he excitedly exclaimed to his mother, "This is a big place!" Besides the swings, slides, and seesaws, the complex includes all kinds of bridges and ramps and tunnels, as well as a large wooden ship, a castlelike structure standing in the midst of a sandbox, a sea horse fountain/pool, and plenty of benches for weary parents.

Back to more mature stuff. Situated in the former ballroom of the now-departed Del Prado Hotel, a Hyde Park landmark of sorts, is the not-for-profit **Hyde Park Art Center** (5307 South Hyde Park Boulevard), which has been around since 1939. In its Ruth Horwich Gallery, the center presents a variety of work by emerging and established artists (such as Chicago painters Ed Paschke and Roger Brown). Numerous classes are also held for everyone from preschoolers to retirees, in such subjects as oil and watercolor painting, Asian ink painting and calligraphy, bookbinding and papermaking, ceramics, black-and-white photography, and stained glass. A nationally recognized outreach program annually serves over 3,000 individuals in schools, nursing homes, and community centers throughout the city. Open Monday through Friday from 9:00 A.M. to 5:00 P.M., Saturday from 10:00 A.M. to 5:00 P.M. Phone (773) 324–5520, or take a look at www.hydeparkart.org.

Promontory Point, known to locals simply as "the Point," is one of Hyde Park's most popular places, a lovely retreat from urban hassles and a spot that offers some of the most magnificent views (on a clear day) of the Chicago skyline. Sitting out on the lake at 55th Street (and reached by a pedestrian Lake Shore Drive underpass), the Point is part of Burnham Park. At the entrance is the David Wallach Fountain (1939), providing drinking opportunities for humans and their pets and incorporating a bronze of a resting doe. Wallach donated money for the "man and beast" fountain, designed by husband-and-wife sculptors Elizabeth and Frank Hibbard. Dominated by a handsome lannon-stone field house that was restored in the late 1980s and is now used for

The Russians Are ... Never Mind

*P*romontory Point is one of Hyde Park's special places, but its recreational use by the public was severely limited in the 1950s because of a lakefront radar site installed by the military south of the Point's field house as a complement to a Nike missile site in nearby Jackson Park. Apparently, there was a fear that the Soviets would try something like—who knows?—lobbing a few missiles onto the roof of the Museum of Science and Industry. Both war-ready sites were removed in the early '70s, when it turned out that the Russians weren't coming after all.

everything from concerts to weddings, the Point was created between the mid-1920s and late 1930s, winding up as a project of President Franklin Roosevelt's Works Progress Administration. It was part of Daniel Burnham's plan for a south lakefront park with lagoons, islands, and promontory. Well, at least the promontory made it; the others were scuttled by legal and political problems. The Point is one of two lakefront promontory landscapes designed by Alfred Caldwell (the other is off Montrose Avenue on the North Side). The last of the great Prairie School designers and a disciple of Jens Jensen, who created natural Midwest landscapes starting in the late 1880s, Caldwell said he wanted the Point to convey "a sense of space and a sense of the power of Nature and the power of the sea."

PLACES TO STAY IN HYDE PARK

Ramada Inn Lake Shore,
4900 South Lake Shore Drive;
(773) 288–5800.
Nicely situated just across the Drive from Lake Michigan, the Ramada, unfortunately, is a long walk from most of the attractions in this chapter, especially those on the University of Chicago campus. (Ask at the desk about hotel or local bus transportation.) But as far as Hyde Park hotels are concerned, this is it. There's an attractive lobby, along with 184 newly renovated rooms and suites, a full-service restaurant and lounge, a conference center, and free parking. Daily scheduled transportation is available to downtown, McCormick Place, the University of Chicago, and the Museum of Science and Industry. Inexpensive.

PLACES TO EAT IN HYDE PARK

Caffé Florian,
5225 South Harper Avenue;
(773) 363–4123.
Established in 1989, this pleasant restaurant is sort of a spruced-up Medici, with exposed brick, wooden booths (but no graffiti), and pop art decorating the walls. Basically a lunch and dinner place— it's open for brunch only Saturday and Sunday from 10:00 A.M. to 3:00 P.M.—it offers a variety of salads, burgers, an assortment of sandwiches, from a Philly beef to a burrito club, deep-dish and thin-crust pizza (including the rather unusual artichoke pesto), several pasta entrees, and other main courses such as grilled chicken Alfredo, lemon pepper catfish, and marinated pork chops. There's cordial service by the staff, which serves coffee in mugs that read "Stolen from Caffé Florian." Open Monday through Thursday from 11:00 A.M. to midnight, Friday from 11:00 A.M. to 1:00 A.M., Saturday from 10:00 A.M. to 1:00 A.M., Sunday from 10:00 A.M. to midnight. Inexpensive.

Calypso Cafe,
5211C South Harper Avenue;
(773) 955–0229.
This Caribbean-style restaurant features a cheery decor—bright-fabric booths, a corrugated tin ceiling, straw-hatted waiters wearing tropical shirts, and uh, bunches of plastic bananas. There's a Cuban black bean soup and Bahamian conch

chowder; appetizers such as coconut-crusted shrimp and plantain nachos; a delicious Caneel Bay spinach chicken salad, with hot, jerked chicken breast; and fanciful-named main dishes like smoked baby back ribs Caribe, Sanibel Island chicken carbonara, and Shrimp St. Barts. Good food, but the service can move along at a tropical pace. Open Sunday through Thursday from 11:00 A.M. to 10:00 P.M., Friday and Saturday from 11:00 A.M. to 11:00 P.M. Inexpensive.

Dixie Kitchen & Bait Shop,
5225 South Harper Avenue; (773) 363–4943.
See page 155 for full description.

La Petite Folie,
1504 East 55th Street; (773) 493–1394.
Incongruously tucked into the Hyde Park Shopping Center, this establishment gives the neighborhood what it has been long lacking: excellent French fare. Chef Mary Mastricola, who also is co-owner with her husband, Michael, is a graduate of Le Cordon Bleu in Paris who obviously did her homework. For lunch, try the splendid peppered salmon with lentils and asparagus, or such selections as beef bourguignon or shrimp and squid sautéed with angel hair pasta in a spicy tomato cream. Dinner appetizers include pan-seared foie gras and terrine of Atlantic smoked salmon, with main dishes ranging from sesame-crusted cod to roasted quail, stuffed saddle of rabbit, and rack of lamb. The decor in the compact space is plain but warm, and when it comes to friendliness, the staff is much more Hyde Parkian than Parisienne. Open for lunch Tuesday through Friday from 11:00 A.M. to 2:00 P.M., and for dinner Tuesday through Sunday from 5:00 P.M. to "whenever." Moderate.

Medici on 57th,
1327 East 57th Street; (773) 667-7394.
See page 146 for full description.

Appendix A: Annual Events

A myriad of special events are scheduled each year in Chicago, and here are some of the leading ones. (Check the Sources of Information for further details.) There are also all kinds of neighborhood events, which run from May through October, sponsored by the Mayor's Office of Special Events (312–744–3370).

January

Chicago Winter Delights. Citywide celebrations and activities for the entire family, including specialty weekends and discounted prices at some local hotels, restaurants, and shops. Sponsored by the Mayor's Office of Special Events, the Chicago Office of Tourism, and the Chicago Convention and Tourism Bureau. (312) 744–3315 or (877) CHICAGO.

February

Chicago Winter Delights. Continues through the end of the month.

February–March

Azalea/Camellia Flower Show. Lincoln Park Conservatory, 2400 North Stockton Drive. (312) 742–7736.

Azalea/Camellia Flower Show. Garfield Park Conservatory, 300 North Central Park Avenue. (312) 746–5100.

March

Chicago Flower and Garden Show. The show features thirty theme gardens that transform Navy Pier's Festival Hall (600 East Grand Avenue) into a botanical wonderland of color. (312) 321–0077.

April

The Chicago International Antiques and Fine Art Fair. Wide range of items, at the Merchandise Mart. (800) 677–6278.

Spring Flower Show. Garfield Park Conservatory. (312) 746–5100.

Spring Flower Show. Lincoln Park Conservatory. (312) 742–7736.

May

Kids and Kites Festival. Free kite-flying clinics, free kite kits, and a demonstration of kite-flying stunts. For children of all ages. At Montrose Harbor. (312) 744–3370.

BIKE Chicago. Monthlong events celebrating the joy of riding bikes. (312) 744–3315.

Chicago Safe Boating and Water Celebration. A celebration of boating activities, at Navy Pier. (773) 768–4093.

June

Taste of Chicago. Music and food festival, continuing into July. Grant Park. (312) 744–3370.

Chicago Gospel Festival. Joyful sounds echo along the lakefront in this event sponsored by the Mayor's Office of Special Events. Petrillo Music Shell, Grant Park. (312) 744–3315.

Chicago Blues Festival. The music in Grant Park changes to the blues, a long-time favorite in "Sweet Home Chicago." Petrillo Music Shell. (312) 744–3315.

Chicago Country Music Festival. Petrillo Music Shell, Grant Park. (312) 744–3315.

57th Street Art Fair. Hyde Park. (773) 493–3247.

Printer's Row Book Fair. Largest outdoor literary event in the Midwest. South Dearborn Street between Congress Parkway and Polk Street. (312) 987–9896.

Park West Antiques Fair. Antiques dealers sell their wares in rented residential garages along Fullerton Avenue in Lincoln Park. Also food and music. (312) 744–3370.

Gay and Lesbian Pride Parade. Known for its spectacular floats, outrageous costumes, and marching units. In Lincoln Park and Lakeview. (773) 348–8243.

Old Town Art Fair. Oldest juried art fair in the United States. In the Old Town Triangle. (312) 337–1938.

July

Venetian Night. A parade of beautifully decorated floats, along with elaborate fireworks synchronized to music. Lake Shore Drive and Congress Parkway. (312) 744–0573.

Sheffield Garden Walk. One of the country's oldest garden walks. At Webster and Sheffield Avenues, Lincoln Park. (773) 929–9225.

August

Chicago Air and Water Show. Featuring civilian and military aircraft (highlighted by a precision-flying squad), as well as various watercraft. Centered along the lakefront from Oak Street Beach to North Avenue Beach. (312) 744–3315.

Viva! Chicago. Latin music festival, Grant Park Petrillo Music Shell. (312) 744–3315.

September

Celtic Fest. The Celtic tradition is celebrated at the Grant Park Petrillo Band Shell. (312) 744–3315.

World Music Festival Chicago. Concerts sponsored by the Department of Cultural Affairs and collaborators. At various locations. (312) 744–6630.

October

Chicagoween. A monthlong celebration of Halloween in the city, with attractions like a haunted village, pumpkin decorating, square dancing, and movies. At various locations. (312) 744–3315.

Edgar Allan Poe Readings. The Metamorphosis Theater brings Poe's words chillingly to life. Glessner House Museum. (312) 329–1480.

Pullman House Tour. Pullman Historic District, centered at 11141 South Cottage Grove Avenue. (773) 785–8901.

Outdoor Chrysanthemum Show. Garfield Park Conservatory. (312) 746–5100.

Chrysanthemum Flower Show. Lincoln Park Conservatory. (312) 742–7736.

November

POW-WOW Festival. Native American traditions sponsored by the American Indian Center, 1630 West Wilson Avenue. (773) 275–5871.

Christmas Around the World/Holidays of Light Festival. A colorful and educational event presented at the Museum of Science and Industry, 5700 South Lake Shore Drive. (773) 684–1414.

Christmas Parade. Various organizations strut their stuff along State Street in the Loop. (312) 744–3370.

Tree Lighting Ceremony. The city marks the official beginning of the Chicago holiday season. At Daley Plaza, Washington Avenue between Clark and Dearborn Streets. (312) 744–3370.

December

Caroling to the Animals. Inhabitants of the Lincoln Park Zoo hear music in the air, whether they want to or not. (312) 742–2000.

Holiday Sports Festival. Various sports tournaments, sponsored by the Mayor's Office of Special Events. (312) 744–3315.

Appendix B: Farther Off The Beaten Path

This appendix covers miscellanous attractions on the West and South Sides in neighborhoods that, because of space limitations, don't have enough visitor sites to warrant a full chapter. These destinations can be reached by car (or taxi). Because some of the areas are "rough," special care must be taken when visiting them.

West Side

The 185-acre **Garfield Park**—situated between South Central Park Boulevard, Fifth Avenue, Hamlin Boulevard, and the Chicago & North Western Railroad tracks—originally was known as Central Park, then renamed in 1881 to honor assassinated President James Garfield.

The park, opened in 1869, was designed by William Le Baron Jenney, who also designed the world's first skyscraper. In 1905 landscape architect Jens Jensen introduced the Prairie School of architecture to the park; he also designed the gardens and the Conservatory.

Jensen conceived the **Conservatory** (300 North Central Park), which opened to the public in 1908, as a series of naturalistic landscapes under glass, a revolutionary idea at the time. It occupies almost two acres, making it one of the largest gardens under glass in the world. Jensen's ideas were realized with the help of Hitchings & Co., an engineering firm that specialized in conservatories. The Conservatory spaces include the Palm House, with palms from around the world; the Show House, which contains flowers, including a formal French garden such as those in the seventeenth and eighteenth centuries; the Desert House, with its various cacti; the large Fern Room, containing a pond and some of the oldest species of plants on earth; and the Children's Garden, complete with playground toys and equipment to help expel all that energy. The Conservatory also presents five annual flower shows. Open every day from 9:00 A.M. to 5:00 P.M. Admission is free, as is year-round trolley service from the Loop. Phone (312) 746–5100.

Only some of the park's buildings remain. One worth checking out is now the *Garfield Fieldhouse* (100 North Central Park Avenue), the so-called Gold Dome Building, featuring a twenty-three-carat gilded dome. Originally known as the West Park Commission Administration Building, built in 1928, it is one of the most lavish buildings on the West Side. The Spanish Revival–style structure has an ornate facade featuring the figure of Robert Cavalier de LaSalle, an explorer of the Upper Midwest, and the interior rotunda includes marble panels by sculptor Richard W. Bock.

Also drive by the nearby *bandstand* (Music Court east of Hamlin Avenue), built in 1896 and designed by Joseph Lyman Silsbee, who also designed the Lincoln Park Conservatory. The white marble octagon structure reportedly could hold a one hundred-piece orchestra on its platform. The park is open daily from 6:00 A.M. to 11:00 P.M. Phone (312) 746–5092.

To reach Garfield Park, take the Eisenhower Expressway (I–290) west from the Loop to the Independence Boulevard exit (3800 West) and head north. Turn east onto Washington Boulevard, then north onto Central Park Avenue.

For nearby breakfast or lunch, a good choice is *Edna's Restaurant* (3175 West Madison Street). Take Madison west from the park. To those Chicago restaurant buffs who have been fortunate to eat at Edna's, there may be a difference in the way they characterize the food. "A lot of people say we serve southern cooking," says owner Edna Stewart. "I just say, basically, that my cooking is from the *soul*. I've been successful because I know how to cook. I can make dumplings that would make you *cry*." In the 1960s, Edna's was unofficial headquarters for many civil rights workers, including staff members for Dr. Martin Luther King, Jr. Her customers over the years have included Jimmy Carter, Rosa Parks, and John Kennedy, Jr. Stewart became the cook in the West Side restaurant that her now-deceased father and ex-husband started at Albany and Madison in 1969, half a block from the present, larger location, which was established in 1991. Asked what dishes she is known for, she doesn't hesitate. "I make the best biscuits on earth. We have the best gravy with our biscuits—the brown gravy, not the white." And don't forget the pork chops, fried chicken, baked catfish, short ribs, and peach cobbler. "People want something that's not greasy," Edna adds. "Well, we don't *have* greasy food." Open from 6:00 A.M. to 9:00 P.M., except Monday. Phone (773) 638–7079. Inexpensive.

Southwest Side

Located near Chicago Midway Airport, the *Balzekas Museum of Lithuanian Culture* (6500 South Pulaski Road) was founded in 1966 and is dedicated to the preservation of Lithuanian art, history, customs, and traditions spanning 1,000 years. Drawing upon everything from old newspaper clippings to vintage currency and medals, the museum is full of historical and cultural photos and items covering such subjects as "The Rise of the Lithuanian State," "The First Lithuanians in America," and "Amber," a semiprecious stone often referred to as "Lithuanian gold." The Women's Guild Room contains native costumes, amber jewelry, textiles, dolls, beautifully decorated eggs, and a display of famous Lithuanian women. The museum also houses a library of over 40,000 volumes, one of the most comprehensive collections on Lithuania and Eastern Europe in the United States, and includes a rare book collection of publications from the sixteenth, seventeenth, and eighteenth centuries. There's also a gift shop on the main floor and an exhibit of artworks on the second. Perhaps the most intriguing section at Balzekas is the Children's Museum of Immigrant History, where youngsters can cross over a "drawbridge" into a "Castle Quest" exhibit, featuring authentic chainmail worn by knights, a 4-foot armor jigsaw puzzle, and medieval-style costumes for transforming oneself into a king or princess. At other locations, there's a Puppet Place and ancient folk instruments. Open daily from 10:00 A.M. to 4:00 P.M. Admission is $3.00 for adults, $2.00 for students and seniors, $1.00 for children under 12. Phone (312) 582–6500.

To get to the museum, take the Stevenson Expressway (I–55), which runs off South Lake Shore Drive near McCormick Place, and get off at the Pulaski exit (3800 South), then head south to 6500.

South Side

For a pleasant drive along the lakefront, take Lake Shore Drive south to *The South Shore Cultural Center* (7059 South Shore Drive), originally designed as the private South Shore Country Club by the architectural firm of Marshall and Fox, best known for their design of the Drake and Blackstone hotels. In 1906 the firm constructed the South Shore Club House in the Italian Resort style, making it look like a summer palace. The only remaining portion is the exquisite ballroom, with its Wedgwood decor. In 1916 the club house was moved to the south section of the grounds and became the golf club (no longer in existence). Marshall and Fox then designed a new Mediterranean-style club house, as well as a garage and stable building. For years the country club was home to Chicago's wealthy types, but in the 1960s it was abandoned and fell into disrepair. Community activists fought to have the club restored, and in 1974 the Chicago Park District bought it for $10 million. In 1975 the site was listed on the National Register of Historic Places, and it has been lovingly restored.

The South Shore Cultural Center is located in a magnificent lakefront setting on about sixty acres, with the grounds including a nine-hole golf course, beach, and a horse stable used by the Chicago Police Department. The center, including its impressive solarium, is the site of banquets, weddings, business meetings, and cultural events. There's an art gallery (open Monday through Friday from 10:00 A.M. to 6:00 P.M., Saturday from 9:00 A.M. to 5:00 P.M.), and the walls in the main-floor corridors are filled with work by black artists in the '30s and '40s that came out of the Federal Art Project of the Works Progress Administration. The center also houses the Paul Robeson Theater series in the theater named for the legendary, politically controversial actor/singer. A small display chronicles Robeson's times in Chicago, including his appearance in the early '40s in *Othello* (opposite Jose Ferrer and Uta Hagen) and his appearance before the stockyard workers. The club is reached by driving along a wonderful colonnaded driveway. Office hours are Monday through Friday from 8:30 A.M. to 6:00 P.M., Saturday from 9:00 A.M. to 5:00 P.M. Phone (312) 747–2536.

Now go back north to 67th Street and take it west to **Oak Woods Cemetery,** the entrance of which is on 67th Street at Greenwood Avenue (1100 East). Though not filled with as nearly as many opulent monuments as Graceland Cemetery on the North Side, it's worth a visit. The office provides a free map to help locate the more prominent folks buried here. Unfortunately, the map can be quite confusing, and you might just end up asking some nice person in the office how to reach your desired stops.

Among the grave sites and monuments in the cemetery, established in 1853, is the Confederate Mound Monument, dedicated to some 6,000 Southern prisoners who died in Chicago's Camp Douglas, mostly of disease. On top of a 12-foot column is a bronze sculpture of a Confederate infantryman. The tallest monument in Oak Woods—no surprise here— is the obelisk over the burial site of William Hale "Big Bill" Thompson, Chicago's notorious two-time mayor (1915–1923 and 1927–1931), whom one historian characterized as "a chauvinistic clown" and who is best known for vehemently opposing U.S. entry into World War I and for presiding over his gangster-ruled city during much of Prohibition.

Others buried here include Harold Washington, Chicago's first African-American mayor; Adrian "Cap" Anson, player and manager of the

Chicago White Stockings (forerunner of the Cubs), whose grave is marked with crossed bats and a ball and the words HE PLAYED THE GAME; and Jesse Owens, the splendid black track star who won three gold medals (broad jump and 100-meter and 200-meter races) in the 1936 Olympics in Berlin—much to Hitler's dismay. ("Athlete and humanitarian," his red granite monument reads. "A master of the spirit as well as the mechanics of sports.") The grounds are open every day from 8:30 A.M. to 4:30 P.M. Office open Monday through Friday from 8:30 A.M. to 4:30 P.M., Saturday from 9:00 A.M. to 3:00 P.M. Phone (773) 288–3800.

If breakfast or lunch hunger pains are striking, the place to go is *Army & Lou's* (422 East 75th Street). Drive south to 75th, then head west just past Martin Luther King Drive. Dependable food, friendly service, and an attractive atmosphere (including distinctive African-American artwork) have made this a longtime citywide Chicago favorite. For over fifty years the restaurant has been a popular meeting place for neighborhood folks, along with business and political leaders, including the late Mayor Harold Washington, an Army and Lou's regular. Southern specialties (also known as soul food) include baby back ribs, pork chops, smothered chicken, fried chicken wings, and fresh mixed greens. Other main dishes range from catfish fillet to Louisiana-style gumbo to salmon croquettes. Try to save room for desserts such as freshly baked peach or apple cobbler, sweet potato pie, and bread pudding. There's also a cozy bar and jazz Friday evenings. Open from 9:00 A.M. to 10:00 P.M.; closed Tuesday. Phone (773) 483–3100. Inexpensive.

At the old Regal Theater on 47th Street and South Park Boulevard (later renamed Martin Luther King Drive), if you were lucky, you would be in attendance on a night when there was amateur talent competition. "Contestants would literally get 'the hook,' if they were really bad," remembers one observer. "I mean, even if a guy was singing 'The Lord's Prayer,' if he was off-key, he'd get that hook." Opening in 1928, the Regal also showcased talented performers such as Duke Ellington, Louis Armstrong, the Ink Spots, Lena Horne, Josephine Baker, Nat King Cole, James Brown, and Stevie Wonder. Hard times forced the theater to close in 1968, and it was demolished five years later. In its ashes in 1987 came the *New Regal Theater* (1645 East 79th Street), housed in the dormant, lavish Avalon movie theater, which theater architect John Eberson had flamboyantly created in 1927 to resemble a Persian temple. In its restored home, with a seating capacity of 2,300, the New Regal has had on its stage folks like Patti Labelle, Gladys Knight and the Pips, and the Isley Brothers. More recent attractions have ranged from Wild & Ruff Blues with Millie Jackson, Clarence Carter, and Mel Waiters, to comedy concerts. In addition, the New Regal Foundation provides children's matinees to Chicago-area school districts, as well as sponsoring a Young Writers' Workshop for high school students and the Ujima Festival Series, a community-wide humanities program focusing particularly on the history and culture of African resettlement. Box office open Monday and Saturday from 10:00 A.M. to 4:00 P.M., Tuesday through Friday from 10:00 A.M. to 6:00 P.M. For schedules and ticket information, call (773) 721–9301. The New Regal is reached by taking South Lake Shore Drive down to Stony Island Avenue. The theater is just east of Stony.

If you're looking for a place to eat, there's a good spot several blocks south. **BJ's Market and Bakery** (8734 South Stony Island) offers "Food for the Soul," and delivers. The most popular offering at the bright and warm, cafeteria-style restaurant is the mustard-fried catfish. "It's a Cajun dish," owner/chef John Meyer said a while back. "We mix a yellow mustard with a Creole mustard, as well as different seasonings." The thing is, Meyer admitted with a grin, "my Mom doesn't really like it. She keeps asking me, 'Why do you put that mustard on it?' " (Well, sometimes mothers *can* be wrong.) Other main dishes include rotisserie smoked chicken, beef short ribs, meatloaf, seafood gumbo, and a vegetarian sampler, with sides ranging from greens with smoked turkey, red beans and rice, candied sweet potatoes, and sweet potato fries. The dessert list includes the ever-popular peach cobbler, along with bread pudding with rum sauce, banana pudding, and sweet potato pie. Open Monday through Thursday from 11:00 A.M. to 9:00 P.M., Friday and Saturday from 11:00 A.M. to 10:00 P.M., Sunday from 11:00 A.M. to 8:00 P.M. Phone (773) 374–4700. Inexpensive.

Finding the **eta Creative Arts Foundation** at 7558 South South Chicago Avenue, can be difficult—a problem not helped by the fact that there are no signs on the building identifying it as such. Take South Lake Shore Drive to Stony Island to 7900 South, where it hits South South Chicago, and follow this diagonal street south a few blocks to 7558. Incorporated as a nonprofit organization in 1971, eta is the only African-American-owned and managed cultural and performing arts complex in the city and one of the few in the country. (*Eta,* pronounced "Et-tah," means "head," derived from the language of the Ewé people of Ghana, West Africa.) The eta offers six mainstage theater productions featuring the works of black playwrights (98 percent of the plays are world premieres); Saturday family matinees, featuring children and teen performers, many of whom are eta students; classes in the performing and technical arts for children, teens, and adults; and a summer cultural arts day camp. The space includes an art gallery and a gift shop, selling

African-American crafts and artworks. For performance times and ticket information—and directions—phone (773) 752– 3955, or log onto www.etacreativearts.org.

You're best advised to stash your car and take a cab down to *The Checkerboard Lounge,* 423 East 43rd Street. (They'll call one when you're ready to leave. The club itself is fine, but the neighborhood can be tough, especially at night.) A South Side blues mecca, this long-established place attracts an interesting mix of neighborhood residents and University of Chicago students. It's the last survivor of a series of clubs that once lined 43rd. Musicians such as Muddy Waters, Junior Wells, Howlin' Wolf, and Magic Slim appeared regularly, and when Chuck Berry and the Rolling Stones were recording for Chess Records, they would get up on the Checkerboard's small stage. In recent years, those who "have a right to sing the blues" have included Vance Kelly & the Backstreet Blues Band and JoJo Murray & the Top Flight Band. There's a modest cover, and there's music only on Thursday, Friday, and Saturday, beginning after 9:30 P.M. Phone (773) 624–3240.

Far South Side

The *Pullman Historic District* (approximately bounded by 103rd and 115th Streets, the Metra railroad, and Langley Avenue), 13 miles south of the Loop, can be reached by taking the Dan Ryan Expressway (I–94) south to the 111th Street exit (#66A), and driving west 4 blocks to Cottage Grove Avenue.

It was called "the world's most perfect town," built for the employees of the Pullman Palace Car Company between 1880 and 1894 and designed by architect Solon S. Beman and landscape architect Nathan F. Barrett. The idea was conceived by manufacturer George M. Pullman, who had introduced the longer, more comfortable railroad sleeping cars in 1859. One of the country's first planned industrial communities, it was home to 12,000 people and contained, among other things, a one-half-million-gallon water tank, stables, hotel, and a wide variety of houses rented to everyone from executives to laborers. Pullman even had its own company marching band. But the image of "perfection" was shattered in 1894 with the infamous Pullman strike, in which Eugene V. Debs's American Railway Union members went on strike—paralyzing rail traffic from Chicago to the Pacific coast—because wages were cut about one-third after the depression of 1893, but rents on the company houses weren't reduced. President Grover Cleveland dispatched bayonet-wielding federal troops on the grounds that the strikers were interfering with transit of the

U.S. mail, and the strike was crushed. In 1907, ten years after Pullman's death, the properties were sold to individual owners following a court order, and Pullman subsequently became a neighborhood of Chicago. It eroded after World War II, but civic organizations fought demolition, and in 1973 the Historic Pullman Foundation was formed to oversee restoration efforts and prevent demolition. Today, residents of the "living community" include third- and fourth-generation Pullmanites, who are restoring the original row houses.

The *Historic Pullman Foundation Visitor Center* (11141 South Cottage Grove Avenue) is a rather ugly structure located in a former American Legion Hall on the site of the Pullman Arcade Building, one of the country's first indoor shopping malls, which contained retail spaces, a theater, and the Pullman bank, library, and post office, and which was demolished in 1927. The center includes a museum filled with old photos, models of the original structures, and a twenty-minute video, shown daily at noon and 1:00 P.M.

Most of the Pullman attractions on a self-guided walking tour are the more than 1,000 original red-brick row houses. Those along *Arcade Row* (the 500 block of 112th Street) originally had nine rooms and were rented by higher-income employees, while the row houses on the 11100 block of St. Lawrence Avenue were considered the more desirable residences. Others include the economical block houses (11100 block of Langley Avenue), intended for unmarried employees, and unskilled laborers' apartments (11300 block of Langley). Also of interest is the Romanesque-style *Greenstone Church* (11211 St. Lawrence Avenue), built in 1882, rented by Presbyterians and sold to Methodists in 1907, and *Arcade Park* (next to the Hotel Florence), redesigned in 1977 to reflect its original appearance. The *Hotel Florence* (1881), closed for extended renovation at this writing, had sixty-five rooms available for $3.00 to $4.00 a night (Pullman himself kept a suite there) and had the only bar in town. Also scheduled for restoration is *Market Hall* (112th Street and Champlain Avenue), used as a produce market with lodge rooms on the upper levels, and gutted by a fire in 1973. Fire also destroyed a major portion of the Pullman Factory/Clock Tower, which had been largely empty for years, in 1998.

The Visitor Center is staffed by volunteers Monday through Friday from noon to 2:00 P.M., Saturday from 11:00 A.M. to 2:00 P.M., Sunday from noon to 3:00 P.M. Guided walking tours are available the first Sunday of the month, May through October, at 12:30 and 1:30 P.M. Group tours arranged by appointment. Phone (773) 785–3828. For information, phone (773) 785–8901.

General Index

Restaurants

Lodgings

About the Author

Cliff Terry is a Chicago-based freelance journalist and former staff writer of the *Chicago Tribune*, where he was a *Sunday Magazine* writer and editor, feature writer, movie critic, and television critic.

He was the first *Tribune* staff writer ever to win a Nieman Fellowship at Harvard University and the first film critic so honored, and he has received writing awards from the Associated Press, as well as the *Tribune*'s Special Writing Award. His work has appeared in such publications as the *New York Times, Washington Post, Los Angeles Times, Boston Globe, TV Guide, Cosmopolitan, Swissair Gazette, Washington Journalism Review, Stagebill, American Cinematographer, The Rotarian,* and *Student Lawyer.*